SwiftUI™

by Wei-Meng Lee

for dummies®

A Wiley Brand

SwiftUI™ For Dummies®

Published by: **John Wiley & Sons, Inc.,** 111 River Street, Hoboken, NJ 07030-5774, www.wiley.com

Copyright © 2020 by John Wiley & Sons, Inc., Hoboken, New Jersey

Published simultaneously in Canada

For general information on our other products and services, please contact our Customer Care Department within the U.S. at 877-762-2974, outside the U.S. at 317-572-3993, or fax 317-572-4002. For technical support, please visit https://hub.wiley.com/community/support/dummies.

Wiley publishes in a variety of print and electronic formats and by print-on-demand. Some material included with standard print versions of this book may not be included in e-books or in print-on-demand. If this book refers to media such as a CD or DVD that is not included in the version you purchased, you may download this material at http://booksupport.wiley.com. For more information about Wiley products, visit www.wiley.com.

Library of Congress Control Number: 2020939546

ISBN 978-1-119-65268-7 (pbk); ISBN 978-1-119-65272-4 (ebk); ISBN 978-1-119-65270-0 (ebk)

Manufactured in the United States of America

SKY10020277_081020

Contents at a Glance

Table of Contents

Introduction

I n 2019, at the Apple Worldwide Developers Conference, Apple announced SwiftUI, a declarative programming framework for developing user interfaces (UIs) for iOS and macOS applications. With SwiftUI, Apple aims to modernize the iOS development experience.

There's no doubt that SwiftUI makes it much easier and more efficient for developers to create apps, but it also means you have to learn something new. That's where *SwiftUI For Dummies* comes in. This book provides you with all the essentials that you need to learn to become a successful iOS developer using SwiftUI.

About This Book

This book covers the basics of SwiftUI. Because SwiftUI supports iOS, iPadOS, macOS, watchOS, and tvOS, it's a really big topic. To narrow the scope, this book focuses on using SwiftUI with iOS, specifically to program iPhone apps.

In this code-intensive book, you're encouraged to try out the examples in each chapter. The chapters are designed to be compact, easy to follow, and easy to understand. However, you don't have to read this book from the first page to the last. Each chapter is designed to be independent, and you're free to start with any chapter to find the topic that you're interested in.

I don't use many special conventions, but here are a couple points you should be aware of: Sidebars (text in gray boxes) and anything marked with the Technical Stuff icon are skippable, and code appears in monofont. Pretty simple, right?

Finally, within this book, you may note that some web addresses break across two lines of text. If you're reading this book in print and want to visit one of these web pages, simply key in the web address exactly as it's noted in the text, pretending as though the line break doesn't exist. If you're reading this as an e-book, you've got it easy — just click the web address to be taken directly to the web page.

Foolish Assumptions

This book is for people who are new (or relatively new) to using SwiftUI for iOS development. Though I do not assume that you're familiar with iOS programming, I do assume the following:

>> You're familiar with the basics of programming.

>> You're familiar with how an iPhone works.

>> You have a Mac that you can use to try out the examples in this book.

>> You don't need an iPhone to test the applications in this book (except for Chapter 12 where I show you how to load your iPhone with the application you've built); the iPhone Simulator will suffice.

Some chapters in this book assume that you're familiar with UIKit programming (the framework used for iOS programming prior to SwiftUI). But this knowledge is not a prerequisite for using this book.

Icons Used in This Book

Like other books in the *For Dummies* series, this book uses icons, or little pictures in the margins, to draw your attention to certain kinds of material. Here are the icons that I use:

REMEMBER

Whenever I tell you something useful or important enough that you'd do well to store the information somewhere safe in your memory for later recall, I flag it with the Remember icon.

TECHNICAL STUFF

The Technical Stuff icon marks text that contains some for-nerds-only technical details or explanations that you're free to skip.

TIP

The Tip icon marks shortcuts or easier ways to do things, which I hope will make your life easier.

WARNING

The Warning icon marks text that contains a friendly but unusually insistent reminder to avoid doing something. You have been warned.

Beyond the Book

In addition to what you're reading right now, this product comes with a free access-anywhere Cheat Sheet that includes information on creating a stacked and table navigation app, creating shake fail feedback using animation, and more. To get this Cheat Sheet, go to www.dummies.com and type **SwiftUI For Dummies Cheat Sheet** in the Search box.

This book includes some downloadable content as well — all the code in the book, as well as the files you need to create the app described in the book. Go to www.dummies.com/go/swiftuifd to download all this great stuff.

Where to Go from Here

The first step to go from here is to prepare your Mac. If you've never programmed an iOS app, now is the time to download and install Xcode (see Chapter 1). If you're a seasoned iOS developer, you'll appreciate the fact that Chapter 1 also compares the old way of doing things using the UIKit and the new way of doing things in SwiftUI.

Chapter 2 provides a quick overview of the Swift programming language, which is the language used in SwiftUI. Learning a new language is not trivial, so I strongly suggest you go through the basics of Swift (even if you're already familiar with it) so that you can learn some of the new language features in the latest version of Swift. You may also want to refer to Apple's documentation on the Swift programming language at https://docs.swift.org/swift-book.

Beyond that, feel free to jump to any chapter that piques your interest. That being said, if you're a SwiftUI newbie, it makes sense to follow the chapters in order.

Finally, my advice to all beginners is: Practice, practice, practice. Type in the code in each chapter and make mistakes. The more mistakes you make, the better you'll understand and remember the topics discussed.

Good luck, and enjoy your newfound knowledge!

1

Getting Started with Swift and SwiftUI

Get a head start in using SwiftUI and build your first iOS app.

Get acquainted with the syntax of the Swift programming language so that you're prepared to dive into the world of SwiftUI.

IN THIS CHAPTER

» Understanding what SwiftUI is

» Getting the tools for SwiftUI

» Comparing UIKit to SwiftUI

» Using the preview canvas and Live Preview

» Understanding the various files in a SwiftUI project

Chapter **1**

Introducing SwiftUI

I know the feeling of being on the verge of learning something new. If you're anything like me, you're eager to try things out and see how it feels. And that's exactly what you do in this chapter!

In this chapter, I explain what SwiftUI is, show you how SwiftUI has changed the user interface (UI) development paradigm, and explain how SwiftUI makes the process easier going forward. Then I tell you how you can get started with the necessary tools. Finally, with the tools that you've installed, you create your first iOS application using SwiftUI, and learn how the various components in your project work together as a whole.

Understanding What SwiftUI Is

SwiftUI is a declarative programming framework for developing UIs for iOS, iPadOS, watchOS, tvOS, and macOS applications. In fact, SwiftUI was invented by the watchOS group at Apple.

Before SwiftUI was introduced, most developers used UIKit and Storyboard (which is still supported by Apple in the current version of Xcode, as of this writing [version 11.4.1]) to design a UI. Using UIKit and Storyboard, developers drag and drop View controls onto View Controllers and connect them to outlets and actions on the View Controller classes. This model of building UIs is known as *Model View Controller* (MVC), which creates a clean separation between UI and business logic.

The following shows a simple implementation in UIKit and Storyboard. Here, a Button and Label view have been added to the View Controller in Storyboard; two outlets and an action have been created to connect to them:

```
class ViewController: UIViewController {

    @IBOutlet weak var lbl: UILabel!
    @IBOutlet weak var button: UIButton!
    @IBAction func btnClicked(_ sender: Any) {
        lbl.text = "Button tapped"
    }
```

For laying out the views, you use auto-layout to position the button and label in the middle of the screen (both horizontally and vertically).

To customize the look and feel of the button, you can code it in the loadView() method, like this:

```
override func loadView() {
    super.loadView()

    // background color
    button.backgroundColor = UIColor.yellow

    // button text and color
    button.setTitle("Submit", for: .normal)
    button.setTitleColor(.black, for: .normal)

    // padding
    button.contentEdgeInsets = UIEdgeInsets(
        top: 10, left: 10, bottom: 10, right: 10)

    // border
    button.layer.borderColor =
        UIColor.darkGray.cgColor
    button.layer.borderWidth = 3.0
```

```
    // text font
    button.titleLabel!.font =
        UIFont.systemFont(ofSize: 26, weight:
        UIFont.Weight.regular)

    // rounder corners
    button.layer.cornerRadius = 10

    // auto adjust button size
    button.sizeToFit()
}
```

Figure 1-1 shows the button that has customized. UIKit is an *event-driven* frame-work, where you can reference each view in your view controller, update its appearance, or handle an event through *delegates* when some events occurred.

FIGURE 1-1:
UIKit is event
driven, and it
uses delegates to
handle events.

In contrast, SwiftUI is a *state-driven*, declarative framework. In SwiftUI, you can implement all the above with the following statements (I explain how to build all these later in this chapter):

```
struct ContentView: View {
    @State private var label = "label"

    var body: some View {
        VStack {
            Button(action: {
                self.label = "Button tapped"
            }) {
                Text("Submit")
                    .padding(EdgeInsets(
                        top: 10, leading: 10,
                        bottom: 10, trailing: 10))
                    .background(Color.yellow)
                    .foregroundColor(Color.black)
                    .border(Color.gray, width: 3)
                    .font(Font.system(size: 26.0))
                    .overlay(
                        RoundedRectangle(cornerRadius: 10)
                            .stroke(Color.gray,
                                lineWidth: 5)
                    )
            }
            Text(label)
                .padding()
        }
    }
}
```

Notice that all the views are now created declaratively using code — no more drag-and-drop in Storyboard. Layouts are now also specified declaratively using code (the VStack in this example stacks all the views vertically). Delegates are now replaced with closures. More important, views are now a function of state (and not a sequence of events) — the text displayed by the Text view is now bound to the state variable label. When the button is tapped, you change the value of the label state variable, which automatically updates the text displayed in the Text view. This programming paradigm is known as *reactive programming*.

Figure 1-2 shows the various views in action.

FIGURE 1-2:
SwiftUI is a
state-driven
declarative
framework.

Getting the Tools

To start developing using SwiftUI, you need the following:

» Xcode version 11 or later

» A deployment target (Simulator or real device) of iOS 13 or later

» macOS Mojave (10.14) or later (Note that if you're running macOS Mojave, you won't be able to use Live Preview and design canvas features; full features are available only in macOS Catalina (10.15) and later.)

To install Xcode, you can install it from the App Store on your Mac (see Figure 1-3).

Alternatively, if you have a paid Apple developer account (you need this if you want to make your apps available on the App Store, but this is not a requirement for trying out the examples in this book), head over to `https://developer.apple.com`, sign in, and download Xcode directly.

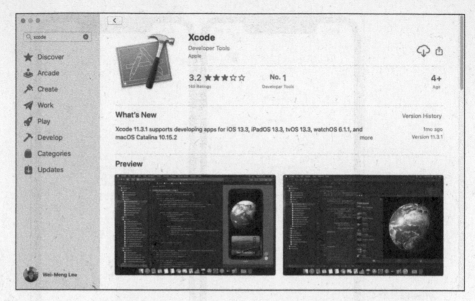

FIGURE 1-3:
Installing Xcode
from the Mac App
Store.

TIP

For this book, our focus is on developing iOS applications for the iPhone. Developing iPad, watchOS, tvOS, and macOS applications using SwiftUI is beyond the scope of this book.

Hello, SwiftUI

After you've installed Xcode, you'll probably be very eager to try out SwiftUI. So, let's take a dive into SwiftUI and see how it works! Follow these steps:

1. Launch Xcode.

2. Click Create a new Xcode project (see Figure 1-4).

3. Select Single View App and click Next (see Figure 1-5).

4. In the Product Name field, enter HelloSwiftUI (see Figure 1-6).

5. In the Organization Name field, enter your name.

6. In the Organization Identifier field, enter a unique identifier, such as the reverse domain name of your company.

7. **From the User Interface drop-down list, select SwiftUI.**

8. **Click Next and save the project to a location on your Mac.**

   You should see the project created for you (see Figure 1-7). The ContentView. swift file contains the UI for your application's main screen.

FIGURE 1-4:
Launching Xcode.

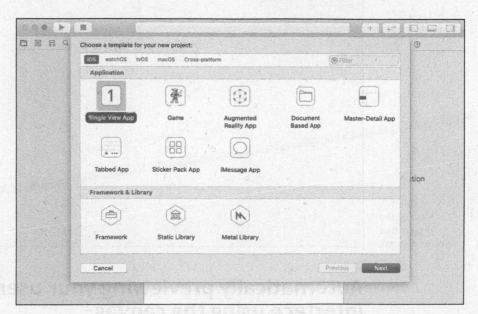

FIGURE 1-5:
Selecting the
Single View App
project type.

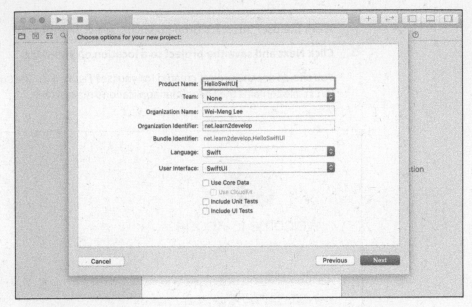

FIGURE 1-6:
Naming the
project.

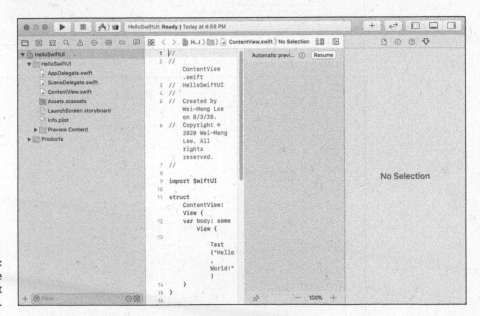

FIGURE 1-7:
Viewing the
project that
you've created.

Automatically previewing your user interface using the canvas

By default, you should see the Inspector window on the right side of the Xcode window. For building your UI using SwiftUI, you usually don't need the Inspector window, so you can dismiss it to gain more screen estate for previewing your UI using the canvas. To dismiss the Inspector window, click the button on the upper-right corner of Xcode (see Figure 1-8).

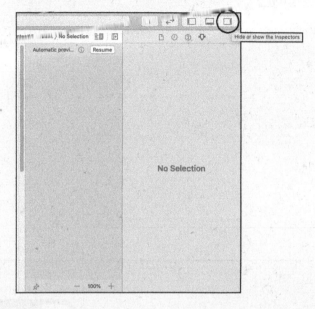

FIGURE 1-8:
Dismissing the
Inspector
window.

With the Inspector window dismissed, you should now see the canvas on the right side of Xcode (see Figure 1-9). The canvas lets you preview the UI of your application without needing to run the application on the iPhone Simulator or a real device.

If you don't see the canvas, you can bring it up again through the Editor ⇨ Canvas menu.

TIP

To preview your UI, click the Resume button on the canvas. You should now be able to see the preview (see Figure 1-10).

If you don't see the Resume button, make sure you're running macOS Catalina (10.15) or later.

TIP

Now let's modify the ContentView.swift file with the code that you've seen earlier (see Figure 1-11).

You may notice that the automatic preview has paused. This sometimes happen when the file you're previewing has some changes that caused the containing module to be rebuilt. When that happens, click the Restore button, and you should see the preview again (see Figure 1-12).

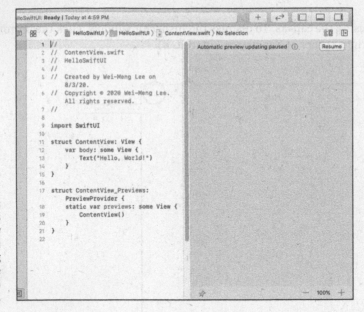

FIGURE 1-9:
The canvas allows you to preview your application without deploying it on the iPhone Simulator or a real device.

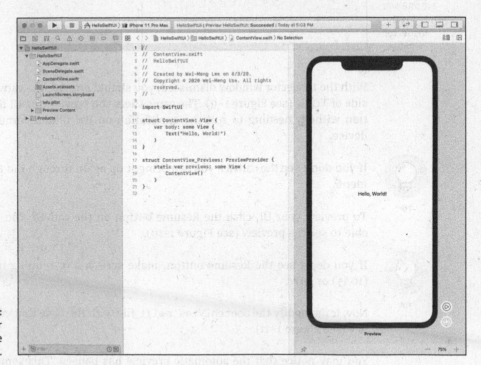

FIGURE 1-10:
Previewing your app on the canvas.

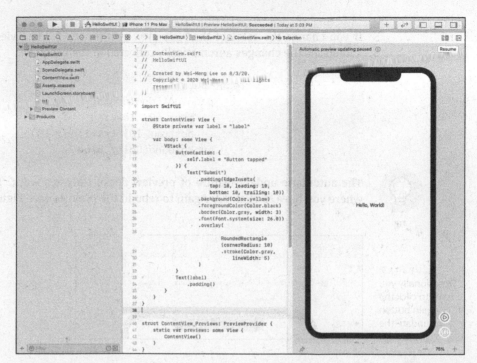

FIGURE 1-11:
Modifying the
`ContentView.
swift` file.

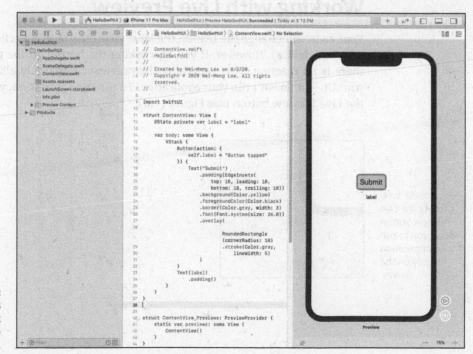

FIGURE 1-12:
The preview is
updated to reflect
the changes in
the code.

If you change the color of the Text view (within the Button view) to blue, you should see the changes automatically reflected in the preview:

```
Text("Submit")
    .padding(EdgeInsets(
        top: 10, leading: 10,
        bottom: 10, trailing: 10))
    .background(Color.blue)
```

TIP

The automatic update feature of preview doesn't always work. There are times where you have to click Try Again to rebuild the preview (see Figure 1-13).

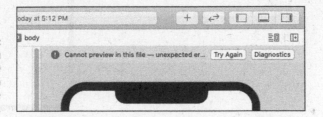

FIGURE 1-13:
Occasionally you have to click the Try Again button to update the preview.

Working with Live Preview

Your code will change the text on the label when the button is clicked (or tapped on a real device). However, if you try clicking the button on the preview canvas, there is no reaction. This is because the preview canvas only allows previewing your UI — it doesn't run your application. To run the application, you need to click the Live Preview button (see Figure 1-14).

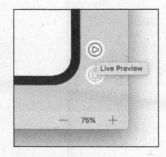

FIGURE 1-14:
Clicking the Live Preview button allows you to run your application directly on the canvas.

When the Live Preview mode is turned on, the background of the simulator will turn dark (see the left side of Figure 1-15). You can now click on the button and the text on the label will be updated (see the right side of Figure 1-15).

Generating different previews

Notice this block of code at the bottom of ContentView.swift?

```swift
struct ContentView_Previews: PreviewProvider {
    static var previews: some View {
        ContentView()
    }
}
```

The ContentView_Previews struct conforms to the PreviewProvider protocol. This protocol produces view previews in Xcode so that you can preview your UI created in SwiftUI without needing to explicitly run the application on the iPhone Simulator or real devices. Essentially, it controls what you see on the preview canvas. As an example, if you want to preview how your UI will look like on an iPhone SE device, you can modify the `ContentView_Previews` struct as follows (see Figure 1-16):

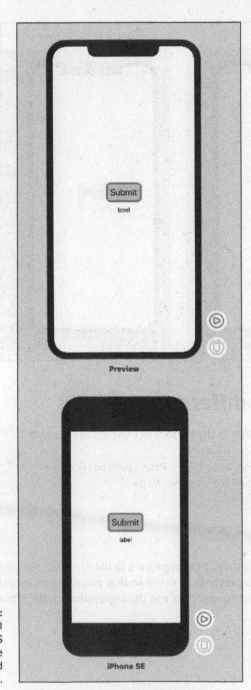

FIGURE 1-16:
Previewing the UI on two iOS devices — the latest iPhone and an iPhone SE.

```
struct ContentView_Previews: PreviewProvider {
    static var previews: some View {
        Group {
            ContentView()
            ContentView()
                .previewDevice(PreviewDevice(
                    rawValue: "iPhone SE"))
                .previewDisplayName("iPhone SE")
        }
    }
}
```

The Gory Details

Now that you've seen how to get started with SwiftUI, let's take a moment to examine the various files created in the project and see how the various parts connect.

In your project, notice that you have the following files created (see Figure 1-17):

» AppDelegate.swift

» SceneDelegate.swift

» ContentView.swift (this is the file that you've been modifying to create the UI of your iOS application)

» Info.plist

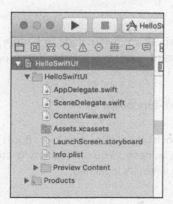

FIGURE 1-17:
The content of
the project
created.

Info.plist

Let's take a look at the `Info.plist` file first (see Figure 1-18). In particular, look at the key named `Application Scene Manifest`.

Within the `Application Scene Manifest` key, you have the following keys:

>> `Enable Multiple Windows`: This is set to NO by default. You can set this to YES if you're building apps for iPadOS and macOS.

>> `Application Session Role`: An array that contains a list of dictionary objects. The default object contains a key named `Delegate Class Name` that points to the `SceneDelegate.swift` file.

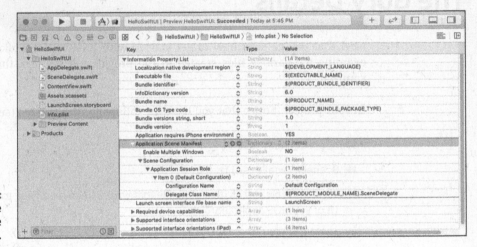

FIGURE 1-18:
Examining the
items in the
`Info.plist` file.

AppDelegate.swift

`AppDelegate.swift` is the place where you write code to handle an application's launch, going into the background, coming to the foreground, and other activities.

`AppDelegate.swift` has three main functions:

>> `application(:didFinishLaunchingWithOptions) -> Bool`: This function is called when the application is launched. You can use this function to perform your setup for the app when it's launched.

» application(: configurationForConnecting:options:) →
UISceneConfiguration: This function is called whenever your app is needed
to supply a new scene. Here, it returns the default item in the dictionary
named Default Configuration:

```
func application(_ application: UIApplication,
    configurationForConnecting connectingSceneSession:
    UISceneSession, options: UIScene.ConnectionOptions) ->
    UISceneConfiguration {

    // Called when a new scene session is being
    //created. Use this method to select a
    //configuration to create the new scene with.
    return UISceneConfiguration(
        name: "Default Configuration",
        sessionRole: connectingSceneSession.role)
}
```

TIP

A *scene* is an object that represents one instance of your app's user interface.

» application(:didDiscardSceneSessions:): This function is called
whenever a user discards a scene (such as swiping it away in the multitasking
window).

SceneDelegate.swift

Whereas the AppDelegate.swift file is responsible for handling your app life
cycle, the SceneDelegate.swift file is responsible for your scene's life cycle.

The SceneDelegate.swift file contains the following default functions:

» scene(_:willConnectTo:options:)

» sceneDidDisconnect(_:)

» sceneDidBecomeActive(_:)

» sceneWillResignActive(_:)

» sceneWillEnterForeground(_:)

» sceneDidEnterBackground(_:)

The scene(_:willConnectTo:options:) function is called when a scene is added
to the app (in simple terms, when your UI is shown). Here, you load the content of

the file named ContentView (which is what you've modified earlier in the ContentView.swift file):

```
func scene(_ scene: UIScene, willConnectTo session:
    UISceneSession, options connectionOptions:
    UIScene.ConnectionOptions) {

    let contentView = ContentView()
    if let windowScene = scene as? UIWindowScene {
        let window = UIWindow(windowScene:
            windowScene)
        window.rootViewController =
            UIHostingController(rootView: contentView)
        self.window = window
        window.makeKeyAndVisible()
    }
}
```

In short, you use AppDelegate.swift to perform setup needed for the duration of the app. You also use it to handle events that focus on the app, as well as registered for external services like push notifications. The SceneDelegate.swift, on the other hand, is designed to handle events for multi-window OS (iPadOS), which supports multiple instances of your app's UI.

Chapter **2**

Basics of the Swift Programming Language

n Chapter 1, I give you a quick look at SwiftUI and explain how it enables you to quickly create the user interface (UI) for your iOS applications. As the name implies, SwiftUI uses the Swift programming language.

This chapter gives you a good overview of the Swift programming language. Although providing an exhaustive discussion of the language in one single chapter isn't possible, I do cover most of the salient points of the language here.

So, should you read through this entire chapter? It depends.

>> **If you're totally new to the Swift programming language,** it makes sense to read this chapter before proceeding with the rest of the book. And while you're reading through the various sections, you should try out the various code samples using Xcode Playgrounds. You can refer to www.hackingwithswift. com/read/0/1/how-to-install-xcode-and-create-a-playground for information on how to get started with Xcode Playgrounds.

>> **If you already have some basic knowledge of Swift,** skim through some topics in this chapter to refresh your knowledge of Swift and see what has changed.

>> **If you're already writing iOS apps using Swift,** use this chapter as a reference so that you can quickly refer to a topic when you need clarification.

Basic Swift Syntax

Swift is a *type-safe language*, which means that the language makes it clear to you the types of values your code is working with. The following sections discuss how to declare constants and variables and how to work with strings and comments.

Constants

In Swift, you create a constant using the let keyword:

```
let radius = 3.45          // Double
let numOfColumns = 5       // Int
let myName = "Wei-Meng Lee"  // String
```

Notice that there is no need to specify the data type — the data types are inferred automatically.

If you want to declare the type of constant, you can do so using the colon operator (:) followed by the data type, as shown here:

```
let diameter:Double = 8
```

After a constant is created, you can no longer change its value. Always use a let when you need to store values that do not change.

Variables

To declare a variable, you use the `var` keyword:

```
var myAge = 25
var circumference = 2 * 3.14 * radius
```

After a variable is created, you can change its value. In Swift, values are never implicitly converted to another type. For example, suppose you're trying to concatenate a string and the value of a variable. In the following example, you need to explicitly use the `String()` function to convert the value of `myAge` to a string value before concatenating it with another string:

```
var strMyAge = "My age is " + String(myAge)
```

REMEMBER

To get the text representation of a value (constant or variable), you can also use the `description` property, like this: `myAge.description`.

Strings

One of the common tasks in programming is inserting values of variables into a string. In Swift, you use *string interpolation* and it has the following format:

```
"Your string literal \(variable_name)"
```

The following statement shows an example:

```
let firstName = "Wei-Meng"
let lastName = "Lee"
var strName = "My name is \(firstName) \(lastName)"
```

You can also use this method to include a `Double` value in your string (or even perform mathematical operations or function calls):

```
var strResult ="The circumference is \(circumference)"
```

Comments

In Swift, as in most programming languages, you insert comments into your code using two forward slashes (//):

```
// this is another comment
```

If you have several lines of comments, it's better to use the /* and */ combination to denote a block of statements as comments:

```
/*
    this is a comment
    this is another comment
*/
```

Basic Data Types

Like most programming languages, Swift provides the following basic data types:

» Integers

» Floating-point numbers

» Booleans

» Tuples

Integers

Integers are whole numbers with no fractional parts. In Swift, integers are represented using the Int type. The Int type represents both positive and negative values. If you only need to store positive values, you can use the unsigned integer UInt type.

In most cases, you use Int for storing signed numbers and UInt if you don't need to store negative values (even if you don't need to store negative numbers, it's still a good idea to use Int for code compatibility). However, if you want to explicitly control the size of the variable used, you can specify one of the various integer types available:

» Int8 and UInt8

» Int16 and UInt16

» Int32 and UInt32

» Int64 and UInt64

Floating-point numbers

Floating-point numbers are numbers with fractional parts. In Swift, there are two floating-point types.

>> Float: Float uses 32 bits for storage and has a precision of at least six decimal digits.

>> Double: Double uses 64 bits for storage and has a precision of at least 15 decimal digits.

When assigning a floating-point number to a constant or variable, Swift always infers the Double type unless you explicitly specify otherwise:

```
var num1 = 3.14          //----num1 is Double---
var num2: Float = 3.14   //----num2 is Float---
```

WARNING

If you try to assign a Double to a Float type, the compiler will flag an error:

```
num2 = num1      //----num1 is Double and num2 is Float----
```

This is because the number stored in a Double type may not be able to fit into a Float type, thereby resulting in an overflow. In order to assign num1 to num2, you need to explicitly cast num1 to a Float, like this:

```
num2 = Float(num1)
```

Booleans

Swift supports the Boolean logic type, Bool. A Bool type can take either a true value or a false value. The following code snippet shows the Bool type in use:

```
var seaIsGreen = false
var areYouKidding:Bool = true
```

One of the common operations with Boolean variables is negating the variable's value. For example, to toggle a button, you usually change the value of a Boolean variable by doing something like this:

```
var startSpinning = true
startSpinning = !startSpinning // ! negates the bool value
```

In Swift 5.1, there is a now a new `toggle()` method that negates the value of a Boolean variable:

```
startSpinning.toggle() // changes true to false and
                       // false to true
```

Tuples

A *tuple* is an ordered collection of values. The values inside a tuple can be of any type; they don't need to be all the same type. Here are some examples of tuples:

```
//---tuple of type (Int, String, String)---
var flight = (7031, "ATL", "ORD")
```

If you want to retrieve the individual values inside a tuple, you can assign it to individual variables or constants:

```
let (flightno, orig, dest) = flight
print(flightno)   //---7031---
print(orig)       //---ATL---
print(dest)       //---ORD---
```

Alternatively, you can access the individual values inside the tuple using the index, starting from 0:

```
print(flight.0)   //---7031---
print(flight.1)   //---ATL---
print(flight.2)   //---ORD---
```

Arrays

An *array* is an indexed collection of objects. The following statement shows two arrays:

```
var names = [String]()                  // empty dictionary
var OSes = ["iOS", "Android", "Windows Phone"]
```

TIP

In Swift, arrays are implemented internally as structures, not as classes.

Retrieving elements from an array

To retrieve the items inside an array, use the subscript syntax, as follows:

```
var item1 = OSes[0]   //"iOS"
```

TIP

Array indices start at 0, not 1. The ordering of objects in an array is important, because you access elements inside an array using their position.

Inserting elements into an array

To insert an element into an array at a particular index, use the `insert()` function:

```
//---inserts a new element into the array at index 2---
OSes.insert("BlackBerry", at: 2)
```

WARNING

You'll get an error if the index is greater than the total element count in the array.

Modifying elements in an array

To change the value of an existing item in the array, specify the index of the item and assign a new value to it:

```
OSes[3] = "WinPhone"
```

TIP

Note that you can only modify values of arrays that were declared using the `var` keyword. If an array is declared using the `let` keyword, its values are not modifiable.

Appending elements to an array

To append an item to an array, use the `append()` function:

```
OSes.append("Tizen")
```

Alternatively, you can also use the `+=` operator to append to an array:

```
OSes += ["Tizen"]
```

You can also append an array to an existing array:

```
OSes += ["Symbian", "Bada"]
```

Removing elements from an array

You can remove elements from an array using the following functions:

```
var os1 = OSes.remove(at: 3)        // removes "WinPhone"
var os2 = OSes.removeLast()         // removes "Bada"


// removes all elements
OSes.removeAll(keepingCapacity: true)
```

TIP

The keepCapacity argument is more for the underlying implementation of the array. Keeping the capacity means that additional elements can be stored later on without needing the array to trigger a reallocation of the backing storage.

Dictionaries

A *dictionary* is a collection of objects of the same type that is identified using a key. Consider the following example:

```
var platforms: Dictionary<String, String> = [
    "Apple": "iOS",
    "Google" : "Android",
    "Microsoft" : "Windows Phone"
]
```

Here, platforms is a dictionary containing three items. Each item is a key/value pair. For example, "Apple" is the key that contains the value "iOS". The declaration specifies that the key and value must both be of the String type.

TIP

Unlike arrays, the ordering of items in a dictionary is not important. This is because items are identified by their keys, not by their positions.

The key of an item in a dictionary is not limited to String. It can be any of the *hashable* types (in other words, it must be uniquely representable).

Retrieving elements from a dictionary

To access a particular operating system (OS) in the preceding example, you would specify the key of the item you want to retrieve, followed by the index of the array:

```
print(platforms["Apple"]!)   //---iOS---
```

Note that you have to use the ! to force-unwrap the value of the dictionary. This is because the dictionary returns you an optional value (it can potentially return you a nil value if you specify a key that does not exist).

TIP

Refer to the "Optional Types" section, later in this chapter, for a discussion on optional values.

Modifying an item in a dictionary

To replace the value of an item inside a dictionary, specify its key and assign a new value to it:

```
platforms["Microsoft"] ="WinPhone"
```

If the specified key doesn't already exist in the dictionary, a new item is added. If it already exists, its corresponding value is updated.

Removing an item from a dictionary

To remove an item from a dictionary, you can simply set it to nil:

```
platforms["Microsoft"] = nil
```

The number of items inside the dictionary would now be reduced by one.

Optional Types

Swift uses a concept known as *optionals*. To understand this concept, consider the following code snippet:

```
let str = "125"
let num = Int(str)
```

Here, str is a string and you use the Int() function to convert a string to an integer. However, the conversion may not always be successful (the string may contain characters that cannot be converted to a number) and, hence, the result returned to num may be an Int value or nil (if the conversion fails).

By type inference, num is assigned a type of Int?. The ? character indicates that this variable can optionally contain a value — or it may not contain a value at all if the conversion is not successful (in which case, num will be assigned a nil value).

In the preceding code snippet, any attempt to use the num variable (such as multiplying it by another variable/constant) will result in a compiler error (Value of optional type 'Int?' must be unwrapped to a value of type 'Int'):

```
let multiply = num * 2   //---error---
```

To fix this, you should use the If statement to determine whether num does, indeed, contain a value. If it does, you need to use the ! character after the variable name to use its value, like this:

```
if num != nil {
    let multiply = num! * 2
}
```

The ! character indicates to the compiler that you know that the variable contains a value and you know what you're doing. The use of the ! character is known as *forced unwrapping* an optional's value.

In the previous example, num is an optional due to type inference. If you want to explicitly declare a variable as an optional type, you can append the ? character to the type name. For example, the following statement declares description to be an optional string type:

```
var description: String?
```

You can then assign a string to description:

```
description = "Hello"
```

You can also assign the special value nil to an optional type:

```
description = nil
```

You cannot assign nil to a nonoptional type.

Working with implicitly unwrapped optionals

In the preceding section, you saw the use of the optional type and the use of the ! character to unwrap the value of an optional variable. The problem with this is that you'll likely end up with a lot of ! characters in your code whenever you access the value of optional variables. To access the value of an optional variable without using the ! character, you can declare an optional type as an *implicitly unwrapped optional*.

Consider the following declaration:

```
//---implicit optional variable---
var str2: String! = "This is a string"
```

Here, str2 is an implicitly unwrapped optional. When you access str2, there is no need to use the ! character because it's already implicitly unwrapped:

```
print(str2) // "This is a string"
```

If str2 is set to nil, accessing the str2 will return a nil:

```
str2 = nil
print(str2) // nil
```

WARNING

For this reason, when using an implicitly unwrapped optional like the preceding, the compiler will always sound the following warning: Coercion of implicitly unwrappable value of type 'String?' to 'Any' does not unwrap optional. This is because the compiler wants you to be absolutely sure that you know what you're getting when you use the variable (you may get the nil value when you aren't expecting to).

TIP

You can fix this warning in one of three ways:

>> Provide a default value in case str2 is nil:

```
print(str2 ?? "Empty String")
```

>> Explicitly unwrap str2 using the ! character (do this if you're really sure str2 is not nil):

```
if str2 != nil {
    print(str2!)
}
```

```
print(str2 as Any)
```

TIP

In Swift, the Any type represents an instance of any type, including function types (discussed later in this chapter).

Using optional binding

Often, you need to assign the value of an optional type to another variable or constant. Consider the following example:

```
var productCode:String? = getProductCode("Diet Coke")
if let tempProductCode = productCode {
    print(tempProductCode)
} else {
    print("Product Code not found")
}
```

In the preceding code snippet, getProductCode() is a function that takes in a product name (of String type) and returns a product code (a String value) or nil if the product cannot be found. As such, the productCode is an optional String.

To assign the value of productCode to another variable/constant, you can use the following pattern:

```
if let tempProductCode = productCode {
```

Here, you're essentially checking the value of productCode. If it isn't nil, you're assigning the value to tempProductCode and executing the If block of statements; if the value is nil, you execute the Else block of statements.

Unwrapping optionals using "?"

Up to this point in this chapter, I show you that you can use the ! character to unwrap an optional type's value. Consider the following scenario:

```
var str:String?
var empty = str!.isEmpty
```

From the preceding code snippet, str is an optional String and isEmpty is a property from the String class. In this example, you want to know if str is empty, so you call the isEmpty property. However, the preceding code will crash, because str contains `nil` and trying to call the `isEmpty` property from `nil` results in a runtime error. The use of the ! character is like telling the compiler: "I am very confident that str is not `nil`, so please go ahead and call the `isEmpty` property." Unfortunately, str is, indeed, `nil` in this case.

To prevent the statement from crashing, you should instead use the ? character, like this:

```
var empty = str?.isEmpty
```

The ? character is like telling the compiler, "I am not sure if str is `nil`. If it is not `nil`, please go ahead and call the `isEmpty` property; if it is `nil`, just ignore it."

Using the nil coalescing operator

Consider the following optional variable:

```
var gender:String?
```

The `gender` variable is an optional variable that can take a `String` value or a `nil` value. Suppose you want to assign the value of `gender` to another variable, and if it contains `nil`, you'll assign a default value to the variable. Your code may look like this:

```
var genderOfCustomer:String

if gender == nil {
    genderOfCustomer = "male"
} else {
    genderOfCustomer = gender!
}
```

Here you check whether `gender` is `nil`. If it is, you assign a default value of `"male"` to `genderOfCustomer`. If `gender` is not `nil`, then its value is assigned to `genderOfCustomer`.

Swift has the *nil coalescing operator*, which has the following syntax: a ?? b. It reads, "Unwrap the value of optional *a* and return its value if it is not `nil`; otherwise, return *b*."

The preceding code snippet can be rewritten in a single statement using the nil coalescing operator:

```
var gender:String?
var genderOfCustomer = gender ?? "male"    //---male---
```

Because gender is `nil`, `genderOfCustomer` is now assigned `male`.

Now if you were to assign a value to gender and execute the preceding statements again, `gender` would be `female`:

```
var gender:String? = "female"
var genderOfCustomer = gender ?? "male"    //---female---
```

Functions

In Swift, a function is defined using the `func` keyword, like this:

```
func doSomething() {
    print("doSomething")
}
```

The preceding code snippet defines a function called `doSomething`. It does not take in any inputs (known as *parameters*) and does not return a value (technically, it does return a `Void` value).

To call the function, simply call its name followed by a pair of empty parentheses:

```
doSomething()
```

Understanding input parameters

A function can also optionally define one or more named typed inputs. The following function takes in one single typed input parameter:

```
func doSomething(num: Int) {
    print(num)
}
```

To call this function, call its name and pass in an integer value (known as an *argument*) with the parameter name, like this:

```
doSomething(num: 5)
```

The following function takes in two input parameters, both of type `Int`:

```
func doSomething(num1: Int, num2: Int) {
    print(num1, num2)
}
```

To call this function, pass it two integer values as the argument:

```
doSomething(num1: 5, num2: 6)
```

Returning a value

Functions are not required to return a value. However, if you want the function to return a value, use the `->` operator after the function declaration. The following function returns an integer value:

```
func doSomething(num1: Int, num2: Int, num3: Int) -> Int {
    return num1 + num2 + num3
}
```

You use the `return` keyword to return a value from a function and then exit it. When the function returns a value, you can assign it to a variable or constant, like this:

```
var sum = doSomething(num1:5, num2:6, num3: 7)
```

TIP

Functions are not limited to returning a single value. In some cases, it's important for functions to return multiple values (or even functions). In Swift, you can use a tuple type in a function to return multiple values.

Flow Control

Swift primarily provides two types of statements for flow control: the `If` statement and the `Switch` statement.

If you've programmed before, you're familiar with the If statement. The If statement enables you to make a decision based on certain conditions. If the conditions are met, the block of statement enclosed by the If statement is executed. If you need to make a decision based on several conditions, you can use the more efficient Switch statement, which enables you to specify the conditions without using multiple If statements.

If-Else statement

Swift supports the traditional C-style If-Else statement construct for decision-making. The If-Else statement has the following syntax:

```
if condition {
    statement(s)
} else {
    statement(s)
}
```

TIP

In Swift, there is no need to enclose the condition within a pair of parentheses (( )).

Ternary conditional operator

Very often, the If-Else statement can be shortened using the ternary conditional operator:

```
variable = condition ? value_if_true : value_if_false
```

It first evaluates the condition. If the condition evaluates to true, the value_if_true is assigned to variable. Otherwise, value_if_false is assigned to variable.

Switch statement

Very often, you need to perform a number of If-Else statements. For this purpose, you should use the Switch statement. The Switch statement has the following syntax:

```
switch variable/constant {
    case value_1:
        statement(s)
```

```
      case value_2:
          statement(s)
      ...

          ...
      case value_n:
          statement(s)
      default:
          statement(s)
  }
```

The value of the variable/constant is used for comparison with the various values specified (value_1, value2, ... value_n). If a match occurs, any statements following the value are executed (specified using the case keyword). If no match is found, any statements specified after the default keyword are executed.

TIP

Unlike C and Objective-C (as well as other programming languages), there is no need to specify a Break statement after the last statement in each case. Immediately after any statements in a case block are executed, the Switch statement finishes its execution. In C, a Break statement is needed to prevent the statements after the current case from execution. This behavior is known as *implicit fallthrough*. In Swift, there is no implicit fallthrough; after the statements in a case are executed, the Switch statement ends.

Every Switch statement must be exhaustive. In other words, the value that you're trying to match must be matched by one of the various cases in the Switch statement. Because it is sometimes not feasible to list all the cases, you would need to use the default case to match the remaining unmatched cases.

Looping

The capability to repeatedly execute statements is one of the most useful features of a programming language. Swift supports the following loop statements:

» For-In

» While

» Repeat-While

For-In loop

Swift supports a loop statement known as the For-In loop. The For-In loop iterates over a collection of items (such as an array or a dictionary), as well as a range of numbers.

The following code snippet prints out the numbers from 0 to 9 using the For-In loop:

```
for i in 0...9 {
    print(i)
}
```

The *closed ranged operator* (represented by . . .) defines a range of numbers from 0 to 9 (inclusive).

While loop

In addition to the For-In loop, Swift also provides the While loop. The While loop executes a block of statements repeatedly as long as the specified condition is true:

```
while condition {
    statement(s)
}
```

Repeat-While loop

A variation of the While loop is the Repeat-While loop. The Repeat-While loop has the following syntax:

```
repeat {
    statement(s)
} while condition
```

Control transfer statements

To exit a loop prematurely, use the `break` statement. To continue with the next iteration of the loop, use the `continue` statement.

Range operators

Swift supports two types of range operators to specify a range of values:

» **Closed range operator** (a . . . b)**:** Specifies a range of values starting from a right up to b (inclusive)

» **Half-open range operator** (a . . <b)**:** Specifies a range of values starting from a right up to b, but not including b

To demonstrate how these range operators work, consider the following example:

```
for num in 5...9 {        // prints all numbers from 5 to 9
    print(num)
}
```

To output only 5 to 8, you can use the half-open range operator:

```
for num in 5..<9 {.        // prints all numbers from 5 to 8
    print(num)
}
```

The half-open range operator is particularly useful when you're dealing with zero-based lists such as arrays. The following code snippet is one good example:

```
//---useful for 0-based lists such as arrays---
var fruits =
    ["apple","orange","pineapple","durian","rambutan"]
for n in 0..<fruits.count {
    print(fruits[n])
}
```

Structures

A *structure* is a special kind of data type that groups a list of variables and places them under a unified name. The group of variables contained within a structure may have diverse data types. Structures are useful for storing related groups of data. For example, consider a scenario in which you're implementing a game of

Go. To represent a stone on the Go board, you can use a structure containing two variables, row and column:

```
struct Go {
    var row = 0        //---0...18---
    var column = 0     //---0...18---
}
```

For structure names, the recommendation is to use UpperCamelCase (such as CustomerAddress, EmployeeCredential, and so on).

The Go structure has two properties called row and column, which are both initialized to 0 (their default values). To create an instance of the Go structure, use the structure's default initializer syntax:

```
var stone1 = Go()
```

The preceding creates an instance of the Go structure, and the instance name is stone1. The properties row and column are both initialized to 0 by default:

```
print(stone1.row)        //---0---
print(stone1.column)     //---0---
```

You access the properties using the dot (.) syntax. Just as you can access the value of the property, you can also change its value:

```
stone1.row = 12          //---change the row to 12---
stone1.column = 16       //---change the column to 16---
```

Memberwise initializers

If the structure has a property that does not have a default value, you can't use the default initializer syntax. In other words, if you don't initialize the value of row or column to some default value, the following statements will fail:

```
struct Go {
    var row:Int          //---no default value---
    var column:Int       //---no default value---
}
var stone1 = Go()        //---error---
```

To rectify this situation, you can use the *memberwise initializer* (which is automatically generated for you when you define a structure) to initialize the properties of a structure with certain values when it's created:

```
var stone1 = Go(row:12, column:16)
```

In the preceding example, when you create an instance of the Go structure, you also set the value for row and column.

Continuing with the Go example, a stone placed on the Go board is either black or white.

Therefore, you can now define a new enumeration called StoneColor and add a color property to the Go structure:

```
enum StoneColor:String {
    case Black = "B"
    case White = "W"
}

struct Go {
    var row:Int              //---0...18---
    var column:Int           //---0...18---
    var color:StoneColor
}
```

The color property is an enumeration of type StoneColor. To create an instance of the Go structure, use the memberwise initializer:

```
var stone1 = Go(row:12, column:16, color:StoneColor.Black)
```

Structures as value types

A structure is a value type. In other words, when you assign a variable/constant of a value type to another variable/constant, its value is copied over to a completely new variable/constant. Consider the following example:

```
var stone1 = Go(row:12, column:16, color:StoneColor.Black)
var stone2 = stone1

print("---Stone1---")
print(stone1.row)
print(stone1.column)
print(stone1.color.rawValue)
```

```
print("---Stone2---")
print(stone2.row)
print(stone2.column)
print(stone2.color.rawValue)
```

In the preceding code snippet, stone1 is assigned to stone2. Therefore, stone2 will now have the same value as stone1. This is evident by the values that are output by the preceding code snippet:

```
---Stone1---
12
16
B
---Stone2---
12
16
B
```

To prove that the value of stone2 is independent of the value of stone1, modify the value of stone1 as follows:

```
stone1.row = 6
stone1.column = 7
stone1.color = StoneColor.White
```

Then print out the values for both stones again. This time, it will print out the following, proving that the values of the two stones are independent of each other:

```
---Stone1---
6
7
W
---Stone2---
12
16
B
```

TIP

In Swift, the String, Array, and Dictionary types are implemented using structures. As such, when they're assigned to another variable, their values are always copied.

Classes

A class is similar to a structure in many ways. Like a structure, a class defines properties to store values, contains initializers to initialize its properties' values, and so on. However, a class has additional capabilities not found in a structure. For example, you can use inheritance on a class to ensure that the class inherits the characteristics of another class, and you can also use de-initializers to free up resources when an instance of a class is destroyed. In this section, I explain the basics of a class and some of the features that are also applicable to structures.

Defining a class

You define a class using the `class` keyword:

```
class MyPointClass {
}
```

When naming classes, the recommendation is to use UpperCamelCase (such as `MyPointClass`, `EmployeeInfo`, `CustomerDetails`, and so on). To create an instance of a class, you call the class name followed by a pair of parentheses (`()`) and then assign it to a variable or constant:

```
var ptA = MyPointClass()
```

Understanding properties

Like structures, classes have properties. In Swift, there are two types of properties:

>> **Stored property:** A constant or variable that is stored within an instance of a class or a structure. When you declare a variable or constant within a class or structure, that is a stored property.

>> **Computed property:** These calculate values and typically return values. They can also optionally store values for other properties indirectly.

Stored properties

You add stored properties to a class by declaring them just as you would normal variables and constants:

```
class MyPointClass {
    var x = 0.0      // variable
```

```
    var y = 0.0       // variable
    let width = 2     // constant
}
```

In Swift, constants and variables that are stored within a class are known as *stored properties*. Like structures, stored properties can also have default values.

Structures also support stored properties.

Computed properties

Whereas stored properties store actual values, computed properties do not. To understand the usefulness of computed properties, consider the following example:

```
class Distance {
    var miles = 0.0
    var km: Double {
        get {
            return 1.60934 * miles
        }
        set (km) {
            miles = km / 1.60934
        }
    }
}
```

In the preceding code snippet, you have the `Distance` class. The `Distance` class has a stored property named `miles`, which enables you to store the distance in miles. You also have a `km` computed property.

The `km` computed property enables you to retrieve the distance in kilometers:

```
var d = Distance()
d.miles  = 10.0
print(d.km)      //---16.0934---
```

It also enables you to store a distance in kilometers:

```
d.km = 20.0
print(d.miles)  //---12.427454732996136---
```

Notice that, in this case, the actual distance in the class is stored in miles, not kilometers. That way, you only need to store the distance once, and you don't have to worry about having additional stored properties to store the distance in other units.

Using methods in classes

In Swift, you define methods just like you define functions. There are two types of methods in Swift:

>> **Instance methods:** Belong to a particular instance of a class

>> **Type methods:** Belong to the class

An instance method is a function that belongs to a particular instance of a class. The following `Car` class has two instance methods, `accelerate()` and `printSpeed()`:

```swift
class Car {
    var speed = 0

    func accelerate() {
        speed += 10
        if speed > 80 {
            speed = 80
        }
        printSpeed()
    }

    func printSpeed() {
        print("Speed: \(speed)")
    }
}
```

To call the methods, you need to first create an instance of the `Car` class:

```swift
var c = Car()
```

After the instance has been created, you can call the methods using dot notation (`.`):

```swift
c.accelerate()    //----10----
```

Methods are not exclusive to classes. Structures can also have methods.

Trying out the self property

Every instance of a class has an implicit property known as self. The self property refers to the instance of the class (hence, its name). Recall from earlier the property named speed:

```swift
class Car {
    var speed = 0

    func accelerate() {
        speed += 10
        if speed > 80 {
            speed = 80
        }
        printSpeed()
    }
    ...
```

Because speed is declared within the class, you can also rewrite the preceding by prefixing speed with self:

```swift
class Car {
    var speed = 0

    func accelerate() {
        self.speed += 10
        if self.speed > 80 {
            self.speed = 80
        }
        printSpeed()
    }
    ...
```

In most cases, prefixing a property using the self keyword is redundant. However, there are cases when this is actually useful and mandatory. Consider the following example:

```swift
class Car {
    var speed = 0

    func setInitialSpeed(speed: Int) {
        self.speed = speed
    }
    ...
```

In this example, the parameter name for the setInitialSpeed() method is also named speed, which is the same as the property named speed. To differentiate between the two, you use the self keyword to identify the property.

Closures

One important feature in Swift is *closure*. Closures are self-contained blocks of code that can be passed to functions to be executed as independent code units. Think of a closure as a function without a name. In fact, functions are actually special cases of closures.

Swift offers various ways to optimize closures so that they're brief and succinct. The various optimizations include the following:

> » Inferring parameter types and return types
> » Implicit returns from single-statement closures
> » Shorthand argument names
> » Trailing closure syntax
> » Operator closure

Understanding closures

The best way to understand closures is to use an example. Suppose you have the following array of integers:

```
let numbers = [5,2,8,7,9,4,3,1]
```

Assume you want to sort this array in ascending order. You can write your own function to perform the sorting, or you can use the sorted() function available in Swift. The sorted() function takes two arguments:

> » An array to be sorted
> » A closure that takes two arguments of the same type as the array and returns a true if the first value appears before the second value

Using functions as closures

In Swift, functions are special types of closures. As mentioned in the preceding section, the `sorted()` function needs a closure that takes two arguments of the same type as the array, returning a `true` if the first value appears before the second value. The following function fulfils that requirement:

```
func ascending(num1:Int, num2:Int) -> Bool {
    return num1<num2
}
```

The `ascending()` function takes two arguments of type `Int` and returns a `Bool` value. If `num1` is less than `num2`, it returns `true`. You can now pass this function to the `sorted()` function, as shown here:

```
var sortedNumbers = numbers.sorted(by: ascending)
```

The `sorted()` function now returns the array that is sorted in ascending order.

TIP

The `sorted()` function does not modify the original array. It returns the sorted array as a new array.

Assigning closures to variables

As mentioned earlier, functions are special types of closures. In fact, a closure is a function without a name. However, you can assign a closure to a variable — for example, the `ascending()` function discussed earlier can be written as a closure assigned to a variable:

```
var compareClosure : (Int, Int)->Bool =
    {
        (num1:Int, num2:Int) -> Bool in
            return num1 < num2
    }
```

To use the `compareClosure` closure with the `sorted()` function, pass in the `compareClosure` variable:

```
sortedNumbers = numbers.sorted(by: compareClosure)
```

Writing closures inline

Earlier, I show you how to pass a function into the `sorted()` function as a closure function, but a better way is to write the closure inline, which obviates the need to define a function explicitly or assign it to a variable.

Rewriting the earlier example would yield the following:

```
sortedNumbers = numbers.sorted(by:
    {
        (num1:Int, num2:Int) -> Bool in
            return num1 < num2
    }
)
```

As you can see, the `ascending()` function name is now gone; all you've supplied is the parameter list and the content of the function.

If you want to sort the array in descending order, you can simply change the comparison operator:

```
sortedNumbers = numbers.sorted(by:
    {
        (num1:Int, num2:Int) -> Bool in
            return num1 > num2
    }
)
```

Understanding type inference

Because the type of the first argument of the closure function must be the same as the type of array you're sorting, it's actually redundant to specify the type in the closure, because the compiler can infer that from the type of array you're using:

```
var fruits = ["orange", "apple", "durian",
              "rambutan", "pineapple"]
print(fruits.sorted(by:
    {
        (fruit1, fruit2) in
            return fruit1<fruit2
    })
)
```

If your closure has only a single statement, you can even omit the return keyword:

```
print(fruits.sorted(by:
    {
        (fruit1, fruit2) in
            fruit1<fruit2
    })
)
```

Using shorthand argument names

In the previous section, names were given to arguments within a closure. In fact, this is also optional, because Swift automatically provides shorthand names to the parameters, which you can refer to as $0, $1, and so on.

The previous code snippet can be rewritten as follows without using named parameters:

```
print(fruits.sorted(by:
    {
        $0<$1
    })
)
```

To make the closure really terse, you can write everything on one line:

```
print(fruits.sorted(by:{ $0<$1 }))
```

Working with the operator function

In the previous section you saw that the closure for the sorted() function was reduced to the following:

```
print(fruits.sorted(by:{ $0<$1 }))
```

One of the implementations of the lesser than (<) operator is actually a function that works with two operands of type String. Because of this, you can actually simply specify the < operator in place of the closure, and the compiler will automatically infer that you want to use the particular implementation of the < operator. The preceding statement can be reduced to the following:

```
print(fruits.sorted(by:<))
```

If you want to sort the array in descending order, simply use the greater than (>) operator:

```
print(fruits.sorted(by:>))
```

Using trailing closures

Consider the closure that you saw earlier:

```
print(fruits.sorted(by:
    {
        (fruit1, fruit2) in
            return fruit1<fruit2
    })
)
```

Notice that the closure is passed in as a second argument of the sorted() function. For long closures, this syntax may be a little messy. If the closure is the final argument of a function, you can rewrite this closure as a trailing closure. A trailing closure is written outside of the parentheses of the function call. The preceding code snippet, when rewritten using the trailing closure, looks like this:

```
print(fruits.sorted()
    {
        (fruit1, fruit2) in
            return fruit1<fruit2
    }
)
```

Using the shorthand argument name, the closure can be shortened to the following:

```
print(fruits.sorted(){$0<$1})
```

Protocols

A *protocol* is a blueprint of methods and properties. It describes what a class (or structure) should have, but it doesn't provide any implementation. A class/structure that *conforms* to a protocol needs to provide the implementation as dictated by the protocol. A protocol can be implemented by a class, a structure, or an enumeration.

TIP

A protocol is similar to what an interface is in Java.

Defining and using a protocol

To define a protocol, use the `protocol` keyword, followed by the name of the protocol:

```
protocol ProtocolName {
    func method1()
    func method2()
}
```

TIP

Methods in a protocol follow the same syntax as normal methods in a class, with one exception: You aren't allowed to specify default values for method parameters.

Here's an example of a protocol:

```
protocol CarProtocol {
    func accelerate()
}
```

The preceding code snippet declares a protocol named `CarProtocol` containing one method: `accelerate()`. A class that wants to implement a car that can accelerate must conform to this protocol.

Conforming to a protocol

To conform to a protocol, specify the protocol name(s) after the class name, as shown here:

```
class ClassName: ProtocolName1, ProtocolName2 {
    ...
}
```

If you're conforming to more than one protocol, separate them using a comma (,). If your class is also extending from another class, specify the protocol name(s) after the class it's extending:

```
class ClassName: BaseClass,
                 ProtocolName1,
                 ProtocolName2  {
    ...
}
```

The following code snippet shows an example of how to conform to a protocol:

```
class Car: CarProtocol {
    ...
]
```

In the preceding code snippet, the Car class is said to "conform to the CarProtocol." Any class that conforms to the CarProtocol must implement the method(s) declared in it.

To conform to the CarProtocol, the Car class might look like this:

```
class Car: CarProtocol {
    var speed = 0

    func accelerate() {
        speed += 10
        if speed > 50 {
            speed = 50
        }
        printSpeed()
    }

    func printSpeed() {
        print("Speed: \(speed)")
    }
}
```

Note that in addition to implementing the accelerate() method that is declared in CarProtocol, the Car class is free to implement other methods as required — in this case, it also implements the printSpeed() method. If any of the method(s) declared in CarProtocol are not implemented in the Car class, the compiler will flag an error.

Using the Codable protocol

In Swift, Codable is a type alias for both the Encodable and Decodable protocols. Suppose you have a struct named Name:

```
struct Name {
    var firstName: String
    var lastName: String
}
```

You can create an instance of the struct like this:

```
var myName = Name(firstName: "Wei-Meng", lastName: "Lee")
```

Suppose you want to encode this struct as a JSON string. To do that, you just need to make the Name struct conform to the Encodable protocol, like this:

```
struct Name: Encodable {
    var firstName: String
    var lastName: String
}
```

To encode the Name struct using JSON, use the JSONEncoder class's encode() function, like this:

```
if let result = try? JSONEncoder().encode(myName) {
    if let jsonString = String(data: result,
        encoding: .utf8) {
        print(jsonString)
    }
}
```

The result is of type Data (byte buffer). To see the JSON as a string, use the String class to convert that into a string. The output will look like this:

```
{"firstName":"Wei-Meng","lastName":"Lee"}
```

To convert the JSON string back into the Name struct, you need to make the Name struct conform to the Decodable protocol:

```
struct Name: Encodable, Decodable {
    var firstName: String
    var lastName: String
}
```

You can now then use the JSONDecoder class's decode() function to decode the JSON string back into the Name struct:

```
if let result = try? JSONEncoder().encode(myName) {
    if let jsonString = String(data: result, encoding: .utf8) {
        print(jsonString)
    }
    if let name = try? JSONDecoder().decode(Name.self,
  from:result){
```

```
        print(name.firstName)
        print(name.lastName)
    }
]
```

The preceding code snippet will produce the following output:

```
Wei-Meng
Lee
```

Using the some keyword

In Chapter 1, I show you how a simple SwiftUI view is created. In particular, I illustrate how the ContentView conforms to the View protocol:

```
struct ContentView: View {
    var body: some View {
        Text("Hello, World!")
    }
}
```

The View protocol requires a body computed property of type some View. So, what is that some keyword?

The some keyword was introduced in Swift 5.1 and is used to define an *opaque type*. An opaque type describes a value in terms of the protocols it supports. Without going into the technical details behind opaque types, you can interpret the following line:

```
var body: some View
```

as "The return type of body must be one of the types that implements the View protocol." Specifically, the body property must return a valid concrete type at compile time.

Let's take a look at an example. The following code snippets return the Image view (this is valid because Image conforms to the View protocol):

```
    var body: some View {
        Image(systemName: "gear")
    }
```

Besides the `Image` view, you can also return a `VStack` view (which is also valid as `VStack` conforms to the `View` protocol):

```
var body: some View {
    VStack {
        Text("Gear Icon")
        Image(systemName: "gear")
    }
}
```

You can even do something like this:

```
var body: some View {
    if x == 1 {
        return Text("Hello, World!")
    } else {
        return Text("Hello, SwiftUI")
    }
}
```

The preceding code snippet is also valid regardless of the outcome of the if statement; you return the `Text` view in either case.

However, the following is invalid:

```
var body: some View {
    if x == 1 {
        return Text("Hello, World!")
    } else {
        return Image(systemName: "gear")
    }
}
```

The preceding code snippet will give the following error message: `Function declares an opaque return type, but the return statements in its body do not have matching underlying types`. This is because, at compile time, the opaque return type cannot be determined. Is the body going to be a `Text` or `Image` view?

Opaque type is an advanced topic in Swift programming, but a basic understanding of the `some` keyword used in SwiftUI programming would be useful.

2

Understanding the Basics of SwiftUI

IN THIS CHAPTER

» **Understanding how SwiftUI views work**

» **Showing an image**

» **Showing a button**

» **Stacking views using** VStack **and** HStack

» **Tying up loose ends**

Chapter **3**

Getting Started with the Basics of SwiftUI

S wiftUI is Apple's latest development framework for creating an application's user interface (UI). It helps you to declaratively create the UI for your iOS applications.

In this chapter, I explain how SwiftUI views work. Then I explain the basic structure of a SwiftUI view through the use of the Text view and the Button view. I show you how to lay out your views using two of the common stacking views, VStack and HStack. Finally, I help you put the finishing touches on the example in this chapter.

Taking a Look at SwiftUI Views

To understand the basics of SwiftUI views, you can use the project you created in Chapter 1. If you haven't created that project yet, using Xcode, create a new Single View App project and name it Hello World.

The `ContentView.swift` file contains the following statements:

```swift
import SwiftUI

struct ContentView: View {
    var body: some View {
        Text("Hello World")
    }
}

struct ContentView_Previews: PreviewProvider {
    static var previews: some View {
        ContentView()
    }
}
```

Now you're ready to dive into the statements in more detail.

Conforming to the View protocol

The `ContentView` struct defines the UI of your screen, and it conforms to the `View` protocol. Because it conforms to the `View` protocol, it must declare a property called `body` of type `View`. This `body` property needs to return a single instance of `View`, which in this case is the `Text` view. The `Text` view is a graphical view that displays one or more lines of read-only text.

TIP

Note that the `body` property implicitly returns the `Text` view without needing to use the `return` keyword. This is one of the new features in Swift 5.1, where single-line function (such as `body`, in this case) can omit the `return` keyword.

Let's now make some changes to the `Text` view:

```swift
struct ContentView: View {
    var body: some View {
        Text("Hello, SwiftUI!")
    }
}
```

Figure 3-1 shows the preview automatically updated to reflect the changes in the `Text` view.

FIGURE 3-1:
The Live Preview dynamically shows the changes made to your ContentView.

Hello, SwiftUI!

The next struct, `ContentView_Previews`, conforms to the `PreviewProvider` protocol. This protocol produces view previews in Xcode so that you can preview your UI created in SwiftUI without needing to run the application on the iPhone Simulator or real devices. Essentially, it controls what you see on the preview canvas. As an example, if you want to preview how your UI will look on an iPhone 8 device, you can modify the `ContentView_Previews` struct as follows:

```
struct ContentView_Previews: PreviewProvider {
    static var previews: some View {
        ContentView().previewDevice("iPhone 8")
    }
}
```

The preview canvas on the right of Xcode will now display your UI on an iPhone 8. I talk more about the `ContentView_Previews` struct in Chapters 5 and 13.

Using modifiers

Now that you've changed the content of the Text view, let's make some cosmetic changes to it:

```
struct ContentView: View {
    var body: some View {
        Text("Hello, SwiftUI!").font(.largeTitle)
    }
}
```

In the preceding statement, you called a function named font(_:). This function is called a *modifier*. A modifier is a function that you apply to a view or the output of another modifier. largeTitle is a property belonging to the Font class; it can be shortened as .largeTitle.

In this example, you chained the Text view to call the font(_:) function. The preceding can also be rewritten as follows:

```
var body: some View {
    let t = Text("Hello, SwiftUI!")
    return (t.font(.largeTitle))
}
```

Notice that this isn't as elegant as the previous statement, where you used chaining to call a modifier after the Text view.

As a convention, you usually put the modifier on a separate line:

```
struct ContentView: View {
    var body: some View {
        Text("Hello, SwiftUI!")
            .font(.largeTitle)
    }
}
```

Stacking modifiers

Every modifier returns a new View instance, so you can chain them. The following example shows how various modifiers can be chained together:

```
Text("Hello, SwiftUI!")
    .font(.largeTitle)
    .bold()
    .foregroundColor(.red)
```

TIP

Besides the modifiers that come with each view, you can also create your own custom modifiers. Chapter 13 discusses this subject in more detail.

Figure 3-2 shows how the Text view looks now.

FIGURE 3-2:
The Text view after applying the chains of modifiers.

Hello, SwiftUI!

Using the Inspector

You can visually inspect each of the views in the preview canvas by ⌘-clicking any of the views. A pop-up appears, as shown in Figure 3-3.

Selecting Show SwiftUI Inspector reveals — drumroll, please — the SwiftUI Inspector (see Figure 3-4).

For example, under the Weight property (in the Font section), you can choose Thin (see Figure 3-5).

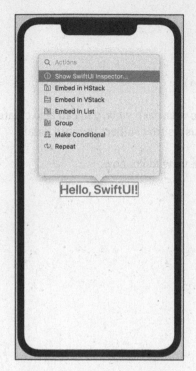

FIGURE 3-3:
Showing the
SwiftUI Inspector.

FIGURE 3-4:
The SwiftUI
Inspector allows
you to customize
the various
properties of the
view.

Using the In...

You can use the inspector to ...
of the view. A few things to note:

» Ctrl-click the Text control ... pop-up pane — the SwiftUI
Inspector (see Figure 3-4).

» For example, under the Weight property in the Font section, you can change
it (see Figure ...).

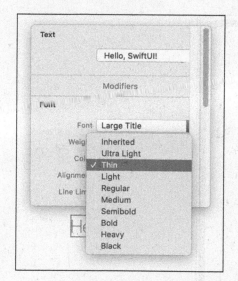

FIGURE 3-5:
Changing the font
weight of the
Text view in the
SwiftUI Inspector.

Xcode automatically modifies your code:

```
Text("Hello, SwiftUI!")
.font(.largeTitle)
.fontWeight(.thin)
.bold()
.foregroundColor(.red)
```

Besides modifying the properties of the view, you can also add modifiers to views visually (see Figure 3-6; be sure to scroll to the bottom of the Inspector).

For example, you can select the modifier named Border, which adds the statements (with the placeholders for the various parameters) shown in Figure 3-7.

You can now double-click the placeholders on the statement and replace them with the values you want. In this example, the border() modifier displays a border around the text (see Figure 3-8).

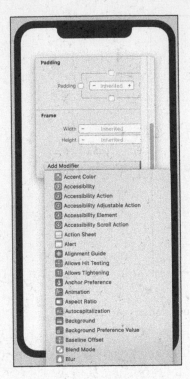

FIGURE 3-6:
You can also add
modifiers to a
view through the
SwiftUI Inspector.

FIGURE 3-7:
Calling the
border()
modifier on the
Text view.

```
struct ContentView: View {
    var body: some View {
        Text("Hello, SwiftUI!")
        .font(.largeTitle)
            .fontWeight(.thin)
            .bold()
            .foregroundColor(.red)
            .border(Color.black, width: 1)|
```

FIGURE 3-8:
Displaying a
border on the
Text view.

Hello, SwiftUI!

Displaying an Image

To display an image in your `ContentView`, you need to use the `Image` view. But before you can do *that*, you need to have an image in your application. The easiest way to add an image to your application is to drag-and-drop one onto the `Assets.xcassets` file (see Figure 3-9). In the example, the image was named `weimenglee`.

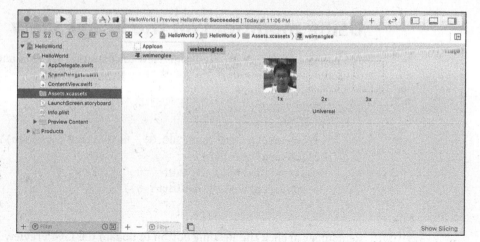

FIGURE 3-9:
Adding an image to the Assets. xcassets file in your Xcode project.

To display the image, use the `Image` view and specify the name of the image located in your `Assets.xcassets` file:

```
var body: some View {
    Image("weimenglee")
}
```

Figure 3-10 shows the image displayed.

FIGURE 3-10:
The `Image` view displaying the image that you've just added to your project.

Using modifiers on the Image view

You can use modifiers on the Image view to customize its look and feel. Consider the following statements:

```
var body: some View {
    Image("weimenglee")
    .frame(width: CGFloat(300.0), height:CGFloat(300))
    .clipShape(Circle())
    .overlay(Circle().stroke(
        Color.black, lineWidth: 5))
}
```

Remember to click the Resume button to update the Live Preview.

REMEMBER

The output is shown in Figure 3-11. Here's what the preceding statements have achieved:

>> Setting a fixed frame of dimension 300 x 300 points

>> Setting a clipping shape for the image, which in this case is a circle

>> Layering a secondary view in front of the image, which draws an outline for the circle with line width of 5 points

If the image is smaller than the dimension of the frame, it's aligned by default to the *center* of the frame. The following makes this clear:

```
Image("weimenglee")
    .frame(width: CGFloat(300), height: CGFloat(300),
        alignment: .center)
    .clipShape(Circle())
    .overlay(Circle().stroke(Color.black, lineWidth: 5))
```

You can set the alignment to something else, like to the bottom right:

```
.frame(width: CGFloat(300), height: CGFloat(300),
    alignment: .bottomTrailing)
```

The image will now appear aligned to the bottom-right corner of the frame, as shown in Figure 3-12.

FIGURE 3-11:
The Image view
displayed with a
circle.

FIGURE 3-12:
Aligning the
image to the
bottom-right
corner of the
frame.

Resizing images

What about stretching the image to fill the frame? In SwiftUI, an image is always fixed in size unless you call the `resizable()` modifier on it, as the following example illustrates:

```
Image("weimenglee")
    .resizable()
```

```
    .frame(width: CGFloat(300), height: CGFloat(300))
    .clipShape(Circle())
    .overlay(Circle().stroke(Color.black, lineWidth: 5))
```

With the `resizable()` modifier, the image will now resize itself to fit the dimension specified by the `frame()` modifier (see Figure 3-13).

A WORD ABOUT THE iOS COORDINATE SYSTEM

In the early days of iPhone development, life was much easier. Back then, there was only one iPhone to support (and, hence, one screen resolution), and everything related to views positioning on the iPhone could be specified in *pixels*.

Today your app needs to run seamlessly on all different devices, so specifying the positions of views in pixels no longer works. In place of pixels, you use *points*. On the original iPhone, 1 point was equivalent to 1 pixel, while on the latest iPhone 11, 1 point is equivalent to 2 pixels. The good news is, as a developer, you don't have to worry about the final pixels your views will take up. You just need to specify everything in points, and iOS automatically manages it for you.

The following table lists all the different iPhone models to date, their screen resolutions, and the corresponding number of pixels per point.

iPhone Model	Screen Resolution (in Pixels)	Pixels per Point
iPhone 3 and older	320 x 480	1
iPhone 4 and 4S	640 x 960	2
iPhone 5, 5S, 5C, and SE	640 x 1,136	2
iPhone 6, 6S, 7, and 8	750 x 1,334	2
iPhone 6 Plus, 6S Plus, 7 Plus, 8 Plus	1,242 x 2,208	3
iPhone X, XS, and 11 Pro	1,125 x 2,436	3
iPhone XR and 11	828 x 1,792	2
iPhone XS Max, 11 Pro Max	1,242 x 2,688	3

FIGURE 3-13:
The image inside the Image view resizing itself to fit the frame.

Displaying a Button

In iOS, buttons look similar to the Text view, except that users can tap them to perform some actions. In SwiftUI, creating a button usually starts with a Text view. You then wrap it with a Button view, like this:

```
Button(action: {
    // the action to perform here
}) {
    Text("This is a button")
}
```

Notice that the Button view has a parameter named action, which uses a closure for its action. You can see how to add some actions to the Button view shortly.

Customizing the button

Like the `Text` view, the `Button` view is customizable. Let's chain some modifiers to the `Text` view located within the `Button` view to make the button look more presentable:

```
Button(action: {

}) {
    Text("This is a button")
    .fontWeight(.bold)
    .font(.title)
    .padding()
    .background(Color.blue)
    .foregroundColor(.white)
    .cornerRadius(CGFloat(10), antialiased: true)
    .padding(10)
    .overlay(
        RoundedRectangle(cornerRadius: 20)
            .stroke(Color.blue, lineWidth: 1)
    )
}
```

Figure 3-14 shows the final look of your customized button.

Remember to click the Resume button.

REMEMBER The preceding statements added the following to the `Text` view:

>> Making the text in the button bold

>> Changing the font using title text style

>> Adding a padding around the text

>> Setting the background color of the text to blue

>> Setting the text color to white

>> Rounding the corner of the rectangle enclosing the text

>> Adding another padding around the rectangle surrounding the text

>> Overlaying a secondary view with a `RoundedRectangle` view with a blue colored stroke of width 1 point

This is a button

FIGURE 3-14:
The customized
version of the
button.

Adding actions

Apparently, the real use of a `Button` view is to perform an action. So, let's now add some action to the button that we've been building:

```swift
Button(action: {
    if let url = URL(string: "https://www.apple.com") {
        UIApplication.shared.open(url)
    }
}) {
    Text("This is a button")
    .fontWeight(.bold)
    .font(.title)
    .padding()
    .background(Color.blue)
    .foregroundColor(.white)
    .cornerRadius(CGFloat(10), antialiased: true)
    .padding(10)
    .overlay(
        RoundedRectangle(cornerRadius: 20)
            .stroke(Color.blue, lineWidth: 1)
    )
}
```

In the preceding, when the action is tapped, you used the open() method from the UIApplication.shared instance to launch a web browser to display Apple's website.

Stacking the Views

In real-life applications, you rarely have a UI with just one view. You're most likely going to have a combination of multiple different types of views, so you need a way to group them together. Plus, the body property of the ContentView must return a single View object, and this is where *stacks* come to the rescue.

In SwiftUI, there are three main types of stacks available to group your UI:

>> HStack: A horizontal stack

>> VStack: A vertical stack

>> ZStack: A depth-based stack

TIP

In this section, you see how the first two types of stacks work. I explain more about the ZStack in Chapter 7, where I cover layouts in more detail.

Suppose you want to build a screen to display a business card. Typically, a business card contains a number of lines of text, with an optional image. In SwiftUI, you can do all this with the following views:

```
Text("Wei-Meng Lee")
Text("Founder")
Text("http://calendar.learn2develop.net")
Text("weimenglee@learn2develop.net")
Text("@weimenglee")
Image("weimenglee")
```

Logically, you might add them to the body property like this:

```
import SwiftUI

struct ContentView: View {
    var body: some View {
        Text("Wei-Meng Lee")
        Text("Founder")
        Text("http://calendar.learn2develop.net")
```

```
            Text("weimenglee@learn2develop.net")
            Text("@weimenglee")
            Image("weimenglee")
        }
    }
```

But remember that the body property needs to return a single view. The preceding code will violate this rule and, hence, result in a syntax error.

VStack

One possible way to group this group of views is to use the VStack view. The VStack view arranges its children views in a vertical line:

```
import SwiftUI

struct ContentView: View {
    var body: some View {
        VStack {
            Text("Wei-Meng Lee")
            Text("Founder")
            Text("http://calendar.learn2develop.net")
            Text("weimenglee@learn2develop.net")
            Text("@weimenglee")
            Image("weimenglee")
        }
    }
}
```

Figure 3-15 shows the views lined up vertically.

The rectangle shown wrapping around the views is not part of the final UI. It is generated in the preview canvas and is shown when you click the VStack view in Xcode. This is a useful feature because it allows you to see the placement of the view with respect to the entire screen.

By default, all the views wrapped within the VStack view are aligned in the center. You can change this default alignment using the alignment parameter. For example, if you want to align the views to the left, you can use the leading property:

```
VStack (alignment: .leading) {
    Text("Wei-Meng Lee")
    Text("Founder")
```

```
        Text("http://calendar.learn2develop.net")
        Text("weimenglee@learn2develop.net")
        Text("@weimenglee")
        Image("weimenglee")
}
```

FIGURE 3-15:
Using the VStack
view to contain a
series of views.

Figure 3-16 shows that the views are all now aligned to the left. You can also use
the following values for the `alignment` parameter:

>> center (default)

>> trailing

HStack

Besides the VStack view, you can also use the HStack view, which aligns views
horizontally. What's more, you can nest the VStack and HStack views together to
create more complex arrangements.

Wei-Meng Lee
Founder
http://calendar.learn2develop.net
weimenglee@learn2develop.net
@weimenglee

FIGURE 3-16:
Aligning the views
contained within
the VStack view
to the left.

Figure 3-17 shows one particular arrangement you can use to create your business card with the HStack and VStack views. It shows that the VStack view is nested within an HStack view. The VStack view itself contains the series of Text views, while the HStack view contains the Image view and the VStack view.

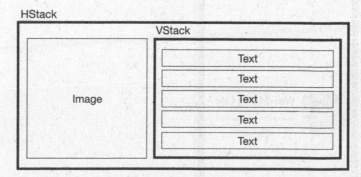

FIGURE 3-17:
Nesting the
various views.

The following statements implement the layout that you've just seen:

```
struct ContentView: View {
    var body: some View {
```

```
HStack {
    Image("weimenglee")
        .resizable()
        .frame(width: CGFloat(120),
               height: CGFloat(120))
        .cornerRadius(CGFloat(15),
            antialiased: true)
    VStack {
        Text("Wei-Meng Lee")
            .font(.largeTitle)
            .bold()
        Text("Founder")
        Text("Developer Learning Solutions")
            .italic()
        Text("http://calendar.learn2develop.net")
        Text("@weimenglee")
    }
}
}
}
```

Figure 3-18 shows how the layout looks now.

FIGURE 3-18:
The HStack view
nesting the
various other
views.

The rectangle surrounding the various views is only a guide shown during the preview. Like the VStack view, the HStack view supports the alignment parameter and can assume the following values:

» bottom

» center

» firstTextBaseline

» lastTextBaseline

» top

The alignment parameter specifies how views *within* the HStack view should be aligned. What if you want the entire HStack to be aligned to, say, the top of the screen? To do so, you can't rely on the alignment parameter in the HStack view; instead, you need to call the frame() modifier on the HStack view and set its alignment as follows:

```
struct ContentView: View {
    var body: some View {
        HStack {
            Image("weimenglee")
                .resizable()
                .frame(width: CGFloat(120),
                       height: CGFloat(120))
                .cornerRadius(CGFloat(15),
                    antialiased: true)
            VStack {
                Text("Wei-Meng Lee")
                    .font(.largeTitle)
                    .bold()
                Text("Founder")
                Text("Developer Learning Solutions")
                    .italic()
                Text("http://calendar.learn2develop.net")
                Text("@weimenglee")
            }
        }.frame(maxWidth: .infinity,
                maxHeight: .infinity,
                alignment: .top)
    }
}
```

The HStack is now aligned to the top of the screen (see Figure 3-19).

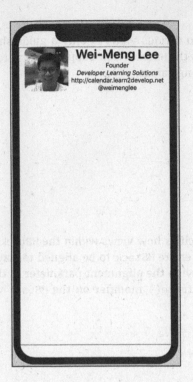

FIGURE 3-19:
Aligning the
entire HStack to
the top of the
screen.

The `alignment` parameter of the `frame()` modifier can assume one of the following values:

- `bottom`
- `bottomLeading`
- `bottomTrailing`
- `center`
- `leading`
- `top`
- `topLeading`
- `topTrailing`

TIP

Embedding a view with `HStack` or `VStack` can also be done visually. In the preview canvas, ⌘-click the specific view and choose either Embed in HStack or Embed in VStack (see Figure 3-20).

FIGURE 3-20:
You can also
visually embed
views in the
HStack or
VStack views.

Putting on the Finishing Touches

To complete this example, you'll make the URL and the Twitter handle of the business card tappable. In other words, tapping the URL or the Twitter handle will launch the web browser on the iOS device and load the appropriate web page. To do so, you just need to wrap the URL and Twitter handle using the Button view:

```swift
struct ContentView: View {
    var body: some View {
        HStack {
            Image("weimenglee").resizable()
                .frame(width: CGFloat(120),
                       height: CGFloat(120))
                .cornerRadius(CGFloat(15),
                              antialiased: true)
            VStack {
                Text("Wei-Meng Lee")
                    .font(.largeTitle)
                    .bold()
                Text("Founder")
                Text("Developer Learning Solutions")
                    .italic()
                Button(action: {
                  if let url = URL(string:
                     "http://calendar.learn2develop.net") {
                        UIApplication.shared.open(url)
```

```
            }
        }) {
            Text("http://calendar.learn2develop.net")
        }
        Button(action: {
            if let url = URL(string:
                "https://twitter.com/weimenglee") {
                    UIApplication.shared.open(url)
                }
        }) {
            Text("@weimenglee")
        }
    }
}.frame(maxWidth: .infinity,
        maxHeight: .infinity,
        alignment: .center)
    }
}
```

To test the buttons, run the application on the iPhone Simulator. Press ⌘+R in Xcode to run the application. Figure 3-21 shows how the application looks (left), the Safari web browser displaying the URL (center), and the Twitter page (right).

FIGURE 3-21:
The final name card with tappable buttons.

Chapter 4

Handling User Inputs and Custom Views

I n this chapter, I introduce you to input views in SwiftUI, which allow you to collect inputs from users. I also explain how you can create your own custom views by grouping all the views available and applying your own layout, so you can reuse them.

Looking at Input Views

Unless you're writing a Hello World application, your app will involve some sort of user inputs. For example, if you're writing a conference app, you need the user to select a particular conference from a list of available conferences. If your app requires the user to log in to a secure service, you need the user to enter her credentials (username and password).

In this section, I walk you through some of the input views in SwiftUI.

TIP
To try out the various input views in the following sections, you can create a Single View App project and type the code snippets into the ContentView. swift file.

TextField

When you need users to enter some text or numbers, you can use the TextField view, which displays an editable text interface. The following code snippet shows a screen containing two TextField views and one Text view, embedded within a VStack view:

```
import SwiftUI

struct ContentView: View {
    @State private var firstName: String = ""
    @State private var lastName: String = ""

    var body: some View {
        VStack {
            TextField("First Name",
                text: $firstName).border(Color.black)
            TextField("Last Name",
                text: $lastName).border(Color.black)
            Text("Your UserID: \(firstName + lastName)")
        }
        .padding()
        .font(.title)
    }
}
```

The first argument to the TextField view is the placeholder text. This provides some hints to the user as to the type of input expected.

Notice that you have two private state variables: firstName and lastName. Each of these two state variables is bound to the TextField object through the text parameter. This is evident from the $firstName and $lastName located within the TextField views. Essentially, you're binding the value of the state variable to the view. As the user types into the TextField view, the value of the state variable is also updated. Conversely, if a state variable is updated, the TextField view that is bound to it will also be updated.

TIP

The $ prefixing the state variable is used to bind the state variable to the view.

To run the code in Xcode, click the Live Preview button (the top button of the two buttons displayed next to the preview). The button turns blue.

As the user types into the two `TextField` views, the two state variables are dynamically updated, and this causes the `Text` object to display whatever the user has typed in. Figure 4-1 shows what the `TextField` and `Text` views look like.

FIGURE 4-1:
The TextField
and Text views
on the screen.

Notice that the `TextField` view has no border by default, which means that when it's loaded, it'll be a bit difficult for the user to locate the view. For this reason, it's always useful to add a border to the `TextField` view.

Figure 4-2 shows the `Text` view displaying the concatenation of the first name and last name that the user typed in.

FIGURE 4-2:
The content of
the Text view is
updated as the
user types in the
two TextField
views.

What if you need to modify the text entered by the user before displaying it in the Text view? For example, on a typical signup page, a user may be asked to enter his name before the system suggests a username based on the name he has entered. In such cases, you can feed the names entered by the user to a function so that it can return a suggested username. The following function named removeSpecialCharsFromString() strips away all the special characters in a string and only returns all the alphanumeric characters in the string. It also converts all the characters to lowercase:

```swift
import SwiftUI

struct ContentView: View {
    @State var firstName: String = ""
    @State var lastName: String = ""

    func removeSpecialCharsFromString(text:String) ->
    String {
        return text.components(separatedBy:
            CharacterSet.alphanumerics.inverted)
            .joined()
            .lowercased()
    }

    var body: some View {
        VStack {
            TextField("First Name",
                text: $firstName).border(Color.black)
            TextField("Last Name",
                text: $lastName).border(Color.black)
            Text(
             "Your UserID: \(removeSpecialCharsFromString(
             text: (firstName + lastName)))")
        }
        .padding()
        .font(.title)
    }
}
```

Figure 4-3 shows the suggested username based on what I've typed for my name.

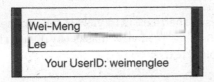

FIGURE 4-3:
The username
created by
removing special
characters from
the first and last
names entered
by the user.

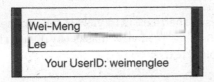

Wei-Meng

Lee

Your UserID: weimenglee

You can also apply styling to the `TextField` views. For example, if you want the `TextField` views to have rounded corners, you can use the `textFieldStyle()` modifier like the following:

```
var body: some View {
    VStack {
        TextField("First Name",
            text: $firstName)
            .textFieldStyle(
                RoundedBorderTextFieldStyle())
        TextField("Last Name",
            text: $lastName)
            .textFieldStyle(
                RoundedBorderTextFieldStyle())
        Text(
          "Your UserID: \(removeSpecialCharsFromString(
          text: (firstName + lastName)))")
    }
    .padding()
    .font(.title)
}
```

Figure 4-4 shows the `TextField` views with rounded corners.

FIGURE 4-4:
The `TextField`
views with
rounded corners.

First Name

Last Name

Your UserID:

SecureField

Almost identical in features to the TextField view is the SecureField view. The only difference is that the SecureField view masks out the user's entry and displays asterisks instead of plain text.

The following code snippet shows how the SecureField view is used:

```
struct ContentView: View {
    @State var username: String = ""
    @State var password: String = ""

    private var enableButton: Bool {
        !username.isEmpty && !password.isEmpty
    }

    var body: some View {
        Group {
            HStack {
                Text("Username").font(.title)
                TextField("Username",
                    text: $username).border(Color.black)
            }
            HStack {
                Text("Password").font(.title)
                SecureField("Password",
                    text: $password).border(Color.black)
            }
            Button("Login") {
                print("Logging in using \(self.username) and \
(self.password)")
            }.disabled(!enableButton)
        }.padding()
        .font(.title)
    }
}
```

Like the TextField view, the SecureField view is bound to a state variable, password. An interesting feature of the preceding code snippet is that the Button view is only enabled when both the username and password state variables are nonempty. As soon as the user types something into both the TextField and SecureField views, the Button view is enabled. Figure 4-5 shows that the Login Button view is disabled when the screen is first loaded.

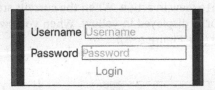

Figure 4-6 shows the Login `Button` view enabled when the user types in both the username and the password. The password entered is masked with the `Secure-Field` view.

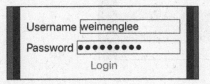

Toggle

To allow users to turn on or off a feature, you can use the `Toggle` view. The `Toggle` view lets users *toggle* (switch) between a true or false state. The following code snippet shows the `Toggle` view in action:

```
struct ContentView: View {
    @State private var showFavorites = true

    var body: some View {
        VStack {
            Toggle(isOn: $showFavorites) {
                Text("Show Favorites").bold()
                }.padding()
                .background(showFavorites ?
                    Color.yellow : Color.gray)
        }
    }
}
```

Like the `TextField` view, the `Toggle` view is bound to a state variable — showFavorites through the isOn parameter. The `Toggle` view comes with a label, which you can supply using a `Text` view. In the preceding code snippet, the background of the `Toggle` view changes depending on the value of its state.

Figure 4-7 shows the `Toggle` view in action. When the current state of the view is `true`, the background color is displayed in yellow. When you switch it to `false`, the background turns gray (see Figure 4-8).

FIGURE 4-7:
The `Toggle` view
with the
background color
of yellow when
it's enabled.

FIGURE 4-8:
The `Toggle` view
with the
background color
of gray when it's
disabled.

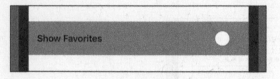

If you want to hide the label, you can use the `labelsHidden()` modifier:

```swift
struct ContentView: View {
    @State private var showFavorites = true
    var body: some View {
        VStack {
            Toggle(isOn: $showFavorites) {
                Text("Show Favorites").bold()
            }.padding()
            .labelsHidden()
        }
    }
}
```

Figure 4-9 shows the `Toggle` view with the label hidden.

FIGURE 4-9:
The `Toggle` view
with the label
hidden.

Slider

If you need the user to select from a bounded linear range of values, the `Slider` view is just the view you need. Using the `Slider` view, you define the minimum and maximum of value that the user can select, and bind it to a state variable.

The following code snippet shows a `Slider` view bound to a state variable, `sliderTemp`:

```swift
struct ContentView: View {
    @State var sliderTemp = 23.0
    var minimumTemp = 20.0
    var maximumTemp = 38.0

    var body: some View {
      VStack {
        HStack {
            Text("\(Int(minimumTemp)) °C")
            Slider(value: $sliderTemp,
                in: minimumTemp...maximumTemp)
            Text("\(Int(maximumTemp)) °C")
        }.padding()
        Text(
          "Temperature Selected: \(Int(sliderTemp)) °C")
      }
    }
}
```

TIP

You don't need to prefix the `sliderTemp` state variable with $ because you're simply reading its value and not binding it to a view.

When the user moves the slider (see Figure 4-10), the value of the `Slider` view is displayed in the `Text` field.

FIGURE 4-10:
As the user moves the `Slider` view, its value is displayed in the `Text` view.

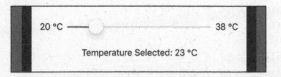

What if you want to implement something like a temperature converter? For example, when you move the slider representing the temperature in degrees Celsius, another slider representing the temperature in degrees Fahrenheit will automatically move its position. Likewise, the user can move the slider representing the temperature in degrees Fahrenheit, and the slider for degrees Celsius will automatically move to represent the temperature in degrees Celsius.

Essentially, you need to bind two state variables to two `Slider` views, and when one state variable changes, it will update the value of another. You can do so through a `Binding` object, which creates a two-way connection between a view and its underlying model.

The following code snippet shows how the `Slider` view is bound to a state variable called `sliderTempC`; whenever the `Slider` is moved, the `sliderTempC` state variable is updated to the new value and at the same time another state variable is also updated, `sliderTempF`.

```
Slider(value:
    Binding(get: {
        self.sliderTempC
    }, set: { (newVal) in
        self.sliderTempC = newVal

        self.sliderTempF =
            self.sliderTempC * 9 / 5 + 32
    }),
    in: minimumTempC...maximumTempC)
```

The following is the full code for the temperature converter:

```
import SwiftUI

struct ContentView: View {
    @State private var sliderTempC = 23.0
    @State private var sliderTempF = 0.0

    var minimumTempC = -17.7778
    var maximumTempC = 50.0

    var minimumTempF = 0.0
    var maximumTempF = 122.0

    init() {
        self._sliderTempF = State(initialValue:
            sliderTempC * 9 / 5 + 32)
    }

    var body: some View {
        VStack {
            Text("Temperature in Degree Celsius").bold()
```

```
        HStack {
            Text("\(String(format: "%.2f",
                minimumTempC)) °C")
            Slider(value:
                Binding(get: {
                    self.sliderTempC
                }, set: { (newVal) in
                    self.sliderTempC = newVal
                    self.sliderTempF =
                        self.sliderTempC * 9 / 5 + 32
                }),
                in: minimumTempC...maximumTempC)
            Text("\(String(format: "%.2f",
                maximumTempC)) °C")
        }.padding()

        Text("\((String(format: "%.2f",
            sliderTempC as Double))) °C").bold()

        Divider()

        Text("Temperature in Fahrenheit").bold()
        HStack {
            Text("\(String(format: "%.2f",
                minimumTempF)) F")
            Slider(value:
                Binding(get: {
                    self.sliderTempF
                }, set: { (newVal) in
                    self.sliderTempF = newVal
                    self.sliderTempC =
                        (self.sliderTempF - 32) * 5 / 9
                }),
                in: minimumTempF...maximumTempF)
            Text("\(String(format: "%.2f",
                maximumTempF)) F")
        }.padding()

        Text("\((String(format: "%.2f",
            sliderTempF as Double))) °C").bold()
        }
    }
}
```

Notice that I only set the initial value of the temperature in degrees Celsius to 23.0 and set the temperature in degrees Fahrenheit to 0:

```
@State private var sliderTempC = 23.0
@State private var sliderTempF = 0.0
```

The equivalent value of the temperature in degrees Fahrenheit is actually set in the initializer:

```
init() {
    self._sliderTempF = State(initialValue:
        sliderTempC * 9 / 5 + 32)
}
```

Figure 4-11 shows the temperature converter in action.

FIGURE 4-11:
The temperature
converter
involving two
Slider views.

Stepper

In the preceding section, you saw how to use the Slider view for users to select a range of linear values. Sometimes you just want the user to increment or decrement a value, such as in a shopping cart, where the user can add an additional item to buy or reduce the quantity of an item. For this, you can use the Stepper view. The Stepper view allows you to set the maximum and minimum value for the user to step through; each tag increases or decreases the count by 1 (this is a default step — it's customizable).

The following code snippet shows the Stepper view in action:

```
struct ContentView: View {
    @State private var qty = 1
    @State private var minimumItems = 0
    @State private var maximumItems = 10

    var body: some View {
        Stepper(value: $qty, in: minimumItems...maximumItems,
          label: {
              Text("Qty: \(qty)")
        }).padding()
    }
}
```

You specify the maximum and minimum values for the Stepper and bind it to the state qty variable. When the user taps the minus (–) or plus (+) button, the value is displayed in the label (see Figure 4-12).

Qty: 1   – +

You can check the value of the qty state variable and display an optional Text view if the current value of the Stepper is at the minimum or the maximum:

```
struct ContentView: View {
    @State private var qty = 1
    @State private var minimumItems = 0
    @State private var maximumItems = 10

    var body: some View {
        VStack{
            Stepper(value: $qty, in:
                minimumItems...maximumItems,
                label: {
                    Text("Qty: \(qty)")
            }).padding()
```

```
            if (qty==maximumItems) {
                Text("Maximum qty reached")
            }
            if (qty==minimumItems) {
                Text("Item will be removed from the cart")
            }
        }
    }
}
```

Figure 4-13 shows the label displayed when the value of the Stepper view reaches 0 (minimum). Figure 4-14 shows the label displayed when the value of the Stepper view reaches 10 (maximum).

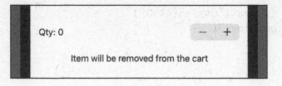

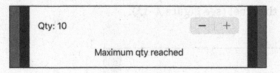

Picker

If you want users to select an item from a set of mutually exclusive values, you can use the Picker view. The following code snippet shows the Picker view showing a list of different types of coffees:

```
import SwiftUI

struct ContentView: View {

    var typesOfCoffee =
        ["Caffè Americano", "Caffè Latte", "Cappuccino",
         "Espresso", "Flat White", "Long Black",
         "Macchiato", "Mochaccino", "Irish Coffee",
         "Vienna", "Affogato"]
```

```
@State private var selectedCoffee = 0

var body: some View {
    VStack{
        Picker(selection: $selectedCoffee,
            label: Text("Types of Coffee").bold()) {
            ForEach(0 ..< typesOfCoffee.count){
                Text(self.typesOfCoffee[$0]).tag($0)
            }
        }
        .padding()
        Text("Coffee selected:
            \(typesOfCoffee[selectedCoffee])")
    }
}
```

Figure 4-15 shows the `Picker` displaying the label and the list of selectable options.

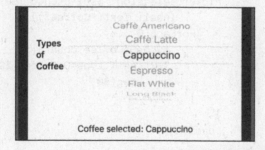

Like the other views (such as the `Stepper`, `Slider`, and `Toggle`), you have to supply a label when using the `Picker` view. To hide it, use the `labelsHidden()` modifier:

```
Picker(selection: $selectedCoffee,
    label: Text("Types of Coffee").bold()) {
    ForEach(0 ..< typesOfCoffee.count){
        Text(self.typesOfCoffee[$0]).tag($0)
    }
}
.padding()
.labelsHidden()
```

Figure 4-16 shows the `Picker` view with the label hidden.

FIGURE 4-16:
Hiding the label
for the Picker
view.

Caffè Americano

Caffè Latte

Cappuccino

Espresso

Coffee selected: Caffè Americano

TIP

If a screen has several views (such as Stepper, Slider, and Toggle) and you want to hide all the labels, you can group them together using a view such as the VStack view and then apply the labelsHidden() modifier to the VStack view instead of applying to the individual views.

The Picker view behaves differently when it's placed into a Form, as the following code snippet shows:

```
var body: some View {
    NavigationView {
        Form {
            Section{
                Picker(selection: $selectedCoffee,
                        label: Text("Coffee")) {
                    ForEach(0 ..<
                        typesOfCoffee.count){
                        Text(self.typesOfCoffee[$0])
                            .tag($0)
                    }
                }
                .padding()
            }
            Text("Coffee selected:
                \(typesOfCoffee[selectedCoffee])")
        }.navigationBarTitle((Text("Types of Coffee")))
    }
}
```

Here, the Picker view is placed inside a Form struct, within a NavigationView struct. When it's loaded, the Picker view will be collapsed into a single row (see Figure 4-17).

When you tap on the Picker view, it navigates to the list of options (see Figure 4-18). Tapping an item in the list of options brings you back to the Picker view.

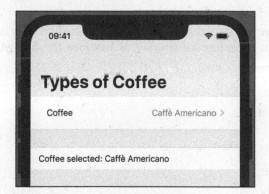

Composing Custom Views

In real life, it's very common to use composition to group various views into a single view. Doing so allows you to reuse the view without needing to manually use the individual views.

In this section, I show you how to create a custom view by combining several other smaller views.

Figure 4-19 shows the view that you'll build. This custom view displays detailed information about a conference speaker. It includes the following information about the speaker:

>> Image

>> Name

>> Title

>> Email address

>> Twitter handle

>> Website

>> Speaker profile

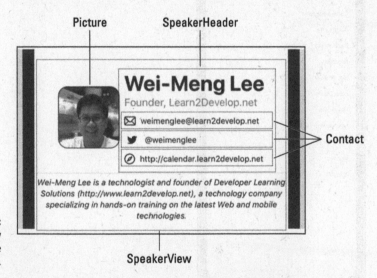

FIGURE 4-19: The custom view that you'll be building.

Composing the custom view

Before you start writing the code for the custom view, the first thing to do is to break it down into smaller parts. As you've seen in Figure 4-19, the custom view is named SpeakerView, and it contains other smaller views:

>> Picture: Displays the image of the speaker with the corner rounded.

>> Contact: Displays an icon followed by the contact details. The icon may be an envelope, the Twitter logo, or a website URL.

» SpeakerHeader: Displays the name of the speaker, along with the speaker's title and a collection of Contact views.

The SpeakerView also contains the speaker's profile information.

You're ready to start writing the code for the various custom views. Follow these steps:

1. **Create a new Xcode project and name it** CustomViews.

2. **Add a new** SwiftUI View **file to your project (see Figure 4-20), and name it** SpeakerView.swift.

   With the SpeakerView.swift file created, you can start coding the custom view.

FIGURE 4-20:
Adding a new
SwiftUI View
file to the project.

3. **Delete the following block of code that is generated for you by default:**

```
struct SpeakerView_Previews: PreviewProvider {
    static var previews: some View {
        SpeakerView()
    }
}
```

4. **Let's start off with the structure for storing the details of a speaker. Add the following statements in bold to the** SpeakerView.swift **file:**

```
import SwiftUI

struct Speaker {
    var name      : String
    var title     : String
    var email     : String
    var twitter   : String
    var URL       : String
    var imageName : String
    var profile   : String
}
```

5. **Define the** Picture **custom view by adding the following statements in bold to the** SpeakerView.swift **file:**

```
import SwiftUI

struct Speaker {
...
}

struct Picture: View {
    var imageFilename: String

    var body: some View {
        Image(imageFilename)
            .resizable()
            .frame(width: 100, height: 100)
            .cornerRadius(15)
    }
}
```

You'll use the Image view to display an image, and set it to a size of 100 x 100 points. You'll also round the corner with a radius of 15 points. Finally, you also want to display a border around the rounded rectangle, so you add a bor-der() modifier:

Image(imageFilename)

.resizable()

.frame(width: 100, height: 100)

```
.cornerRadius(15)
```

.border(Color.black)

This will result in the border displayed in Figure 4-21, with the border surrounding the rectangle instead of the rounded edges.

FIGURE 4-21: Applying border to a rounded Image view.

To fix this, the easiest way to is add an extension function to the View class:

```
import SwiftUI

extension View {
    public func addBorder<S>(_ content: S,
        width: CGFloat = 1, cornerRadius: CGFloat) ->
        some View where S : ShapeStyle {
        return overlay(RoundedRectangle(
            cornerRadius: cornerRadius).strokeBorder(
                content, lineWidth: width))
    }
}
```

The preceding code snippet adds the addBorder() function to the View class. You can now call it via a modifier to the Image object:

```
struct Picture: View {
    var imageFilename: String

    var body: some View {
        Image(imageFilename)
            .resizable()
            .frame(width: 100, height: 100)
```

```
          .cornerRadius(15)
          .addBorder(Color.black, width: 1,
                     cornerRadius: 15)
    }
}
```

The rounded corners are now displayed with the correct border (see Figure 4-22).

FIGURE 4-22:
Displaying a
border on the
corner-rounded
Image view.

6. **Define the** Contact **view by adding the following statements in bold to the** SpeakerView.swift **file:**

```
import SwiftUI

extension View {
    ...
}

struct Speaker {
    ...
}

struct Picture: View {
    ...
}

struct Contact: View {
    var detail: String
    var imageType: String
    var imageName: String
```

```
    var body: some View {
        HStack {
            if (imageType=="System"){
                Image(systemName: imageName)
            } else {
                Image(imageName).resizable()
                    .frame(width: 25, height: 25)
            }
            Text(detail).font(.footnote)
        }
    }
}
```

The Contact view will display an icon followed by the speaker's contact information, such as email address, Twitter handle, or website URL. The Image view allows
you to load icons from the Apple's San Francisco Symbol set using the systemName
parameter. For email addresses and website URLs, you can use the "envelope" and
"safari" icons. But for Twitter, you'll load the Twitter icon from your assets file.

TIP

If you want to learn more about Apple's San Francisco Symbol set, go to
https://developer.apple.com/design/human-interface-guidelines/
sf-symbols/overview/.

7. Define the SpeakerHeader **view by adding the following statements in**
bold to the SpeakerView.swift file:

```
import SwiftUI

extension View {
    ...
}

struct Speaker {
    ...
}

struct Picture: View {
    ...
}

struct Contact: View {
    ...
}

struct SpeakerHeader: View {
    var speaker: Speaker
```

```
    var body: some View {
        VStack(alignment: .leading) {
            Text(speaker.name)
                .font(.largeTitle)
                .foregroundColor(.primary)
                .bold()
            Text(speaker.title)
                .foregroundColor(.secondary)
            Contact(detail: speaker.email,
                    imageType: "System",
                    imageName: "envelope")
            Contact(detail: speaker.twitter,
                    imageType: "nil",
                    imageName: "twitter")
            Contact(detail: speaker.URL,
                    imageType: "System",
                    imageName: "safari")
        }
    }
}
```

The SpeakerHeader view displays the speaker's name and title; it uses the Contact view to display the speaker's contact information.

8. **Put everything together through the** SpeakerView **view:**

```
struct SpeakerView: View {
    var speaker: Speaker

    var body: some View {
        VStack{
            HStack {
                Picture(imageFilename:
                    speaker.imageName)
                SpeakerHeader(speaker: speaker)
            }
            Spacer().frame(height: 15)
            Divider()
            Text(speaker.profile)
                .font(.footnote)
                .italic()
                .multilineTextAlignment(.center)
        }
    }
}
```

The SpeakerView view takes in a Speaker struct and then uses the information to populate the various views.

Using the custom view

You're now ready to use the custom view that you created in the preceding section. But before you do that, you need to add two images into the Assets.xcassets file in your project.

Add two images named twitter.png and wei-meng lee.png into the Assets.xcassets file, as shown in Figure 4-23.

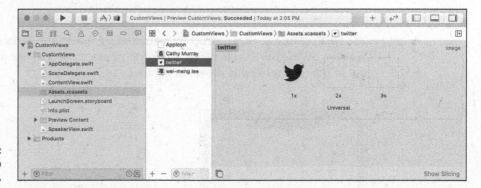

FIGURE 4-23:
Adding images to
the Xcode project.

TIP

You can get the images from the book's support web page at www.dummies.com/go/swiftuifd.

In the ContentView.swift file, add the following statements in bold:

```
import SwiftUI

struct ContentView: View {

    let speaker = Speaker(
        name: "Wei-Meng Lee",
        title: "Founder, Learn2Develop.net",
        email: "weimenglee@learn2develop.net",
        twitter: "@weimenglee",
        URL: "http://calendar.learn2develop.net",
        imageName: "wei-meng lee",
        profile: "Wei-Meng Lee is a technologist and
                 founder of Developer Learning Solutions
                 (http://www.learn2develop.net), a
```

```
                    technology company specializing in
                    hands-on training on the latest Web and
                    mobile technologies.")

        var body: some View {
            SpeakerView(speaker: speaker)
        }
    }

    struct ContentView_Previews: PreviewProvider {
        static var previews: some View {
            ContentView()
        }
    }
}
```

You first create a Speaker struct by instantiating it with the various details of the speaker. To use the SpeakerView, you simply pass it the Speaker struct. The output of the custom view is shown in Figure 4-24.

FIGURE 4-24: Using the custom view that you've created.

IN THIS CHAPTER

» **Displaying collections of items using the** List **view**

» **Programmatically generating rows in a** List **view**

» **Adding, deleting, and moving rows**

» **Displaying items in sections**

» **Previewing your user interface in Light and Dark modes**

Chapter **5**

Displaying Lists of Items

O ne common task a mobile app developer needs to do is display a list of items. In SwiftUI, the List view is a container that displays rows of items arranged in a single column.

In this chapter, I show you how to use the List view to display a list of items. I also explain how to dynamically populate a list, add items to a list, remove items from a list, as well as rearrange the position of items in the list. Finally, I explain how you can preview your user interface (UI) using Apple's new support for Light and Dark modes.

Using the List View to Display Items

In this section, you create a very simple list with a couple of items. In SwiftUI, the List view presents rows of data displayed in a single column. The following code snippet shows the List view displaying a list of country names:

```
struct ContentView: View {
    var body: some View {
        List {
```

```
            Text("Australia")
            Text("Belgium")
            Text("Canada")
            Text("Denmark")
            Text("Finland")
            Text("Germany")
            Text("Japan")
            Text("United States of America")
        }
    }
}
```

Figure 5-1 shows what the list looks like.

FIGURE 5-1:
The List view
displaying a list of
items

Customizing the rows

In the previous example, each row is displayed using the Text view. However, you're free to create your own custom view if you need to display more information. Typically, you can use either an HStack or VStack view as a container to display additional views, such as in the following example, where you use the HStack view to contain Image and Text views:

```
struct ContentView: View {
    var body: some View {
        List {
            HStack{
                Image("Australia")
                Text("Australia")
            }
            HStack{
                Image("Belgium")
                Text("Belgium")
            }
            HStack{
                Image("Canada")
                Text("Canada")
            }
            HStack{
                Image("Denmark")
                Text("Denmark")
            }
            HStack{
                Image("Finland")
                Text("Finland")
            }
            HStack{
                Image("Germany")
                Text("Germany")
            }
            HStack{
                Image("Japan")
                Text("Japan")
            }
            HStack{
                Image("United States of America")
                Text("United States of America")
            }
        }
    }
}
```

TIP

The string within the Image view refers to an image that you've added to the Assets.xcassets file in your project (see Figure 5-2). You can find the images at www.iconfinder.com/iconsets/flags_gosquared.

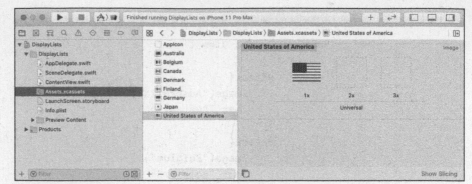

FIGURE 5-2:
For this example
to work, you need
to add the
various flag
images to the
Assets.
xcassets file in
your project.

Figure 5-3 shows each row showing the flag of the country, along with the country name.

FIGURE 5-3:
Each row showing
the flag of the
country and the
country's name.

Adding rows programmatically

Usually, you add rows to a List view programmatically instead of hard-coding the items. And you usually bind it to a state variable, so that the items in the List view can be updated dynamically.

The following code snippet contains a state variable named `countries`, which itself is a list of country names:

```
struct ContentView: View {
    @State private var countries = [
        "Australia", "Belgium", "Canada", "Denmark",
        "Finland", "Germany", "Japan",
        "United States of America"]

    var body: some View {
        List {
            ForEach(countries, id: \.self) { (country) in
                Text(country)
            }
        }
    }
}
```

Within the `List` view, you use the `ForEach` view in SwiftUI. The `ForEach` view lets you pass a collection of data to its initializer and then creates multiple subviews.

You need to tell `ForEach` how to uniquely identify each item it generates through the `id` parameter. In the preceding code snippet, the `\.self` indicates that each string in the `countries` state variable will be used as the identifier for each row that it generates.

Here is another example of using the `ForEach` view. This time, the following code snippet creates ten rows, with the content from 1 to 10 (see Figure 5-4 for the output):

```
struct ContentView: View {
    var body: some View {
        List {
            ForEach((1...10), id: \.self) { (num) in
                Text("\(num)")
            }
        }
    }
}
```

FIGURE 5-4:
Generating a list of items from 1 to 10 in a List view using the ForEach view.

Back to the original example on the list of countries. You can create a struct named country to store the name of a country and the name of the image representing the country's flag, like this:

```
import SwiftUI

struct country {
    let name: String
    let flag: String
}
```

The countries state variable can now be used to store a list of country structs. The countries state variable can now be used by the ForEach view:

```
struct ContentView: View {
    var countries = [
        country(name: "Australia", flag: "Australia"),
        country(name: "Belgium", flag: "Belgium"),
        country(name: "Canada", flag: "Canada"),
        country(name: "Denmark", flag: "Denmark"),
        country(name: "Finland", flag: "Finland"),
        country(name: "Germany", flag: "Germany"),
        country(name: "Japan", flag: "Japan"),
        country(name: "United States of America",
                flag: "United States of America"),
    ]
```

```
        var body: some View {
            List {
                ForEach(countries, id: \.self) { (country) in
                    HStack {
                        Image(country.flag)
                        Text(country.name)
                    }
                }
            }
        }
    }
```

The preceding code snippet generates an error. The ForEach view requires that the country struct conforms to the Hashable protocol. Hence, you need to add the following statement to the country struct:

```
struct country:Hashable {
    let name: String
    let flag: String
}
```

Alternatively, you can use the name attribute of the country struct as the identifier in the ForEach view without making the country struct conform to the Hashable protocol:

```
    ForEach(countries, id: \.name) { (country) in
```

Alternative way to generate rows in a List view

Another way to generate rows in a List view is to bind the variable directly to the List view, like the following:

```
struct ContentView: View {
    var countries = [
        country(name: "Australia", flag: "Australia"),
        country(name: "Belgium", flag: "Belgium"),
        country(name: "Canada", flag: "Canada"),
        country(name: "Denmark", flag: "Denmark"),
        country(name: "Finland", flag: "Finland"),
        country(name: "Germany", flag: "Germany"),
        country(name: "Japan", flag: "Japan"),
```

```
            country(name: "United States of America",
                    flag: "United States of America"),
    ]

    var body: some View {
        List (countries, id:\.name) {(country) in
            HStack {
                    Image(country.flag)
                    Text(country.name)
            }
        }
    }
}
```

However, for the rest of this chapter, you won't be using this approach. This is because when it comes to deleting and moving rows (more on these in later sections), modifiers such onDelete() and onMove() only work on ForEach views.

Displaying the List within a NavigationView

List view usually appears in a NavigationView, where users can view a list of items, tap an item, and then display the details on another page. To display the List view within a NavigationView, wrap it within the NavigationView struct and set the title using the navigationBarTitle() method:

```
    var body: some View {
        NavigationView{
            List {
                ForEach(countries, id: \.name) {
                    (country) in
                    HStack {
                            Image(country.flag)
                            Text(country.name)
                    }
                }
            }
            .navigationBarTitle("List of Countries")
        }
    }
```

Figure 5-5 shows the `List` view enclosed within the `NavigationView` with the bar title set.

FIGURE 5-5:
The `List` view enclosed within the `NavigationView`.

Making the items tappable

The advantage of wrapping the `List` view within the `NavigationView` is that you can navigate to another page when an item in the `List` is tapped. To enable items in the `List` to be tappable, add a `NavigationLink()` function to the `ForEach` view:

```
var body: some View {
    NavigationView{
        List {
            ForEach(countries, id: \.name) {
                (country) in
                NavigationLink(destination:
                    VStack{
                        Text(country.name).bold()
                        Image(country.flag)
                    }
                ) {
```

```
                    HStack {
                        Image(country.flag)
                        Text(country.name)
                    }
                }
            }
        }
        .navigationBarTitle("List of Countries")
    }
}
```

The NavigationLink() function takes in an argument of type View. In the preceding example, you simply create a VStack view containing a Text view and an
Image view. You can also link it to another View (saved in another SwiftUI view
file) if you want to.

Figure 5-6 shows the view that is displayed when the last item ("United States of
America") in the List is tapped.

FIGURE 5-6:
Tapping the last
item in the List
and displaying
the item selected
on another
screen.

Adding rows

Many times, you may allow users to add additional rows to the List view. You can do that by appending a new item to the countries variable. One very important point to take note of is that, because you're using the ForEach view together with the countries variable, any attempt to modify the countries variable will incur the error Cannot use mutating member on immutable value: 'self' is immutable. This means that the countries variable's value cannot be altered. To solve this, you need to convert it into a state variable, like this:

```
struct ContentView: View {
    @State private var countries = [
        country(name: "Australia", flag: "Australia"),
        country(name: "Belgium", flag: "Belgium"),
        country(name: "Canada", flag: "Canada"),
        country(name: "Denmark", flag: "Denmark"),
        country(name: "Finland", flag: "Finland"),
        country(name: "Germany", flag: "Germany"),
        country(name: "Japan", flag: "Japan"),
        country(name: "United States of America",
                flag: "United States of America"),
    ]
```

To allow the user to add new rows to the List, add a navigation bar item (Button) to the upper-right corner (trailing) of the NavigationView, and specify the action of the button to point to a function to add a new item to the countries state variable:

```
var body: some View {
    NavigationView{
        List {
            ForEach(countries, id: \.name) {
                (country) in
                NavigationLink(destination:
                    VStack{
                        Text(country.name).bold()
                        Image(country.flag)
                    }
                ) {
                    HStack {
                        Image(country.flag)
                        Text(country.name)
                    }
                }
```

```
                }
            }
            .navigationBarTitle("List of Countries")
            .navigationBarItems(
                trailing: Button(action: addCountry,
                    label: { Text("Add") }
                )
            )
        }
    }

    func addCountry() {
        countries.append(
            country(name: "Norway", flag: "Norway")
        )
    }
}
```

As soon as a new country struct is added to the countries state variables, the new
row will be added to the List view (see Figure 5-7).

FIGURE 5-7:
Adding a new row
to the List view.

Using the Identifiable protocol

Recall that the ForEach view uses the name attribute of the country struct as the unique identifier for each row:

```
ForEach(countries, id: \.name) { (country) in
```

What happens if you click the Add button multiple times? In this case, the country Norway would be added multiple times, and the key for the additional row would no longer be unique:

```
countries.append(
    country(name: "Norway", flag: "Norway")
)
```

Although the List view will let you add the row without any complaints, problems would arise later when you're trying to delete rows. If you delete a row where the identifier is not unique, the List view will always delete the last item from rows that have identical keys.

To solve this problem, you need to make sure that each row added to the List view has a unique identifier. The easiest way to fix this in this example is to add a unique identifier to the country struct. You can do it this way:

```
struct country: Identifiable {
    let id = UUID()
    let name: String
    let flag: String
}
```

Here, you are making country conform to the Identifiable protocol. This protocol requires the struct to implement a property named id, which can be of any type as long as it's hashable. For simplicity, you'll use the UUID() function to generate a universally unique identifier every time you create an instance of the country struct.

Finally, update the ForEach view so that you don't have to use the name attribute as the identifier anymore. Instead, because the country struct conforms to the Identifiable protocol, the List view will automatically make use of id as the identifier for the rows:

```
var body: some View {
    NavigationView{
        List {
            ForEach(countries) {
```

```
                (country) in
                NavigationLink(destination:
                    VStack{
                        Text(country.name).bold()
                        Image(country.flag)
                    }
                ) {
                    HStack {
                        Image(country.flag)
                        Text(country.name)
                    }
                }
            }
        }
        .navigationBarTitle("List of Countries")
        .navigationBarItems(
            trailing: Button(action: addCountry,
                label: { Text("Add") }
            )
        )
    }
}
```

Deleting rows

Another common operation with List is deleting rows. To delete a row, you typi-cally swipe an item to the left and a Delete button will display on the right side of the item. To allow an item to be deleted, simply use the onDelete() modifier and pass a function to its perform parameter:

```
var body: some View {
    NavigationView{
        List {
            ForEach(countries) {
                (country) in
                NavigationLink(destination:
                    VStack{
                        Text(country.name).bold()
                        Image(country.flag)
                    }
                ) {
```

```
                    HStack {
                        Image(country.flag)
                        Text(country.name)
                    }
                }
            }
            .onDelete(perform: delete)
        }
        .navigationBarTitle("List of Countries")
        .navigationBarItems(
            trailing: Button(action: addCountry,
                label: { Text("Add") }
            )
        )
    }
}

func delete(at offsets: IndexSet) {
    countries.remove(atOffsets: offsets)
}

func addCountry() {
    countries.append(
        country(name: "Norway", flag: "Norway")
    )
}
```

The delete() function takes in an argument — offsets, of type IndexSet. An IndexSet is a collection of unique integer values that represent the indices of elements in another collection. In the case of the delete() function, the offsets argument contains the positions of all the items in the ForEach view that should be removed. You can pass the offsets argument to the remove() function of the countries state variables to remove the specific row.

Figure 5-8 shows the Delete button showing when you swipe an item to the left.

TIP

The delete() modifier only works for the ForEach view. Hence, it's important that you generate the rows in your List view using the ForEach view if you want to let the user remove a row during runtime.

FIGURE 5-8:
Deleting a row
from the List
view.

Editing rows

Apart from swiping each item in a List individually, you can also switch the List to edit mode so that each item displays a Delete icon. You can delete an item quickly by simply tapping the Delete icon. The following statement adds an EditButton view to the top-right corner (trailing) of the NavigationView and moved the Add button to the upper-left corner (leading):

```
var body: some View {
    NavigationView{
        List {
            ForEach(countries) { (country) in
                NavigationLink(destination:
                    VStack{
                        Text(country.name).bold()
                        Image(country.flag)
                    }
                ) {
                    HStack {
                        Image(country.flag)
                        Text(country.name)
                    }
                }
            }
            .onDelete(perform: delete)
        }
        .navigationBarTitle("List of Countries")
        .navigationBarItems(
            leading: Button(action: addCountry,
                label: { Text("Add") }
            ),
```

```
            trailing: EditButton()
        )
    }
}
```

Figure 5-9 shows the Edit button.

Tapping the Edit button reveals the Delete icon on the left of each item (see Figure 5-10).

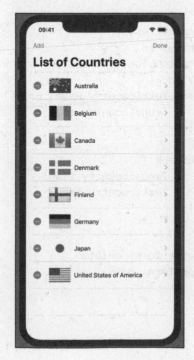

When you tap the Delete icon, the Delete button will appear on the right of the row (see Figure 5-11). Tapping the Delete button deletes the row.

FIGURE 5-11: The Delete button appears when you tap the Delete icon.

Moving rows

You can also let the users rearrange the positions of the various rows in a List view. This is done by attaching the onMove() modifier to the end of the ForEach view:

```
var body: some View {
    NavigationView{
        List {
            ForEach(countries) {
                (country) in
                NavigationLink(destination:
                    VStack{
                        Text(country.name).bold()
                        Image(country.flag)
                    }
                ) {
                    HStack {
                        Image(country.flag)
                        Text(country.name)
                    }
                }
            }
            .onDelete(perform: delete)
            .onMove(perform: move)
        }
```

```
            .navigationBarTitle("List of Countries")
            .navigationBarItems(
              leading: Button(action: addCountry,
                  label: { Text("Add") }
              ),
              trailing: EditButton()
            )
        }
    }

    func move(from source: IndexSet, to destination: Int){
        countries.move(fromOffsets: source,
                      toOffset: destination)
    }

    func delete(at offsets: IndexSet) {
        countries.remove(atOffsets: offsets)
    }

    func addCountry() {
        countries.append(
            country(name: "Norway", flag: "Norway")
        )
    }
```

The preceding code snippet calls the move() function when the user moves the
row in the List view. The move() function takes in two arguments: an IndexSet
and an Int. The first argument contains the indices of the items to move, and the
second argument is the index of the final position to move to.

In order to allow the user to move the items in the List, you need to ensure that
you have an EditButton added to the navigation bar; if you don't, there is no way
for the user to move the items.

Figure 5-12 shows that after the user taps the Edit button, the drag handle for
each item appears.

Using the handle, the user can drag and move the item to the new position (see
Figure 5-13).

FIGURE 5-12:
The drag handle
of each item
allows you to
rearrange the
items.

FIGURE 5-13:
Rearranging an
item in the List
view.

The preceding code snippet calls the `onMove` method to let the user move the row in the `List`. The `onMove` function takes in two arguments: an `IndexSet` and an `Int`. The first argument `IndexSet` contains the items to move, and the second argument is the index or location of position.

In order to allow the user to move rows in the `List`, you need to ensure that you have an Edit button added to the navigation bar. Otherwise, there is no way for the user to move the items.

Figure 5-12 shows that after the app is run, each row has a drag handle for rearrangement, as shown in the figure.

Using the handle, the user can drag and move the item to a new position (see Figure 5-13).

Displaying Sections

Up to this point, you've displayed a flat list of items using the `List` view. One of the powerful features of the `List` view is its support for displaying items in sections. For example, you may want to group related items in separate sections. A good example of sections in iOS is the Settings app on your iPhone (see Figure 5-14).

FIGURE 5-14: The Settings app in iOS uses the List view.

To display sections in the `List` view, use the `Section` struct, like this:

```swift
import SwiftUI

struct ContentView: View {

    var body: some View {
        List {
            Section(header: Text("Section I")) {
                Text("Item 1")
                Text("Item 2")
            }
```

```
            Section(header: Text("Section II")) {
                Text("Item 1")
                Text("Item 2")
            }
        }
    }
}
```

The Section struct allows you to create hierarchical view content. In the preceding code snippet, there are two Section structs, and you supply a Text view to display as the header for each section. Figure 5-15 shows the output.

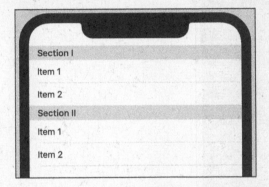

FIGURE 5-15:
The List view displays two sections, each with two items.

Displaying sections from a dictionary

A much more common scenario is that your data is stored in a dictionary. Consider the following state variable named countries:

```
@State private var countries = [
    "Africa": ["Algeria", "Angola"],
    "Asia": ["China", "Cyprus"],
    "Europe":["Lithuania","Luxembourg"],
    "North America":["Costa Rica","Cuba"],
    "South America":["Brazil ","Peru"],
    "Oceania/Australia":["Fiji ","New Zealand"],
]
```

Each key in the state variable represents a continent, and the value for each key contains a couple of countries in each continent. Using the Section struct, you can display all the countries under each continent, like this:

```
struct ContentView: View {
    @State var countries = [
        "Africa": ["Algeria", "Angola"],
        "Asia": ["China", "Cyprus"],
        "Europe":["Lithuania","Luxembourg"],
        "North America":["Costa Rica","Cuba"],
        "South America":["Brazil ","Peru"],
        "Oceania/Australia":["Fiji ","New Zealand"],
    ].sorted{$0.key < $1.key}

    var body: some View {
        List {
            ForEach(countries, id: \.0) { index, item in
                Section(header: Text(index)) {
                    ForEach (item, id: \.self) {
                        (country) in
                        Text(country)
                    }
                }
            }
        }
    }
}
```

An important point to note is that the ForEach view generates each row and monitors them for changes, such as when new rows are inserted or existing rows are moved or updated. In particular, the order of the rows is important.

WARNING

For a dictionary, the items are not ordered. As such, if you're binding a dictionary object to the ForEach view, it will cause the following error: Referencing initializer 'init(_:id:content:)' on 'ForEach' requires that '[String : [String]]' conform to 'RandomAccessCollection'.

To solve this problem, you need to ensure that the items in the dictionary maintain their order. Thus, you need to sort the items, like this:

```
@State var countries = [
    "Africa": ["Algeria", "Angola"],
    "Asia": ["China", "Cyprus"],
    "Europe":["Lithuania","Luxembourg"],
    "North America":["Costa Rica","Cuba"],
```

```
    "South America":["Brazil ","Peru"],
    "Oceania/Australia":["Fiji ","New Zealand"],
].sorted{$0.key < $1.key}
```

Figure 5-16 shows all the countries displayed in sections, grouped by continent.

Changing the style of the List view

You can change the style of the List view to GroupedListStyle:

```
var body: some View {
    List {
        ForEach(countries, id: \.0) { index, item in
            Section(header: Text(index)) {
                ForEach (item, id: \.self) { (country) in
                    Text(country)
                }
```

```
            }
        }
    }.listStyle(GroupedListStyle())
}
```

Figure 5-17 shows the updated `List` style.

FIGURE 5-17:
Showing
the List view in
Grouped
ListStyle.

If you do not want any section headers, use an `EmptyView` instead of the `Text` view:

```
var body: some View {
    List {
        ForEach(countries, id: \.0) { index, item in
            Section(header: EmptyView()) {
                ForEach (item, id: \.self) {
                    (country) in
```

```
                    Text(country)
                }
            }
        }
    }.listStyle(GroupedListStyle())
}
```

Figure 5-18 shows the `List` view displayed without any section headers.

FIGURE 5-18:
Sections are
displayed without
any headers.

Previewing in Light and Dark Modes

SwiftUI natively supports the new Light and Dark modes in Apple iOS. There are two ways to test out your application in both modes: during runtime and during design time.

During runtime

When your application is running on the iPhone Simulator, you can go to the Debug area of Xcode and click the Environment Overrides button (see Figure 5-19).

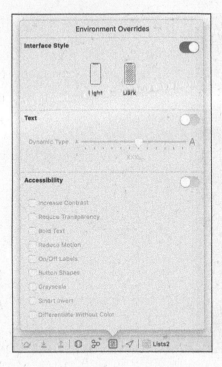

FIGURE 5-19:
The Environment
Overrides section
on Xcode allows
you to switch
between Light
and Dark modes.

Switch the Interface Style to On and you can toggle between Light and Dark modes. Figure 5-20 shows the List view displayed in Dark mode.

TIP

Another way to switch between Light and Dark modes is to go to the iPhone Simulator, select Settings, select Developer, and then turn on Dark Appearance.

During design time

If you want to preview your UI during design time, you can simply use the `environment()` modifier on the `ContentView` struct:

```
struct ContentView_Previews: PreviewProvider {
    static var previews: some View {
        ContentView()
        .environment(\.colorScheme, .dark)
    }
}
```

FIGURE 5-20:
The List view
displayed in Dark
mode.

The preceding code snippet changes the preview layout to use Dark mode. If you want to preview both the Light and Dark modes at the same time, use the `Group` struct to contain both `ContentView` structs, like this:

```
struct ContentView_Previews: PreviewProvider {
    static var previews: some View {
        Group {
            ContentView()
                .environment(\.colorScheme, .light)

            ContentView()
                .environment(\.colorScheme, .dark)
        }
    }
}
```

Xcode will now display two previews (see Figure 5-21).

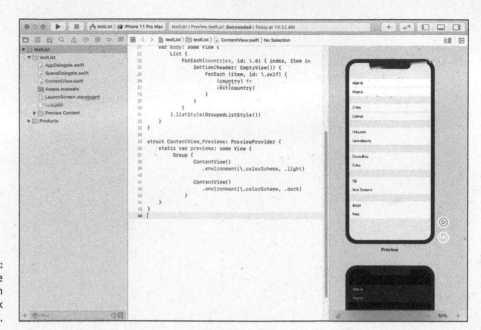

FIGURE 5-21:
Viewing the
preview in both
Light and Dark
modes.

Chapter **6**

Creating Navigation and Tabbed Applications

W hen it comes to mobile app user interface (UI) designs, two common patterns stand out:

» Navigation style

» Tabbed style

Navigation style is most often used in applications where users follow through a sequence of screens in order to complete a task. It's most commonly used together with the List view (see Chapter 5), where users can select from a list of items and view the details of the selected item on another screen. The navigation style provides an easy way for users to move to the next screen, or navigate back to the previous screen. Figure 6-1 provides the conceptual overview of a navigation-style app.

The tabbed style, on the other hand, places several buttons at the bottom of the screen. These buttons are always visible and users can quickly decide which button has the content they want. Figure 6-2 shows the conceptual overview of a tabbed-style application.

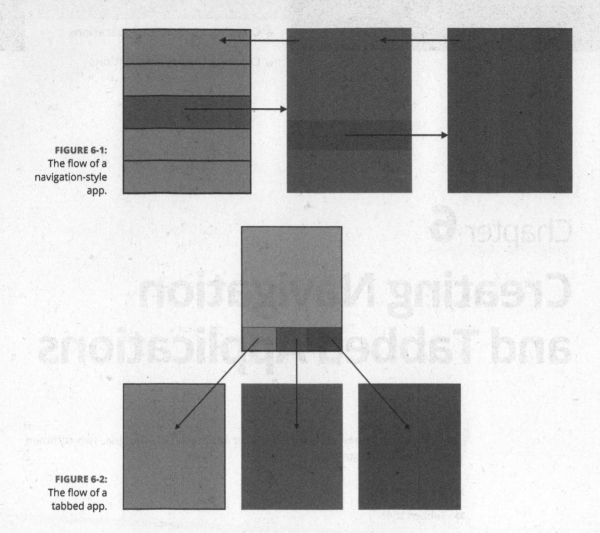

FIGURE 6-1:
The flow of a navigation-style app.

FIGURE 6-2:
The flow of a tabbed app.

In this chapter, I explain how to build both navigation and tabbed applications using the various views in SwiftUI.

Creating Navigation Apps

The first type of application you build in this section is the navigation app. You find out how to create a master/detail app and use the various techniques to navigate to a detail page and back. Then I show you how to build a real-world application — a news reader application that allows you to display a news feed where the users can navigate to view the details of the news items.

Working with the two key views in navigation-style apps

In SwiftUI, navigation-style apps are created with the help of two key views:

>> NavigationView

>> NavigationLink

In this section, I show you how these views work together.

NavigationView

The NavigationView allows you to present content, and at the same time handle navigation between views. In addition, it also places a navigation bar at the top of the screen.

The simplest way to understand the use of the NavigationView is to embed a Text view within it:

```
import SwiftUI

struct ContentView: View {
    var body: some View {
        NavigationView {
            Text("This is a Text view")
        }
    }
}
```

Figure 6-3 shows the NavigationView displaying a string using the Text view.

Notice that the navigation bar (at the top of the screen) is empty. If you want to display a string on the navigation bar, you can use the navigationBarTitle() modifier on the content within the NavigationView, like this:

```
struct ContentView: View {
    var body: some View {
        NavigationView {
            Text("This is a Text view")
                .navigationBarTitle(Text("Nav Bar Title"))
        }
    }
}
```

This is a Text view

Working with the Two Types of Views in navigation-style apps

FIGURE 6-3:
A Text view
wrapped within a
NavigationView.

Figure 6-4 shows the navigation bar now displaying a title.

The `navigationBarTitle()` modifier takes in a `Text` field. But because what it really displays is a string, you can directly pass in a string, like this:

```
.navigationBarTitle("Nav Bar Title")
```

By default, the title in the navigation bar is displayed in large format (through the `displayMode` parameter), like this:

```
.navigationBarTitle("Nav Bar Title", displayMode: .large)
```

If you want to make the title a little smaller, you can use the `inline` mode, like this:

```
.navigationBarTitle("Nav Bar Title", displayMode: .inline)
```

Figure 6-5 shows the title displayed in `inline` mode.

FIGURE 6-4: Displaying the navigation bar title.

FIGURE 6-5: Displaying the navigation bar title in `inline` display mode.

NavigationLink

To navigate to another screen, use the `NavigationLink` within the `NavigationView`. The following shows a simple example:

```
struct ContentView: View {
    var body: some View {
        NavigationView {
            NavigationLink(destination:
                Text("This is the destination view")) {
                Text("This is a Text view")
            }
            .navigationBarTitle("Nav Bar Title", displayMode:
    .large)
        }
    }
}
```

In this example, the destination is the `Text` view. Figure 6-6 shows what happens when you click the This Is a Text View link.

To return to the previous screen, simply tap the back button (labeled < Nav Bar Title, as shown in Figure 6-7).

FIGURE 6-6:
Clicking the This
Is a Text View link
navigates to
another screen
(Text view in this
example).

FIGURE 6-7:
The back button
to return to the
previous screen

Navigating to a page

The previous section showed the `NavigationLink` navigating to another view. In real life, it's more common to navigate to another screen saved as a separate Swift file. For this, add a new SwiftUI file to the project by choosing File⇨ New⇨ File⇨ SwiftUI View. Name the new file `DetailView.swift`.

Add the following statement in bold to the `DetailView.swift` file:

```
import SwiftUI

struct DetailView: View {
    var body: some View {
        Text("This is the destination view")
    }
}


struct DetailView_Previews: PreviewProvider {
    static var previews: some View {
        DetailView()
    }
}
```

Back in the `ContentView.swift` file, replace the `Text` view with that of the `DetailView()` instance:

```
struct ContentView: View {
    var body: some View {
        NavigationView {
            NavigationLink(destination:
                DetailView()) {
                Text("This is a Text view")
            }
            .navigationBarTitle("Nav Bar Title", displayMode:
            .large)
        }
    }
}
```

The result will be the same as that as shown in Figure 6-6.

Navigating programmatically

So far in the examples I've shown, all navigations are performed by the `NavigationLink`. In addition to using the `NavigationLink`, you can navigate programmatically. In this section, I show you how this is done.

Let's modify the `DetailView.swift` file first:

```swift
import SwiftUI

struct DetailView: View {
    @Binding var showView : Bool

    var body: some View {
        VStack{
            Text("This is the destination view")
            Button(
                action: {
                    self.showView = false
                },
                label: {
                    Text("Back")
                }
            )
        }
    }
}

struct DetailView_Previews: PreviewProvider {
    static var previews: some View {
        DetailView(showView: .constant(false))
    }
}
```

Notice that you have a `Binding` property named `showView`. You also added a `VStack` and a `Button` view. When the button is tapped, the `showView` binding variable is set to `false`. The `Binding` property provides two-way binding — changing the variable changes the state of the view it's bounded to, and changing the state of the view changes the variable.

In the `ContentView.swift` file, add the following statements in bold:

```swift
import SwiftUI

struct ContentView: View {
    @State var displayView = false

    var body: some View {
        NavigationView {
            VStack{
```

```
            NavigationLink(destination:
                DetailView(showView: $displayView),
                    isActive: $displayView)
            {
                Text("This is a Text view")
            }
            Button(
                action: {
                    self.displayView = true
                },
                label: {
                    Text("Next")
                }
            )
        }.navigationBarTitle("Nav Bar Title",
            displayMode: .large)
    }
  }
}
```

Here, you add a state variable named `displayView` and initialize it to `false`. You then bind it to the `showView` binding property from `DetailView`. The `isActive` parameter of the `NavigationLink` button sets whether the destination view should be visible (this is why you initialize `displayView` to `false` initially). You also add a `VStack` and a `Button` view. When the button is tapped, you set the `displayView` state variable to `true`.

When the button in the `DetailView` is tapped, the `showView` binding variable will be set to `false`. This will also change the value of `displayView` and, hence, cause the `DetailView` to disappear.

Now you can navigate between the screens using the Next and Back buttons (see Figure 6-8).

Creating a news reader application

The `NavigationView` is often paired together with the `List` view to display a master-detail interface. So, in this section, you build a news reader application to download the news headlines, display them in a `List` view, and allow the user to tap a particular news item to read more about the news.

Examining the structure of the news headline feed

For this example, you use the free service provided by News API (`https://newsapi.org`). This is a JSON-based application programming interface (API) that provides you with breaking news headlines and allows you to search for articles from more than 30,000 news sources and blogs.

JSON stands for JavaScript Object Notation.

To register for your own API key, go to `https://newsapi.org/register`.

For your project, you'll retrieve all the top business headlines in the United States. The URL looks like this: `https://newsapi.org/v2/top-headlines?country=us&category=business&apiKey=<API_KEY>`.

The news headline API returns a JSON string containing the details of the news headlines. You can paste the URL into a web browser and obtain the content. When the JSON content is displayed in your browser, copy and paste it into a JSON validator website, such as `http://jsonlint.com`. You'll have a good idea of the structure of the JSON content. Figure 6-9 shows the structure of a sample of the JSON content.

```
{
    "status": "ok",
    "totalResults": 70,
    "articles": [{
        "source": {
            "id": "cnbc",
            "name": "CNBC"
        },
        "author": "Elliot Smith",
        "title": "Deutsche Bank posts net loss of 5.3 billion euros for 2019 amid major restructuring - CNBC",
        "description": "Deutsche Bank on Thursday posted a full-year net loss of 5.3 billion euros for 2019, mis
        "url": "https://www.cnbc.com/2020/01/30/deutsche-bank-earnings-q4-2019.html",
        "urlToImage": "https://image.cnbcfm.com/api/v1/image/104047038-RTSQ0LQ.jpg?v=1529452164",
        "publishedAt": "2020-01-30T06:03:00Z",
        "content": "Deutsche Bank on Thursday posted a full-year net loss of 5.3 billion euros ($5.8 billion) an
    }, {
        "source": {
            "id": "cnn",
            "name": "CNN"
        },
        "author": "Sherisse Pham, CNN Business",
```

FIGURE 6-9:
The structure of the JSON content displayed using www.jsonlint.com.

Notice that the value of the `articles` key is an array of items, each containing the details of each article. In each article, you would want to retrieve the following details:

>> `title`: The title of the news item

>> `url`: The link containing the details of the news item

>> `description`: A synopsis of the news item

>> `urlToImage`: The link containing the image for the article

Now you're ready to start coding. Using Xcode, create a Single View App application and name it `NewsReader`.

To extract the items from JSON into structures in Swift, create the following structs:

```swift
struct Result: Codable {
    var articles: [Article]
}

struct Article: Codable {
    var url: String
    var title: String
    var description: String?
    var urlToImage: String?
}
```

TIP Chapter 2 provides more details on the `Codable` protocol.

Fetching the JSON string

Before you see how to fetch the news headlines from the web, let's define a state variable named `articles`. This state variable will store all the decoded JSON content; you'll also use it to bind to your `List` view for display:

```
private let url = "https://newsapi.org/v2/top
        headlines?country=us&category=business&apiKey=
        <API_KEY>"

@State private var articles = [Article]()
```

To fetch the news headlines, you'll define the `fetchData()` function:

```
func fetchData() {
    guard let url = URL(string: url) else {
        print("URL is not valid")
        return
    }

    let request = URLRequest(url: url)

    URLSession.shared.dataTask(with: request) {
        data, response, error in
        if let data = data {   // data is Optional, so
                               // you need to unwrap it
            if let decodedResult = try?
               JSONDecoder().decode(
                 Result.self, from: data) {
                 // decoding is successful
                 DispatchQueue.main.async {
                     // assign the decoded articles to
                     // the state variable
                     self.articles =
                         decodedResult.articles
                 }
                 return
            }
        }
        print("Error: \(error?.localizedDescription ??
            "Unknown error")")
    }.resume()
}
```

You use the `dataTask()` method of the `URLSession.shared` object instance to fetch the news headlines. When the JSON content is downloaded, you use the `JSONDecoder()` object's `decode()` function to convert the JSON content into the `Result` struct that you defined earlier. When the conversion is done, you assign the result to the `articles` state variable.

Defining the view

Now you can define the view. You'll use a `List` view to display the list of articles:

```
var body: some View {
    List(articles, id: \.url) { item in
        VStack(alignment: .leading) {
            Text(item.title)
                .font(.headline)
            Text(item.description ?? "")
                .font(.footnote)
        }
    }.onAppear(perform: fetchData)
}
```

The `List` view is bound to the `articles` state variable, and you use a `VStack` view to display the `title` and `description` of the article. The `onAppear()` modifier to the `List` view specifies that the `fetchData()` function be called when the `List` view first appears.

For your reference, here is the content of the `ContentView.swift` file:

```
import SwiftUI

struct Result: Codable {
    var articles: [Article]
}

struct Article: Codable {
    var url: String
    var title: String
    var description: String?
    var urlToImage: String?
}

struct ContentView: View {
    private let url = "https://newsapi.org/v2/top-
        headlines?country=us&category=business&apiKey=
        <API_KEY>"
```

```
@State private var articles = [Article]()

func fetchData() {
    guard let url = URL(string: url) else {
        print("URL is not valid")
        return
    }

    let request = URLRequest(url: url)

    URLSession.shared.dataTask(with: request) {
        data, response, error in
        if let data = data {  // data is Optional, so
                              // you need to unwrap it
            if let decodedResult = try?
                JSONDecoder().decode(
                    Result.self, from: data) {
                // decoding is successful
                DispatchQueue.main.async {
                    // assign the decoded articles to
                    // the state variable
                    self.articles =
                        decodedResult.articles
                }
                return
            }
        }
        print("Error: \(error?.localizedDescription ??
            "Unknown error")")
    }.resume()
}

var body: some View {
    List(articles, id: \.url) { item in
        VStack(alignment: .leading) {
            Text(item.title)
                .font(.headline)
            Text(item.description ?? "")
                .font(.footnote)
        }
    }.onAppear(perform: fetchData)
}
```

Figure 6-10 shows how the app looks when you run the Live Preview on Xcode.

FIGURE 6-10:
Displaying the news headlines using the List view.

Displaying images remotely

So far, the news headlines are displayed nicely using the List view. However, it would be much nicer if you were able to display an image for each news headlines. As the saying goes, a picture is worth a thousand words.

In Chapter 3, you learn about using the Image view to display images. The one key problem with the Image view is that it's only capable of displaying local images (that is, images that are bundled locally with the application). If you want to display an image that is located on the web, you're out of luck.

One way to fix this is to create your own Image view to load images remotely. But there are already solutions developed by others. So you can just make use of one of them. For this purpose, you'll use the URLImage view located at https://github.com/dmytro-anokhin/url-image.

To make use of the URLImage view, you need to add its package to your project. You can do so by going to Xcode and following these steps:

1. **Choose File ⇨ Swift Packages ⇨ Add Package Dependency.**

2. **Enter this URL** https://github.com/dmytro-anokhin/url-image **(see Figure 6-11).**

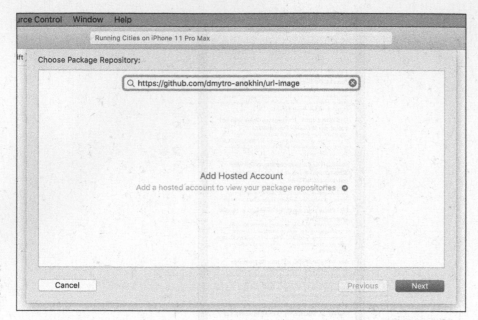

FIGURE 6-11:
Adding a package
to your XCode
project.

3. **Click Next.**

4. **Click Next.**

5. **Click Finish.**

   The package will be added to the project.

With the `URLImage` package added to the project, add the following statements in bold to the `ContentView.swift` file:

```swift
import SwiftUI
import URLImage

...

    var body: some View {
        List(articles, id: \.url) { item in
            HStack(alignment: .top) {
                URLImage(
                    (( URL(string:item.urlToImage ??
                                "https://picsum.photos/100")
                            ?? nil
                    )!),
                    delay: 0.25,
                    processors:
```

```
                        [Resize(size:
                            CGSize(width: 100.0,
                                    height: 100.0),
                                scale:
                                    UIScreen.main.scale)],
                    content: {
                        $0.image
                        .resizable()
                            .aspectRatio(contentMode:
                                            .fit)
                        .clipped()
                    }
                ).frame(width: 100.0, height: 100.0)

                VStack(alignment: .leading) {
                    Text(item.title)
                        .font(.headline)
                    Text(item.description ?? "")
                        .font(.footnote)
                }
            }
        }.onAppear(perform: fetchData)
    }
}


struct ContentView_Previews: PreviewProvider {
    static var previews: some View {
        ContentView()
    }
}
```

The preceding statements add the URLImage view (of size 100 x 100) to each row in the List view. You need to check whether each news headline contains an image (through the urlToImage property). If no image is available, you'll make use of a sample image provided by https://picsum.photos/. The URL https://picsum.photos/100 indicates to the site to return an image of size 100 x 100 pixels.

For more information on how to use the URLImage view, check out https://github.com/dmytro-anokhin/url-image.

TIP

Figure 6-12 shows the image displayed next to each news headline.

FIGURE 6-12:
Displaying an
image next to
each news
headline.

Wrapping the List view in a NavigationView

Now that you've managed to populate the List view with the various news headlines, you can wrap the List view in a NavigationView:

```
var body: some View {
    NavigationView {
        List(articles, id: \.url) { item in
            HStack (alignment: .top) {
                URLImage(((URL(string:item.urlToImage ??
                    "https://picsum.photos/100")
                    ?? nil)!),
                    delay: 0.25,
                    processors:
                        [Resize(size:
                            CGSize(width: 100.0,
                                height: 100.0),
                            scale:
                            UIScreen.main.scale)],
                content: {
                    $0.image
```

```
                        .resizable()
                            .aspectRatio(contentMode:
                                        .fit)
                        .clipped()
                    }
                ).frame(width: 100.0, height: 100.0)

                VStack(alignment: .leading) {
                    Text(item.title)
                        .font(.headline)
                    Text(item.description ?? "")
                        .font(.footnote)
                }
            }
        }.onAppear(perform: fetchData)
        .navigationBarTitle("News Headlines")
    }
}
```

Figure 6-13 shows the `List` view displayed within a `NavigationView` with the navigation bar title set.

FIGURE 6-13:
Displaying
the navigation
bar title.

You can make the text in the navigation bar title smaller by setting its display mode to `inline`:

```
.navigationBarTitle("News Headlines",
                    displayMode: .inline)
```

Figure 6-14 shows reduced font size of the navigation bar title.

FIGURE 6-14: Reducing the font size of the navigation bar title.

Creating the details page

When the user taps a row in the `List` view, you should display the content of the news on another page. The details of the news can be obtained through its `url` property of the `Article` struct.

To display the news using its URL, you need to use a web browser. In the current version of SwiftUI, not all the views are implemented yet, and this includes the implementation of the web browser, which is available in the existing WebKit framework and known as the `WebView`. So what you need to do now is make use of the `WebView` in your SwiftUI application.

To do so, let's add a new SwiftUI View file to the project and name it `NewsView.swift`. Add the following statements in bold to the `NewsView.swift` file:

```
import SwiftUI
import WebKit


struct WebView: UIViewRepresentable {
    let request: URLRequest
```

```
    func makeUIView(context: Context) -> WKWebView  {
        return WKWebView()
    }

    func updateUIView(_ uiView: WKWebView, context: Context) {
        uiView.load(request)
    }
}

struct NewsView: View {
    let url: String

    var body: some View {
        WebView(request: URLRequest(url: URL(string:
            url)!))
    }
}

struct NewsView_Previews: PreviewProvider {
    static var previews: some View {
        NewsView(url: "https://www.dummies.com")
    }
}
```

The `UIViewRepresentable` protocol allows you to create and manage a `UIView` object in your SwiftUI application. By conforming to this protocol, you need to implement the following methods:

➤ `makeUIView`: Creates the view object.

➤ `updateUIView` Updates the state of the view object.

The `UIViewRepresentable` protocol is discussed in more detail in Chapter 9.

When the WebView is created, you can use it by passing in the URL of the page to load. For the preview, you load the web page shown in Figure 6-15.

FIGURE 6-15:
Previewing the
details page.

Once the details page is created, you're ready to link it with the ContentView. Add
the following statements in bold to the ContentView.swift file:

```swift
var body: some View {
    NavigationView {
        List(articles, id: \.url) { item in
            NavigationLink(destination:
                NewsView(url:item.url)
            ) {
                HStack (alignment: .top) {
                    URLImage(
                        ((URL(string:item.urlToImage ??
                            "https://picsum.photos/100")
                            ?? nil)!),
                        delay: 0.25,
                        processors:
                            [Resize(size:
                                CGSize(width: 100.0,
                                    height: 100.0),
                                scale:
                                    UIScreen.main.scale)],
```

```
                    content: {
                        $0.image
                        .resizable()
                            .aspectRatio(contentMode:
                                            .fit)
                        .clipped()
                    }
                ).frame(width: 100.0, height: 100.0)

                VStack(alignment: .leading) {
                    Text(item.title)
                        .font(.headline)
                    Text(item.description ?? "")
                        .font(.footnote)
                }
            }
        }
    }.onAppear(perform: fetchData)
        .navigationBarTitle("News Headlines",
displayMode: .inline)
    }
}
}
```

Figure 6-16 shows how the application works. Tap a row in the List view and the details will be loaded on the details page.

What if you want to display the navigation bar title in large text? Well, you can set it as follows in the ContentView.swift file:

```
var body: some View {
    NavigationView {
        List(articles, id: \.url) { item in
            NavigationLink(destination:
                NewsView(url:item.url)
            ) {
                ...
        }.onAppear(perform: fetchData)
            .navigationBarTitle("News Headlines")
    }
}
```

However, you'll soon realize that when you navigate to the details page, there is a large empty space below the navigation bar in the details page (see Figure 6-17).

To resolve this, you need to set the navigation bar title in the NewsView.swift to display in inline mode:

```swift
struct NewsView: View {
    let url: String
    var body: some View {
        WebView(request: URLRequest(url: URL(string:
            url)!))
        .navigationBarTitle("News Details",
            displayMode: .inline)
    }
}
```

FIGURE 6-17:
The details page
with an empty
space below the
navigation bar.

Figure 6-18 shows the details view now showing the content without the empty space. In addition, the navigation bar also displays a title.

FIGURE 6-18:
The empty space
below the
navigation bar is
gone.

If you don't want the title, simply pass in an empty string to the `navigation BarTitle()` modifier:

```
.navigationBarTitle("",
    displayMode: .inline)
```

Creating Tabbed Applications

Besides building navigation applications, another type of UI that is very popular is the tabbed application. A tabbed application is an application that has a little tab bar at the bottom of the screen. The tab bar contains tab items that display different screens when tapped. It's a quick way for users to switch between screens providing different functionalities.

SwiftUI provides the `TabView` that allows you to create tabbed applications quickly and easily.

Using the TabView

To create tabs on your screen, you use the `TabView`. `TabView` is a view that allows you to switch between multiple child views. A `TabView` contains a collection of `View` items, so the first thing you need to do is to create your `View`. The following example shows two `View` items: `TabView1` and `TabView2`:

```
import SwiftUI

struct ContentView: View {
    var body: some View {
        ...
    }
}

struct TabView1: View {
    var body: some View {
        Text("This is Tab View 1")
    }
}

struct TabView2: View {
    var body: some View {
        Text("This is Tab View 2")
    }
}
```

You can now put the two `View` items inside the `TabView`, like this:

```
import SwiftUI

struct ContentView: View {
    var body: some View {
        TabView {
            TabView1()
                .tabItem {
                    Image(systemName: "doc.richtext")
                    Text("News")
                }
```

```
        TabView2()
            .tabItem {
                Image(systemName. "Info.circle")
                Text("About")
            }
        }
    }
}
```

The tabItem() modifier customizes the content of the tab bar item of each tab. Here, you added an icon and a Text view to each tab item. Figure 6-19 shows how the tabbed application looks.

FIGURE 6-19:
Displaying a
TabView with two
screens.

Selecting TabViews programmatically

Sometimes you want a specific TabView to be active when the screen is loaded. In this case, you need to use the tag() modifier with a unique identifier and add it to each view in the `TabView`. You can then use a state variable and bind it to the `TabView`, like this:

```
struct ContentView: View {

    @State var selectedTabView = 1

    var body: some View {
        TabView(selection:$selectedTabView) {
            TabView1()
                .tabItem {
                    Image(systemName: "doc.richtext")
                    Text("News")
                }.tag(0)

            TabView2()
                .tabItem {
                    Image(systemName: "info.circle")
                    Text("About")
                }.tag(1)
        }
    }
}
```

The preceding code snippet makes the second tab view (with tag 1) the default active view. In other words, the `TabView2` will be displayed when the application is loaded.

What if you needed to change the tab view during runtime when the user is interacting with your app? In this case, you can make use of a `Binding` property. For example, say in `TabView1` you have a button that when tapped, brings the user to `TabView2`. In this case, add a `Binding` property to `TabView1` and change its value when the button is tapped:

```
struct TabView1: View {

    @Binding var selectedTabView: Int

    var body: some View {
        VStack {
            Text("This is Tab View 1")
```

```
            Button(
                action: {
                    self.selectedTabView = 1
                },
                label: {
                    Text("Display TabView2")
                }
            )
        }

    }
}
```

In the main `ContentView`, pass the state variable `selectedTabView` to `TabView1`, so that changes to the state variable `selectedTabView` will cause the `TabView2` to be displayed:

```
struct ContentView: View {
    @State var selectedTabView = 1

    var body: some View {
        TabView(selection:$selectedTabView) {
            TabView1(selectedTabView: $selectedTabView)
                .tabItem {
                    Image(systemName: "doc.richtext")
                    Text("News")
                }.tag(0)

            TabView2()
                .tabItem {
                    Image(systemName: "info.circle")
                    Text("About")
                }.tag(1)
        }
    }
}
```

Figure 6-20 shows that when you click the Display TabView2 button, the `TabView2` will be loaded.

FIGURE 6-20:
Programmatically
displaying the
TabView2.

IN THIS CHAPTER

» **Laying out your views**

» **Justifying views**

» **Inserting spacing between views**

» **Animating with** ZStack

» **Displaying views for collecting user inputs**

» **Logically grouping views**

Chapter **7**

Formatting Your User Interface

I n the previous chapters, I show you how the various views in SwiftUI help you to create compelling user interfaces (UIs) in your iOS apps. I also show you a few ways to lay out your views using the VStack, HStack, and ZStack views. In this chapter, I explain these views in more detail and tell you how they allow you to lay out your UI in different ways.

Laying Out Views Using Stacks

In SwiftUI, you describe your app's UI in the view's body property:

```
struct ContentView: View {
    var body: some View {
        // your UI here
    }
}
```

The body property only returns a single view, so no matter how complex your UI is, it needs to return only one *single* view. To create a compelling UI, you combine and embed different views using VStack, HStack, or ZStack.

VStack

The VStack view is no stranger to you if you've read the previous chapters. The VStack arranges its children in a vertical column. Here's one example of a VStack containing a Rectangle view:

```
struct ContentView: View {
    var body: some View {
        VStack {
            Rectangle()
                .fill(Color.yellow)
                .frame(width: 100, height: 100)
        }
    }
}
```

TIP

When you have only a single element in a VStack, it makes no difference whether you use a VStack or an HStack.

Figure 7-1 shows the rectangle displayed in the center of the screen.

At this moment, the VStack contains only one view, the Rectangle, so the size of VStack will also assume the size of Rectangle (which is 100 x 100 points). By default, the VStack is always positioned in the center of the screen, vertically and horizontally. To prove this, add a border to the VStack view:

```
var body: some View {
    VStack {
        Rectangle()
            .fill(Color.yellow)
            .frame(width: 100, height: 100)
    }
    .border(Color.black, width:1)
}
```

TIP

Adding a border to container views such as VStack or HStack is a great way to troubleshoot layout issues.

Figure 7-2 shows the rectangle from Figure 7-1 displayed with a black border.

FIGURE 7-1:
The rectangle is displayed in the center of the screen.

FIGURE 7-2:
Showing the rectangle with a border.

Let's now add another Rectangle to the VStack view:

```
var body: some View {
    VStack {
        Rectangle()
            .fill(Color.yellow)
            .frame(width: 100, height: 100)
        Rectangle()
            .fill(Color.red)
            .frame(width: 200, height: 100)
    }
    .border(Color.black, width:1)
}
```

Now you can see that VStack has expanded in size to accommodate the second rectangle (see Figure 7-3) and that both rectangles are stacked vertically.

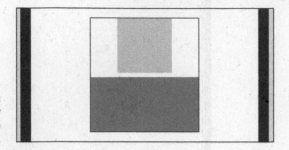

FIGURE 7-3:
The VStack view now contains two rectangles.

TIP

Notice that there is a default spacing (8 points) between the two Rectangle views within the VStack view. You can get rid of this spacing by using the spacing attribute in the VStack view, like this:

```
VStack (spacing:0) {
```

Alignment

The VStack contains two views, and its size has expanded to accommodate the two views. Setting a border to the VStack makes it easy to see this.

You can see that the yellow rectangle (the top one) is centered horizontally. This is the default behavior of views that are contained within the VStack view. You can change this behavior through the use of the alignment parameter:

```
struct ContentView: View {
    var body: some View {
        VStack (alignment: .trailing) {
            Rectangle()
                .fill(Color.yellow)
                .frame(width: 100, height: 100)
            Rectangle()
                .fill(Color.red)
                .frame(width: 200, height: 100)
        }
        .border(Color.black, width:1)
    }
}
```

Here, you're setting the horizontal alignment for all the views contained within the VStack view. Figure 7-4 shows both the rectangles aligned to the right side of the VStack.

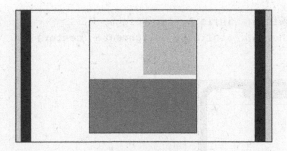

FIGURE 7-4:
Aligning both rectangles to the right.

The `alignment` parameter for the VStack view can take in one of the following values (of type `HorizontalAlignment`):

>> center

>> leading

>> trailing

As mentioned, the VStack view by default takes on the size of its containing views. However, you can change its size if you want:

```
struct ContentView: View {
    var body: some View {
        VStack (alignment: .leading) {
            Rectangle()
                .fill(Color.yellow)
                .frame(width: 100, height: 100)
            Rectangle()
                .fill(Color.red)
                .frame(width: 200, height: 100)
        }
        .border(Color.black, width:1)
        .frame(maxWidth: .infinity, minHeight: 0,
               maxHeight: .infinity, alignment: .center)
        .border(Color.black)
    }
}
```

The preceding code sets up the VStack view to occupy the entire screen (see Figure 7-5) through the use of the frame() modifier. Notice that now the views contained in VStack are centered horizontally and vertically (the default alignment):

```
.frame(maxWidth: .infinity, minHeight: 0,
       maxHeight: .infinity, alignment: .center)
```

FIGURE 7-5:
The VStack views now occupy the entire screen.

If you want to align the views horizontally to the left, you can set the alignment parameter of the frame() modifier to leading:

```
.frame(maxWidth: .infinity, minHeight: 0,
       maxHeight: .infinity, alignment: .leading)
```

The left of Figure 7-6 shows the views aligned to the left, and the right of Figure 7-6 shows the views aligned to the right when the alignment parameter is set to trailing.

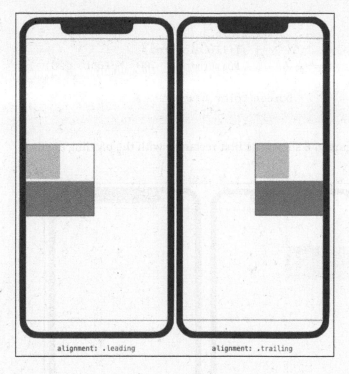

alignment: .leading   alignment: .trailing

FIGURE 7-6:
Aligning the
content of the
VStack using the
leading and
trailing options.

You can also set the views to align to the top left and bottom right of the screen, as shown in Figure 7-7. Besides all these alignments, you also have:

» .bottom

» .bottomLeading

» .topTrailing

Padding

Often, you'll want views to be spaced out with a margin so that they aren't sticking to one another. This is the job of the padding() modifier. Using the same example that I use earlier, let's add the padding() modifier to the first rectangle:

```
var body: some View {
    VStack (alignment: .leading) {
        Rectangle()
            .fill(Color.yellow)
            .frame(width: 100, height: 100)
            .padding()
```

```
        Rectangle()
            .fill(Color.red)
            .frame(width: 200, height: 100)
    }
    .border(Color.black)
}
```

Figure 7-8 shows the first rectangle with the padding applied.

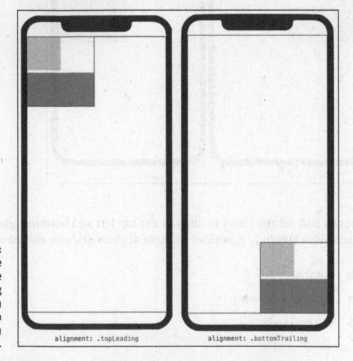

FIGURE 7-7:
Aligning the
content of the
VStack using
the topLeading
and bottom
Trailing
options.

alignment: .topLeading   alignment: .bottomTrailing

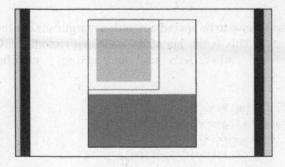

FIGURE 7-8:
Applying padding
to the first
rectangle.

The blue line surrounding the yellow rectangle is drawn by the preview canvas in Xcode to highlight the padding. It isn't visible when the app is deployed. By default, calling the `padding()` modifier without any argument is equivalent to:

```
.padding([.all])
```

The `all` argument indicates that the padding is applied to all four edges of the view. Figure 7-9 shows the different arguments that you can pass to the `padding()` modifiers and their respective effects.

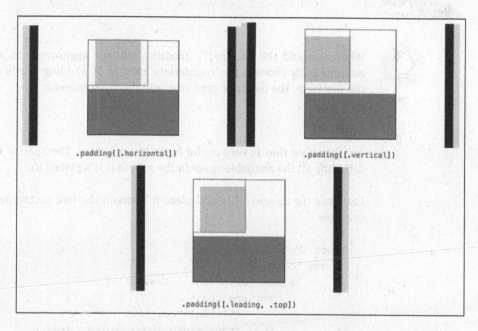

FIGURE 7-9:
Applying padding
with the various
specified options.

The order in which you apply the `padding()` modifier to a view is important. The left of Figure 7-10 shows that the padding is applied to the top rectangle first, followed by the frame size. The final size of the rectangle, 100 x 100, is inclusive of the padding applied.

On the other hand, the top rectangle on the right of Figure 7-10 has the frame size applied first, before applying the padding. The final size of the rectangle is 100 x 100, plus the padding around its four sides.

TIP

If you find the sequences of the modifiers hard to visualize, try reading them from the bottom to the top. In the left of Figure 7-10, you apply the frame to the padding, while on the right of Figure 7-10, you apply the padding to the frame.

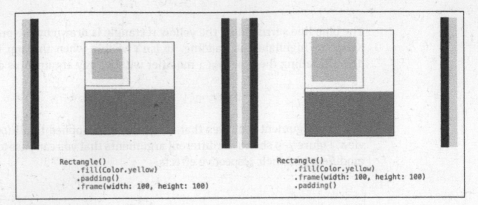

FIGURE 7-10:
The order of
applying the
modifiers matter.

```
Rectangle()
    .fill(Color.yellow)
    .padding()
    .frame(width: 100, height: 100)
```

```
Rectangle()
    .fill(Color.yellow)
    .frame(width: 100, height: 100)
    .padding()
```

TIP

When you add the `padding()` modifier without arguments to a view, SwiftUI automatically chooses the appropriate amount of padding that's appropriate for the platform, the dynamic type size, and the environment.

Spacer

Another view that is very useful is the Spacer view. The Spacer view automatically fills all the available space in the axis that it's placed in.

Let's use the Spacer view and place it between the two rectangles in our earlier example:

```
struct ContentView: View {
    var body: some View {
        VStack (alignment: .leading) {
            Rectangle()
                .fill(Color.yellow)
                .frame(width: 100, height: 100)
            Spacer()
                .frame(height: 50)
            Rectangle()
                .fill(Color.red)
                .frame(width: 200, height: 100)
        }
        .border(Color.black)
    }
}
```

Figure 7-11 shows that there is a gap of 50 points between the two rectangles.

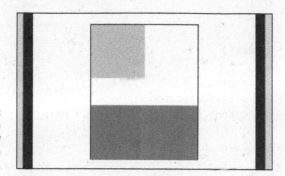

FIGURE 7-11:
Applying a
Spacer view
between the two
rectangles.

If you leave the `frame()` modifier out of the `Spacer` view, the `Spacer` view will fill up all the space between the two rectangles (see Figure 7-12):

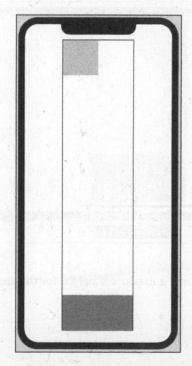

FIGURE 7-12:
The Spacer view
expanding to fill
up the space
between the two
rectangles.

```
var body: some View {
    VStack (alignment: .leading) {
        Rectangle()
            .fill(Color.yellow)
            .frame(width: 100, height: 100)
```

```
            Spacer()

        Rectangle()
            .fill(Color.red)
            .frame(width: 200, height: 100)
    }
    .border(Color.black)
}
```

When the phone is switched to the landscape mode, the Spacer view automatically adjusts its heights (see Figure 7-13).

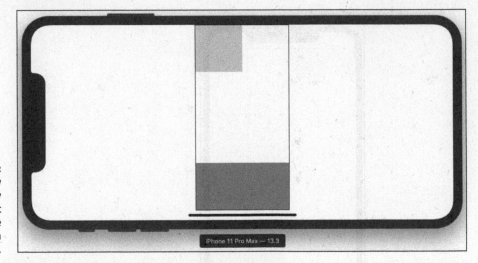

iPhone 11 Pro Max — 13.3

FIGURE 7-13:
The Spacer view automatically adjusts its height based on the screen orientation.

You can set a minimum height and a maximum height for the Spacer view using the frame() modifier:

```
var body: some View {
    VStack (alignment: .leading) {
        Rectangle()
            .fill(Color.yellow)
            .frame(width: 100, height: 100)

        Spacer()
            .frame(minHeight: 350,
                    maxHeight:450)
```

```
        Rectangle()
            .fill(Color.red)
            frame(width: 200, height: 100)
    }
        .border(Color.black)
    }
```

Figure 7-14 shows the Spacer view having a maximum height of 450 points while the phone is in portrait orientation and a minimum height of 350 points when in landscape orientation.

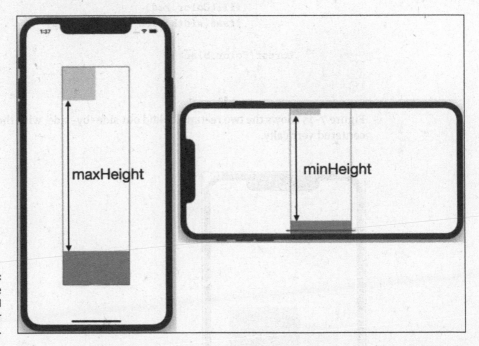

Note that if the minimum height exceeds the available height of the screen (such as when the device is in landscape orientation), the two rectangles will be pushed out of the screen.

HStack

The HStack view is very similar to the VStack view, except that instead of laying out the views vertically, it lays them out horizontally. Here's an example:

```
struct ContentView: View {
    var body: some View {
        HStack {
            Rectangle()
                .fill(Color.yellow)
                .frame(width: 100, height: 100)
            Rectangle()
                .fill(Color.red)
                .frame(width: 200, height: 200)
        }
        .border(Color.black)
    }
}
```

Figure 7-15 shows the two rectangles laid out side-by-side, with the first rectangle centered vertically.

FIGURE 7-15:
Using the HStack view to contain the two rectangles.

Like the VStack, you can place a Spacer view between views contained in an HStack view (see Figure 7-16):

```
var body: some View {
    HStack {
        Rectangle()
            .fill(Color.yellow)
            .frame(width: 100, height: 100)
        Spacer()
            .frame(width: 50)
        Rectangle()
            .fill(Color.red)
            .frame(width: 200, height: 200)
    }
    .border(Color.black)
}
```

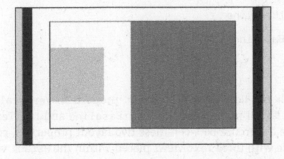

FIGURE 7-16:
Using the Spacer view in the HStack view.

To control the alignment for the views contained within the HStack view, use the alignment parameter:

```
var body: some View {
    HStack (alignment: .bottom) {
        Rectangle()
            .fill(Color.yellow)
            .frame(width: 100, height: 100)
        Spacer()
            .frame(width: 50)
        Rectangle()
            .fill(Color.red)
            .frame(width: 200, height: 200)
    }
    .border(Color.black)
}
```

Figure 7-17 shows the first rectangle aligned to the bottom of the HStack view.

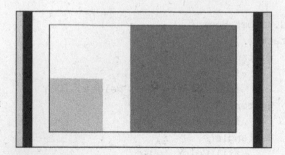

FIGURE 7-17:
Aligning the first rectangle to the bottom of the HStack view.

The alignment can take one of the following VerticalAlignment properties:

>> bottom

>> center

>> firstTextBaseline

>> lastTextBaseline

>> top

Compared with the HorizontalAlignment properties, VerticalAlignment has two additional layout properties: firstTextBaseline and lastTextBaseline. To understand the difference between these two layout properties, consider the following example with three Text views placed within the HStack view:

```
struct ContentView: View {
    var body: some View {
        HStack {
            Text("SwiftUI")
                .font(.caption)
            Text("For")
                .font(.title)
            Text("Dummies")
                .font(.largeTitle)
        }
    }
}
```

The three Text views of different sizes are centered vertically, as shown in Figure 7-18.

FIGURE 7-18:
The three Text
views are
centered
vertically within
the HStack view.

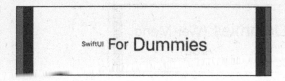

Figure 7-19 shows how the Text views are aligned using the various Vertical Alignment options.

FIGURE 7-19:
The various
alignment
options applied
to the views
contained within
the HStack view.

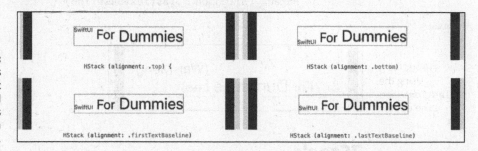

However, the last two options (firstTextBaseline and lastTextBaseline) do not seem to differ. To see the difference, let's add another Text view to the HStack view:

```swift
struct ContentView: View {
    var body: some View {
        HStack (alignment:.firstTextBaseline) {
            Text("SwiftUI")
                .font(.caption)
            Text("For")
                .font(.title)
            Text("Dummies")
                .font(.largeTitle)
            Text("(Wei-Meng Lee)")
                .font(.title)
        }
    }
}
```

You can now see that all four Text views are aligned based on the first line within each view (see Figure 7-20).

FIGURE 7-20:
Using the
firstTextBase
line option.

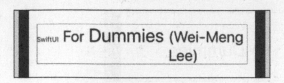

If you now use the lastTextBaseline option, the alignment will be based on the last line within each view (see Figure 7-21):

```
HStack (alignment:.lastTextBaseline) {
```

FIGURE 7-21:
Using the
lastTextBase
line option.

(Wei-Meng
SwiftUI For Dummies Lee)

ZStack

If you want to stack views on top of one another, you can use the ZStack view. The ZStack view overlays its children views, aligning them in both axes.

Let's take a look at an example:

```
struct ContentView: View {
    var body: some View {
        ZStack {
            Image("pdf")
                .resizable()
                .frame(width: 256, height: 256.0)
            Text("Watermark")
                .font(.largeTitle)
                .foregroundColor(.gray)
                .opacity(0.5)
                .rotationEffect(.degrees(-45))
        }
    }
}
```

This example shows the ZStack view containing an Image view and a Text view. The Image view shows an image named pdf (stored in the Assets.xcassets folder). The Text view displays the word *Watermark* rotated 45 degrees counter-clockwise. Because the Text view comes after the Image view, it's stacked on top of the Image view (see Figure 7-22).

FIGURE 7-22:
Stacking the Text
view over the
Image view in the
ZStack view.

The order of the views placed within the ZStack determines how views are displayed. Views are drawn on top of the previous view in the order in which they appear in the ZStack. If you want to override this (for example, to bring a view to the top), you can use the zIndex() modifier with a number. By default, all views have a default value of 0 for the zIndex. But if you set the zIndex for certain views, they're displayed in order based on the zIndex (in ascending order) or the order in which they appear (if the zIndex is not set).

The following shows the Text view placed before the Image view, but because its zIndex is set to 1, it's drawn last. The effect is still the same as the previous code snippet:

```
var body: some View {
    ZStack {
        Text("Watermark")
            .font(.largeTitle)
            .foregroundColor(.gray)
            .opacity(0.5)
            .rotationEffect(.degrees(-45))
            .zIndex(1)
        Image("pdf")
            .resizable()
            .frame(width: 256, height: 256.0)
    }
}
```

TIP

The zIndex() modifier works with negative numbers as well. Views have a default zIndex of 0, but you can provide positive or negative values that position them on top of or below other views respectively.

Using ZStack

Here's an example of a good use of the ZStack view:

```
ZStack {
    Image(systemName: "bubble.right")
        .resizable()
        .frame(width: 200.0, height: 200.0)
    Text("Hello, SwiftUI")
}
```

This code snippet shows an Image view showing a conversation bubble and a Text view overlaid on top of it showing the text of the conversation (see Figure 7-23).

FIGURE 7-23:
Overlaying the
Image view with
the Text view.

Notice that the Text view is not really centered vertically within the rectangle of the bubble. This is because the height of the Image also includes the pointed tip at the bottom of the rectangle. To fix this, you can make use of the VStack and Spacer views (see the previous sections):

```
ZStack {
    Image(systemName: "bubble.right")
        .resizable()
        .frame(width: 200.0, height: 200.0)
    VStack{
        Text("Hello, SwiftUI")
        Spacer()
        .frame(height: 30)
    }
}
```

The text should now appear centered in the rectangle of the bubble (see Figure 7-24).

FIGURE 7-24:
Using a Spacer
view in the
ZStack view.

Animating within a ZStack

The ZStack view is very useful when you want to show some simple animation. For example, you can create a series of images showing a horse in motion, like the famous series of photographs by Eadweard Muybridge (see Figure 7-25).

THE HORSE IN MOTION.

Illustrated by
MUYBRIDGE.

"SALLIE GARDNER," owned by LELAND STANFORD; running at a 1.40 gait over the Palo Alto track, 19th June, 1878.

FIGURE 7-25:
*The Horse in
Motion* by
Eadweard
Muybridge.

Source: https://en.wikipedia.org/wiki/The_Horse_in_Motion

You can then put all these images within the ZStack view. To make the horse "move," you can change the zIndex of the images programmatically so that each image can move to the top, creating the impression that the horse is galloping.

For this section, you use a simpler example — one image showing a button and another image showing the same button depressed.

Here's the code that makes this happen:

```
struct ContentView: View {
    @State private var currentState = true
    let timer =
        Timer.publish(every: 1.0, on: .main, in: .common)
            .autoconnect()

    var body: some View {
        ZStack{
            Image("up")
                .resizable()
                .frame(width: 150.0, height: 150.0)
                .zIndex(currentState ? 1:0)
            Image("down")
                .resizable()
                .frame(width: 150.0, height: 150.0)
                .zIndex(currentState ? 0:1)
        }
        .onReceive(timer) { input in
            self.currentState.toggle()
        }
    }
}
```

I'll dissect the code to show you how it works:

» You place two Image views in the ZStack view.

» Each of the two Image views has the zIndex() modifier applied. (Strictly speaking, for this example, you only need to apply the zIndex() modifier to one Image view.)

» The zIndex of each Image view is bound to the currentState state variable. Based on the value of currentState, the zIndex of each Image view is set appropriately.

» You use a Timer class to run some code at a regular time interval. In this example, the Timer object will trigger the onReceive() closure every 1 second, which toggles the currentState variable.

» The Timer class's publish() method sets the timer to fire every 1 second, use the main run-loop option, and use the common mode to run alongside other common events.

Figure 7-26 shows the button in its original state.

FIGURE 7-26:
The button in its
original state.

One second later, the button will be "depressed" (see Figure 7-27).

FIGURE 7-27:
The button in its
depressed state.
(Poor button.)

And 1 second later, the button will go back to its original state, and the process repeats forever, simulating a button being pressed and released repeatedly.

TIP

This is just a simple demonstration for using the ZStack view for some simple animation. Chapter 11 discusses more animation techniques.

Using Container Views

One of the most common things users do in an application is fill up forms. Whether you're filling details on a signup page or viewing the preferences of an app, you need to edit or fill in information of some sort. Creating the UI of a form may not be difficult, but it actually gets quite mundane and laborious when you have a number of forms to create.

Consider the following example where you want to create a preferences page for your application (say, a conference app). You want the preferences page to display the following:

>> A toggle to enable/disable your favorited conference session to be shared with your peers

>> A picker to select whether a notification should be sent for all commencing sessions or only favorited sessions

» A label to display the name of your app

» A label to display the version of your app

» A label to display the author of the app

You could implement the preceding using the various views that I cover in the previous few chapters, and arrange them using a combination of VStack and HStack views:

```
import SwiftUI

struct ContentView: View {

    @State private var shareFavoritedSessions = false
    @State private var notifMode = 0

    var modes = ["All Sessions", "Favorited Sessions"]

    var body: some View {
        NavigationView {
            VStack{
                Toggle(isOn: $shareFavoritedSessions) {
                    Text("Share Favorited Sessions")
                }
                Picker(selection: $notifMode,
                    label: Text(
                        "Display Notifications for")) {
                    ForEach(0..<modes.count) {
                        Text(self.modes[$0])
                    }
                }
                HStack {
                    Text("Name")
                    Spacer()
                    Text("DLS Conferences")
                }
                HStack {
                    Text("Version")
                    Spacer()
                    Text("1.0.1")
                }
                HStack {
                    Text("Developed by")
                    Spacer()
```

```
                    Text("Wei-Meng Lee")
                }
            }
            .padding()
            .navigationBarTitle("Preferences")
        }
    }
}
```

Figure 7-28 shows how the view would look.

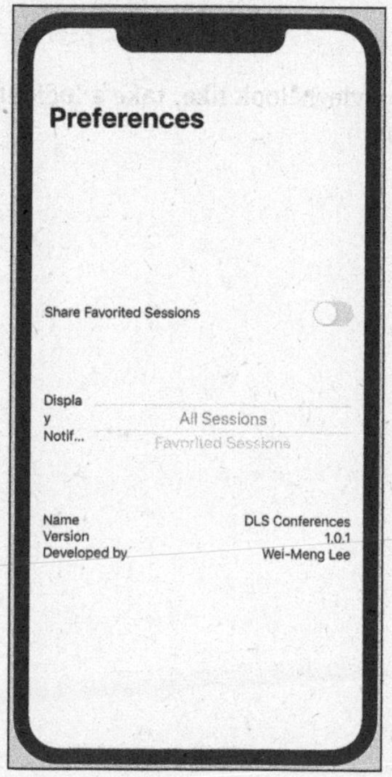

FIGURE 7-28:
The views need
some serious
layout to make
this look
professional.

Obviously, while functional, they need some sort of layout to make it more presentable. What if there were a better way to do all this?

Form and Section

Fortunately, SwiftUI makes it easy to lay out your views in a form. You can use the `Form` view, together with the `Section` view, like this:

```
Form {
    Section(header: Text("Section Header 1")) {

    }
    Section(header: Text("Section Header 2")) {

    }
}
```

To see what the `Form` and `Section` views look like, take a look at the Settings app on your iPhone (see Figure 7-29).

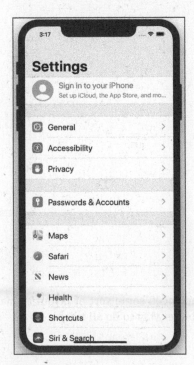

FIGURE 7-29:
The Settings app
on the iPhone.

Let's put all these views into the Form and Section views, like the following:

```swift
struct ContentView: View {

    @State private var shareFavoritedSessions = false
    @State private var notifMode = 0
    var modes = ["All Sessions", "Favorited Sessions"]

    var body: some View {
        NavigationView {
            Form {
                Section(header: Text("Sessions")) {
                    Toggle(isOn: $shareFavoritedSessions){
                        Text("Share Favorited Sessions")
                    }
                    Picker(selection: $notifMode,
                        label: Text(
                        "Display Notifications for")) {
                        ForEach(0..<modes.count) {
                            Text(self.modes[$0])
                        }
                    }
                }
                Section(header: Text("About this App")) {
                    HStack {
                        Text("Name")
                        Spacer()
                        Text("DLS Conferences")
                    }
                    HStack {
                        Text("Version")
                        Spacer()
                        Text("1.0.1")
                    }
                    HStack {
                        Text("Developed by")
                        Spacer()
                        Text("Wei-Meng Lee")
                    }
                }
            }
            .navigationBarTitle("Preferences")
        }
    }
}
```

Figure 7-30 shows the views formatted nicely.

FIGURE 7-30:
The views laid out
using the Form
and Section
views.

Group

The Group view doesn't have a visible appearance — it's used to logically group views together (hence, the name). To understand how it works, consider the following example:

```
struct ContentView: View {
    var body: some View {
        VStack {
            Text("User 1")
                .font(.largeTitle)
            Text("Emma")

            Text("User 2")
                .font(.largeTitle)
            Text("Olivia")

            Text("User 3")
```

```
                                    .font(.largeTitle)
                Text("Ava")

                Text("User 4")
                    .font(.largeTitle)
                Text("Isabella")

                Text("User 5")
                    .font(.largeTitle)
                Text("Sophia")
            }
        }
    }
```

This example has a VStack view containing ten Text views (see Figure 7-31).

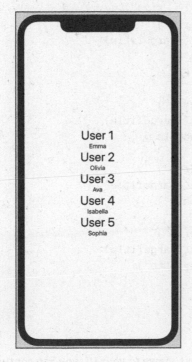

FIGURE 7-31:
All container
views in SwiftUI
can contain, at
most, ten views.

Now if you want to add more Text views to your UI, you can continue to add them to the VStack or create additional Stack views to contain them.

In SwiftUI, all container views can contain a maximum of ten views. If you have more than ten views in the VStack view, an error will occur. To solve this limitation, use the Group view to group views into groups of no more than ten views, like this:

```
struct ContentView: View {
    var body: some View {
        VStack {
            Group {
                Text("User 1")
                    .font(.largeTitle)
                Text("Emma")

                Text("User 2")
                    .font(.largeTitle)
                Text("Olivia")

                Text("User 3")
                    .font(.largeTitle)
                Text("Ava")
            }
            Group {
                Text("User 4")
                    .font(.largeTitle)
                Text("Isabella")

                Text("User 5")
                    .font(.largeTitle)
                Text("Sophia")

                Text("User 6")
                    .font(.largeTitle)
                Text("Charlotte")
            }
        }
    }
}
```

Now if you want to add more Text views to your UI, you can continue to add them to the VStack or create additional Group views to contain them.

Divider

The Divider view draws a line on your UI, allowing you to visually separate views or groups of views.

TIP

The Divider view displays a horizontal line when it isn't in a stack.

The following code snippet contains a series of Image views:

```
struct ContentView: View {
    var body: some View {
        HStack() {
            Image(systemName: "text.alignleft")
            Image(systemName: "text.aligncenter")
            Image(systemName: "text.alignright")
            Image(systemName: "text.alignright")
            Image(systemName: "increase.indent")
            Image(systemName: "decrease.indent")
            Image(systemName: "decrease.quotelevel")
        }
        .padding()
        .border(Color.black)
        .frame(maxWidth: .infinity, minHeight: 0,
               maxHeight: 50, alignment: .center)
    }
}
```

The top of Figure 7-32 shows all the images grouped together. Separating the images based on functionality would be useful. Hence, you can use the Divider view to draw a line that separates them (see the bottom of Figure 7-32):

```
HStack() {
    Image(systemName: "text.alignleft")
    Image(systemName: "text.aligncenter")
    Image(systemName: "text.alignright")
    Image(systemName: "text.alignright")
    Divider()
    Image(systemName: "increase.indent")
    Image(systemName: "decrease.indent")
    Image(systemName: "decrease.quotelevel")
}
```

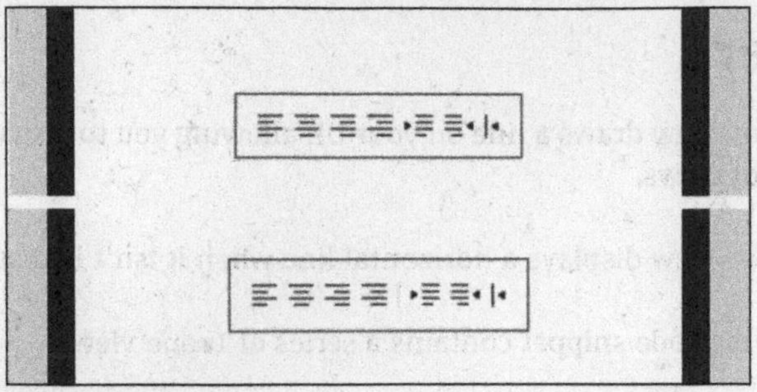

FIGURE 7-32:
All the images grouped together (top) and with a divider inserted between them (bottom).

3
Exploring with SwiftUI in More Detail

IN THIS PART . . .

Understand the fundamentals of statement management in SwiftUI.

Use the legacy UIKit views and view controllers together with SwiftUI views.

IN THIS CHAPTER

» Understanding how a property
  wrapper works

» Working with state variables

» Binding state variables

» Managing state from external objects

» Sharing objects

» Accessing built-in environment
  variables

Chapter **8**

Understanding State Management in SwiftUI

I f you've read this book from the beginning and arrived at this chapter, you
should have a good understanding of how SwiftUI works. SwiftUI builds your
user interface (UI) declaratively, and it relies heavily on the concept of state
variables to keep its UI updated. Besides @State, there are a number of other
mechanisms for state management in SwiftUI. These mechanisms are the focus of
this chapter.

Using a Property Wrapper

SwiftUI 5.1 introduced a new feature to the language: the *property wrapper*. A property wrapper is a generic data structure that has read/write capabilities, while at
the same time providing and enforcing additional functionalities. As its name
implies, a property wrapper "wraps" a property in order to attach additional logic
to it. The property wrapper is best explained using a simple example.

Suppose you want to store some string values in your app — say, email addresses. One criteria is that the email addresses must be in lowercase. Instead of checking this rule every time an email is stored, it would be easier if this rule could be enforced programmatically. Using a property wrapper, you can do this.

In order to enforce this lowercase rule, you can define a struct — say AllLower Cased — with the @propertyWrapper attribute. You would also need to have a property called wrappedValue. Here is an example of the AllLowerCased struct:

```
@propertyWrapper struct AllLowerCased {
    var wrappedValue: String {
        didSet {
            wrappedValue = wrappedValue.lowercased()
        }
    }

    init(wrappedValue: String) {
        self.wrappedValue = wrappedValue.lowercased()
    }
}
```

Here, in addition to the wrappedValue property, you also have an initializer. When a string value has been assigned (either through the wrappedValue property or through the initializer), it will be changed to lowercase using the lowercased() function.

To use the AllLowerCased property wrapper, consider the following User struct:

```
struct User {
    var userName: String
    @AllLowerCased var email: String
}
```

TIP

A property wrapper is what allows @State to work. Whenever the value of a state variable is changed, the property wrapper allows the associated logic to fire, thereby triggering updates to the UI.

Notice that the email property has been declared with the @AllLowerCased property wrapper. This means that the value of the email property will be converted to lowercase automatically.

To prove this, create an instance of the User struct and initialize it with a username and email address. Then display the username and email address using two Text views:

```
struct ContentView: View {
    var user = User(userName: "Wei-Meng Lee",
                    email: "WeiMengLee@gmail.com")
    var body: some View {
        VStack {
            Text(user.userName)
            Text(user.email)
        }
    }
}
```

Figure 8-1 shows the value displayed. Notice that the email address is in all lowercase.

FIGURE 8-1: Displaying an email address in lowercase.

Maintaining State Using State Variables

In the previous few chapters in this book, I show you how state variables help your UI get updated automatically. In this section, I examine this in more detail.

A state variable is a property that is marked with the @State keyword. The @State keyword is known as a property wrapper (see the preceding section). When you mark a property as a state variable, SwiftUI starts monitoring the state variable's value. When a View reads a value from a state variable, SwiftUI ensures that this View is updated whenever the value of the state variable changes.

Following is an example of the use of a state variable to display an Alert view in SwiftUI.

In iOS, an Alert view is a pop-up that conveys important information to the user. Often, it requests feedback from the user, such as confirming an action to be performed. An alert often comes with one or two buttons, allowing the user to dismiss the alert or respond to an action.

```
import SwiftUI

struct ContentView: View {
    @State private var displayAlert = false

    var body: some View {
        VStack {
            Button(action: {
                self.displayAlert = true
            }) {
                Text("Display Alert")
            }
            .alert(isPresented: $displayAlert) {
                Alert(
                  title: Text(
                    "Do you want to delete this account?"),
                  message: Text(
                    "You cannot undo this action"),
                  primaryButton: .cancel(Text("Cancel")),
                  secondaryButton:
                    .destructive(Text("Delete"), action:{
                        print("Delete")
                    })
                )
            }
            Toggle(isOn: $displayAlert) {
                Text("Show Alert").bold()
            }.padding()
```

```
                    .background(displayAlert ?
                    Color.yellow : Color.gray)
        }
    }
}
```

In this example, you have a state variable, displayAlert, which is initially set to false.

To display an alert in SwiftUI, you use the Alert structure:

```
Alert(
    title: Text(
        "Do you want to delete this account?"),
    message: Text(
        "You cannot undo this action"),
    primaryButton: .cancel(Text("Cancel")),
    secondaryButton:
        .destructive(
            Text("Delete"), action:{
                print("Delete")
            })
)
```

The primaryButton and secondaryButton parameters allow you to specify up to two buttons to display in the Alert view. You can display the following types of buttons in an Alert view:

>> default(): The button is displayed in normal font.

>> cancel(): The button is displayed in bold font.

>> destructive(): The button is displayed in normal font but in red.

In order to display the Alert view, you need a context to bind so that the Alert view can be displayed. In this example, you use the alert() modifier on the Button view to display the alert. This alert is controlled by the isPresented parameter, whose value is bound to the displayAlert state variable.

For this example, you also bind the displayAlert state variable to a Toggle view.

When the button is tapped, the displayAlert state variable is changed to true, and the Alert view is displayed (see Figure 8-2). Notice that the Toggle view changes its background color, because the state variable has changed its value.

FIGURE 8-2:
Displaying the
Alert view
through the use
of a state
variable.

Tapping either button in the Alert view dismisses the Alert view and automatically causes the displayAlert state variable to be set to false. This happens because you're binding the displayAlert state variable to the Alert view (notice the $ prefix in $displayAlert). Internally within the Alert structure, the value of the state variable changes to false when the Alert view is dismissed.

Figure 8-3 shows the Toggle view with its background changed to gray when the Alert view was dismissed.

For the cancel button in the Alert, notice that you supplied a Text view to the cancel() button, like this:

```
primaryButton: .cancel(Text("Cancel")),
```

You can also simply omit the Text view and the alert will still display the cancel button:

```
primaryButton: .cancel(),
```

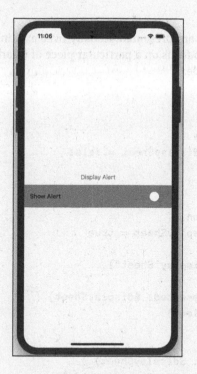

FIGURE 8-3:
The Toggle view
changes its color
when the Alert
view is dismissed.

TIP

SwiftUI adopts the philosophy of a "single source of truth." The key idea behind this philosophy is that every piece of data that you use in your view has a source of truth. This source of truth may be the state of a button highlight or the caption of a Text label. But regardless of where the source of truth lives, you must always have a single source of truth. If there are multiple (or duplicated) sources of truth, this will easily lead to data inconsistency. You can think of @State as the single source of truth for your view. The state of your view depends on the value of your state variable. If the value of the state variable changes, the state of the view automatically reflects the changes.

Binding State Variables

In the example in the preceding section, I show you how the state variable helps to display the Alert view. I also show you how dismissing the Alert view automatically sets the bound state variable to false. So, how does the Alert view automatically set the state variable?

The answer to this question lies with the concept known as *binding*. And the best way to illustrate this concept is to use the sheets in SwiftUI.

TIP

SwiftUI sheets are views that are presented modally over existing ones. They're useful when you want users to focus on a particular piece of information, such as showing a ticket with a QR code.

```swift
import SwiftUI

struct ContentView: View {
    @State private var displaySheet = false

    var body: some View {
        VStack{
            Button(action: {
                self.displaySheet = true
            }) {
                Text("Display Sheet")
            }
            .sheet(isPresented: $displaySheet) {
                TicketView()
            }

            Toggle(isOn: $displaySheet) {
                Text("Display Sheet").bold()
            }.padding()
             .background(displaySheet ?
                Color.yellow : Color.gray)
        }
    }
}

struct TicketView: View {
    var body: some View {
        VStack{
            Text("Your ticket")
        }
    }
}
```

The preceding example contains two views — one ContentView and the other TicketView. Like the previous example, you have a state variable to display the sheet. To display a sheet, you use the sheet() modifier and attach it to the Button view. The sheet to display is TicketView, which contains a Text view.

You bind the displaySheet state variable to the isPresented parameter of the sheet() modifier. When the state variable is set to true, the sheet is displayed as shown in Figure 8-4.

FIGURE 8-4:
Displaying a
sheet in iOS.

To dismiss the sheet, you simply drag it downward, and it's gone. What about programmatically dismissing it? To do that, you can add a Button view in the TicketView and bind it to a state variable, like this:

```
struct TicketView: View {
    @State var isPresented:Bool

    var body: some View {
        VStack{
            Text("Your ticket")
            Button("Dismiss Sheet") {
                self.isPresented = false
            }
        }
    }
}
```

In the ContentView, you can now pass in the displaySheet state variable when calling TicketView:

```
struct ContentView: View {
    @State private var displaySheet = false

    var body: some View {
        VStack{
            Button(action: {
                self.displaySheet = true
            }) {
                Text("Display Sheet")
            }
            .sheet(isPresented: $displaySheet) {
                TicketView(isPresented:
                    self.displaySheet)
            }

            Toggle(isOn: $displaySheet) {
                Text("Display Sheet").bold()
            }.padding()
             .background(displaySheet ?
                Color.yellow : Color.gray)
        }
    }
}
```

The button on the TicketView now appears in the sheet (see Figure 8-5). However, clicking the button does not dismiss the sheet. This is because changing the state variable in TicketView doesn't reflect the changes back to the ContentView.

To fix this, you need to use a *binding variable* in TicketView, instead of a state variable:

```
struct TicketView: View {
    @Binding var isPresented: Bool

    var body: some View {
        VStack{
            Text("Your ticket")
```

```
                    Button("Dismiss Sheet") {
                        self.isPresented = false
                    }
                }
            }
        }
    }
}
```

FIGURE 8-5:
Clicking the
Dismiss Sheet
button does not
dismiss the sheet.

You can now bind the `displaySheet` state variable with the `isPresented` binding variable in `TicketView`:

```
struct ContentView: View {
    @State private var displaySheet = false

    var body: some View {
        VStack{
            Button(action: {
                self.displaySheet = true
            }) {
                Text("Display Sheet")
            }
```

```
                .sheet(isPresented: $displaySheet) {
                    TicketView(isPresented:
                        self.$displaySheet)
                }


                Toggle(isOn: $displaySheet) {
                    Text("Display Sheet").bold()
                }.padding()
                    .background(displaySheet ?
                        Color.yellow : Color.gray)
            }
        }
    }
```

TIP

Besides binding a @Binding object to a @State object, it can also bind to @Binding and ObservableObject objects. (Say that ten times fast.)

When the isPresented binding variable is changed in TicketView, the change is also reflected back in ContentView, which will now dismiss the sheet.

Figure 8-6 summarizes how the binding works.

```
                                              (1)
                                    displaySheet is bound to isPresented
struct ContentView: View {
    @State private var displaySheet = false

    var body: some View {
        VStack{
            Button(action: {
                self.displaySheet = true        struct TicketView: View {
            }) {                                    @Binding var isPresented: Bool
                Text("Display Sheet")               var body: some View {
            }                                           VStack{
            .sheet(isPresented: $displaySheet) {            Text("Your ticket")
                TicketView(isPresented:                     Button("Dismiss Sheet") {
                    self.$displaySheet)                         self.isPresented = false
            }                                               }
                                                        }
            Toggle(isOn: $displaySheet) {           }
                Text("Display Sheet").bold()    }
            }.padding()
                .background(displaySheet ?
                    Color.yellow : Color.gray)
        }                                               (2)
    }                                       Changes to isPresented will affect displaySheet too
}
```

FIGURE 8-6:
How binding
works.

Managing State from External Objects

In the previous section, I explain how the @Binding property wrapper allows you to bind state variables of primitive types to properties in another view. If you want to bind more complex objects, you should use another property wrapper, @ObservedObject.

TIP

You use @State for controlling the state of a view (say, a Button view). However, if you want to observe changes made to an object, you should use @ObservedObject.

Suppose you have a page (with a link) that shows the search engine you've selected. When you tap the link, it navigates to another screen where you can change the search engine (see Figure 8-7).

FIGURE 8-7:
Selecting from a
list of search
engines.

When the search engine has been changed, going back to the previous screen displays the updated search engine (see Figure 8-8).

Using the ObservableObject protocol and @Published

So, how can this be implemented?

FIGURE 8-8:
Selecting a search engine will automatically update the ContentView.

First, let's add a new Swift file to the project and name it `SearchEngine.swift`. Populate it with the following statements in bold:

```swift
import Foundation

class SearchEngineChoice: ObservableObject {
    var searchEngines = ["Google","Yahoo","Bing"]
    @Published var engine = "Google"
}
```

In this file, you have a class named `SearchEngineChoice`, and it conforms to the `ObservableObject` protocol. The `ObservableObject` protocol allows you to track changes made to members of a class (hence, its name).

Within this class, you have a property named `searchEngines`, which contains an array of search engines that users can choose from. The second property, `engine`, has a `@Published` prefix. This means that any view that is bound to this property will automatically be notified when the property's value changes. For now, you'll initialize this value to `Google`.

Figure 8-9 summarizes the use of the `ObservableObject` protocol and the `@Published` property wrapper.

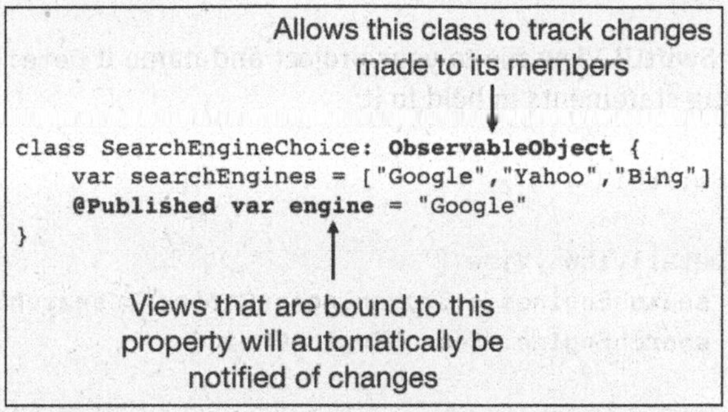

FIGURE 8-9: How the Observable Object protocol works.

Using the @ObservedObject

In the ContentView.swift file, let's display the currently selected search engines. Add the following statements in bold to the ContentView.swift file:

```swift
import SwiftUI

struct ContentView: View {
    @ObservedObject var searchEngine = SearchEngineChoice()

    var body: some View {
        NavigationView{
            VStack {
                NavigationLink (destination:
                    (DetailView(searchEngine:
                        searchEngine))) {
                    Text("Your search engine is " +
                        "\(searchEngine.engine)")
                }
            }
        }
    }
}
```

First, you have a property named searchEngine, which is of type SearchEngineChoice. Notice that it has the @ObservedObject prefix, which indicates that it will be observing the changes made to this property.

You then used the NavigationView and the NavigationLink so that when the user taps the Text view, it will navigate to another screen. Here, the Text view shows the search engine currently selected (through the searchEngine.engine property). The searchEngine is then passed to the DetailView (which you define next).

Add a new SwiftUI View file to your project and name it `DetailView.swift`. Add the following statements in bold to it:

```swift
import SwiftUI

struct DetailView: View {
    var searchEngines = SearchEngineChoice().searchEngines
    var searchEngine: SearchEngineChoice

    @State var selectedEngine = SearchEngineChoice().engine

    var body: some View {
        List {
            ForEach (searchEngines, id: \.self) {
                (engine) in
                Button(action: {
                    self.searchEngine.engine = engine
                    self.selectedEngine = engine
                }) {
                    HStack{
                        Text(engine)
                        Image(systemName:
                            self.selectedEngine == engine ?
                            "checkmark.square" : "square")
                    }
                }
            }
        }
    }
}

struct DetailView_Previews: PreviewProvider {
    static var previews: some View {
        DetailView(searchEngine: SearchEngineChoice())
    }
}
```

First, you get the list of search engines available from `SearchEngineChoice().searchEngines`. You also create a property named `searchEngine`, whose value is passed in from `ContentView`.

Next, you create a state variable called `selectedEngine`, which is used to bind to the individual rows in the `List`. When a row in the `List` view is tapped, it will change two variables:

» The observed property `engine` in the `SearchEngineChoice` object

» The state variable `selectedEngine`

Each row in the `List` displays the search engine name, as well as an image containing either a checked box (`checkmark.square`) or an empty square box (`square`). The `Image` view is bound to the `selectedEngine` state variable, and changes to the state variable will cause the image to be updated.

When the `engine` property is modified:

```
self.searchEngine.engine = engine
```

Views that are bound to this property in `ContentView` will be notified immediately. Figure 8-10 summarizes how the notifications of the `@ObservedObject`'s property works.

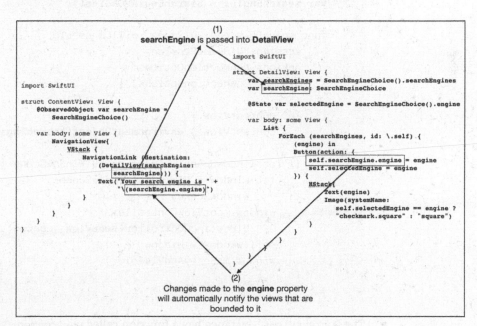

FIGURE 8-10: How the ObservedObject property works.

Sharing Objects

So far, you saw how `@Binding` and `@ObservedObject` allow you to bind objects between views. But sometimes, you just want to share your data with all the views in your entire app, not just between two views.

For this purpose, you can use the @EnvironmentObject property wrapper. The @EnvironmentObject allows you to share data anywhere in your views, and at the same time it keeps your view updated whenever the data is changed.

Using the same example in the preceding section, let's modify the app so that instead of creating a navigation application you create a tabbed application.

In the SceneDelegate.swift file, add the following statements in bold:

```
import UIKit
import SwiftUI

class SceneDelegate: UIResponder, UIWindowSceneDelegate {

    var window: UIWindow?

    var searchEngine = SearchEngineChoice()

    func scene(_ scene: UIScene, willConnectTo
        session: UISceneSession,
        options connectionOptions:
        UIScene.ConnectionOptions) {

        let contentView =
            ContentView().environmentObject(searchEngine)

        if let windowScene = scene as? UIWindowScene {
            let window = UIWindow(windowScene:
                windowScene)
            window.rootViewController =
                UIHostingController(rootView: contentView)
            self.window = window
            window.makeKeyAndVisible()
        }
    }
```

The ContentView() instance has a function called environmentObject(), which allows you to pass in an instance of the SearchEngineChoice object. This function supplies an ObservableObject object to a view subhierarchy, and this object can be read by any child by using @EnvironmentObject.

To use this @EnvironmentObject, add the following statements in bold to the ContentView.swift file and remove the statement containing the ObservedObject:

```
import SwiftUI

struct ContentView: View {
    // @ObservedObject var searchEngine = SearchEngineChoice()

    @EnvironmentObject var
        searchEngine: SearchEngineChoice


    var body: some View {
        TabView {
            NavigationView{
                VStack {
                    NavigationLink (
                        destination: DetailView()) {
                        Text("Your search engine is " +
                            "\(searchEngine.engine)")
                    }
                }
            }
            .tabItem {
                Image(systemName: "magnifyingglass")
                Text("Search")
            }

            DetailView()
            .tabItem {
                Image(systemName:
                    "magnifyingglass.circle.fill")
                Text("Search Engines")
            }
        }
    }
}
```

In the preceding example, you used the TabView to embed the original
NavigationView, and at the same time added another view containing DetailView.

Any changes made to searchEngine is now visible to all the views in the entire
app. Likewise, changes made to seachEngine elsewhere in the app will also be
reflected here.

Make the following changes in bold to the `DetailView.swift` file:

```swift
import SwiftUI

struct DetailView: View {
    var searchEngines = SearchEngineChoice().searchEngines

    @EnvironmentObject var
        searchEngine : SearchEngineChoice

    @State var selectedEngine =
        SearchEngineChoice().engine

    var body: some View {
        List {
            ForEach (searchEngines, id: \.self) {
                (engine) in
                Button(action: {
                    self.searchEngine.engine = engine
                    self.selectedEngine = engine
                }) {
                    HStack{
                        Text(engine)
                        Image(systemName:
                            self.selectedEngine == engine
                            ? "checkmark.square" :
                                "square")
                    }

                }
            }
        }
    }
}

struct DetailView_Previews: PreviewProvider {
    static var previews: some View {
        DetailView()
    }
}
```

Figure 8-11 shows that when the app is loaded, you can click the Search Engine tab item and select a search engine.

Select a search engine, and when you go back to the `ContentView`, the search engine selected is automatically updated (see Figure 8-12).

FIGURE 8-11:
Selecting a tab page to select the search engine.

FIGURE 8-12:
Selecting a search engine will automatically update the ContentView.

REMEMBER

The @EnvironmentObject is useful if you want to share data anywhere in your views (especially when you have more than two views that need to share the same data). This example shows only two views sharing the same data using the @EnvironmentObject, but in a real-world situation, if you have only two views, you're better off using @Binding.

Accessing Built-in Environment Variables

In the preceding section, I show you how to use environment objects to share objects with all the views in your application. Besides sharing your own objects, there is a set of built-in environment variables in SwiftUI that you can access.

Here are examples of built-in environment variables accessible from SwiftUI:

>> colorScheme: The color scheme of the current display

>> lineLimit: The number of lines used to render text in the available space

>> locale: The current locale that views should use

>> presentationMode: The current presentation mode of a view

You can make use of these environment variables through the @Environment property wrapper. Let's see an example of how it works. The following code snippet references the colorScheme environment variable as colorScheme:

```
import SwiftUI

struct ContentView: View {
    @Environment(\.colorScheme) var colorScheme

    var body: some View {
        Text(colorScheme == .dark ?
            "Dark Mode" : "Light Mode")
    }
}
```

The colorScheme environment variable allows you to know whether the iOS device is currently displaying in Dark or Light mode. Using this information, you can display custom text depending on the mode that the iOS device is displaying in. Figure 8-13 shows the device in Light mode.

FIGURE 8-13:
The view in Light
mode.

To switch the iPhone Simulator to Dark mode, go to Settings, tap Developer, and turn on Dark Appearance. Switch back to your app and see that the text is now changed to Dark mode (see Figure 8-14).

A practical use of the `colorScheme` environment variable might be to vary the font color of views in different modes. The following code snippet shows that the text in the `Text` view will be displayed in green when in Dark mode and in blue when in Light mode:

```
struct ContentView: View {
    @Environment(\.colorScheme) var colorScheme

    var body: some View {
        Text(colorScheme == .dark ?
            "Dark Mode" : "Light Mode")
            .foregroundColor(colorScheme == .dark ?
            .green: .blue)
    }
}
```

FIGURE 8-14:
The view in Dark
mode.

Defining your own environment keys

The environment variables that you can access are not limited to the one defined by the system — you can define your own environment variables so that they can be used throughout your app.

To define your own environment variables, you need to create a struct that conforms to the `EnvironmentKey` protocol. This creates an environment key. The following code snippet creates two custom environment keys, `AppName EnvironmentKey` and `AppTitleSizeEnvironmentKey`:

```swift
import SwiftUI

struct AppNameEnvironmentKey: EnvironmentKey {
    static var defaultValue: String = "DLS"
}

struct AppTitleSizeEnvironmentKey: EnvironmentKey {
    static var defaultValue: CGFloat = 25.0
}
```

Each of these two structs has the `defaultValue` property, which defines the type and default value for the environment variable.

You then need to create an extension on the `EnvironmentValues` struct, name your environment variables, and implement the setters and getters for each variable:

```
extension EnvironmentValues {
    var appName : String {
        set { self[AppNameEnvironmentKey.self] = newValue }
        get { self[AppNameEnvironmentKey.self] }
    }

    var appTitleSize : CGFloat {
        set { self[AppTitleSizeEnvironmentKey.self] = newValue }
        get { self[AppTitleSizeEnvironmentKey.self] }
    }
}
```

The preceding code snippet creates two environment variables, `appName` and `appTitleSize`.

Using your own environment keys

You can now make use of the two custom environment variables in a custom view:

```
struct CompanyLabel: View {
    @Environment(\.appName) private var appName
    @Environment(\.appTitleSize) private var appTitleSize

    var body: some View {
        Text(appName)
            .font(.system(size: appTitleSize))
            .bold()
    }
}
```

The `CompanyLabel` view displays a `Text` view and makes use of the two environment variables to display the content of the `Text` view, as well as set the size of the text.

The following code snippet shows two instances of `CompanyLabel` placed within the `ContentView`:

```
struct ContentView: View {
    @Environment(\.colorScheme) var colorScheme
    var body: some View {
        VStack {
            CompanyLabel()
                .environment(\.appName,
                    "Learn2Develop.net")
                .environment(\.appTitleSize, 35)
            CompanyLabel()
        }
    }
}
```

The first `CompanyLabel` view has the environment variable values overridden. The second `CompanyLabel` view uses the default value in the environment variables. Figure 8-15 shows the output.

FIGURE 8-15: Overriding the custom environment variable values for a particular view.

When overriding the values of the environment variables, the changes are applied to a view and all its children. The following demonstrates this.

```
struct ContentView: View {
    @Environment(\.colorScheme) var colorScheme
    var body: some View {
        VStack {
            CompanyLabel()
            CompanyLabel()
                .environment(\.appName,
                    "Learn2Develop.net")
        }
        .environment(\.appTitleSize, 35)
    }
}
```

The first CompanyLabel view retains its default value for the appName environment variable, while the second view is overridden. However, because the environment() modifier is applied to the VStack view, the new appTitleSize value will be applied to all the views in the VStack. This explains why the two CompanyLabel views have the same font size (see Figure 8-16).

FIGURE 8-16: Overriding the custom environment variable values for all views.

Chapter **9**

Using Legacy UIKit Views and View Controllers in SwiftUI

S
wiftUI comes with a number of views that make creating user interfaces (UIs) for your applications very easy. It is, nevertheless, still in its early days. A number of popular views and view controllers still have not been ported over to SwiftUI. For example, the Activity Indicator and WebView views in `UIKit` and the Image Picker and Contacts Picker view controllers are just some of the views and view controllers that have yet to port to SwiftUI.

Fortunately, SwiftUI works seamlessly with the existing `UIKit` frameworks on all Apple platforms — you can place `UIKit` views and view controllers within SwiftUI views and vice versa.

In this chapter, I show you how to use the existing `UIKit` views and view controllers in SwiftUI. I recap the way things are done in `UIKit`, so if you're a new iOS developer, don't worry if certain concepts are new to you — I explain them in an easy-to-understand way.

Using UIKit in SwiftUI

When you develop iOS apps using Storyboard in Xcode, you use the `UIKit` for all UI matters. `UIKit` is the framework that forms the core components of all iOS applications. Among all the classes in the `UIKit`, view and view controllers are the most commonly used classes.

View controllers (`UIViewController`) play a crucial role in your apps — they act as the skeleton of your application. A view controller is basically a class that manages a set of views (to display to the user), while coordinating with model (data) objects.

TECHNICAL STUFF

Because the view controller is connected to your Storyboard (an external file), it has very little control of what's happening on the view side of things (and vice versa). You may be familiar with this — connect an event in your Interface Builder to a function in your code in Swift and then later on you delete the function. However, the Interface Builder doesn't know that your function is now gone, and all hell will break loose when that event is invoked during runtime. This problem is precisely what SwiftUI tries to resolve.

The various widgets — such as `Button`, `Label`, `TextField`, and `Switch` — are represented by the subclasses of `UIView`.

TIP

This chapter discusses how to use `UIKit` within a SwiftUI project, but the converse is also true — you would also want to use SwiftUI in an existing `UIKit` project. For more information on this topic, refer to www.answertopia.com/swiftui/integrating-swiftui-with-uikit. Note that after you add SwiftUI to your `UIKit` project, your apps will only run on iOS 13.0 and later, macOS 10.15 and later, tvOS 13.0 and later, and watchOS 6.0 and later.

Figure 9-1 shows a `UIViewController` instance containing a number of `UIView` instances.

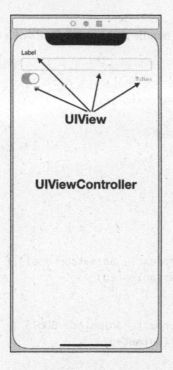

FIGURE 9-1:
Legacy View
controller and
views.

Understanding the UIKit View Controller life cycle

In order to handle the various states of a view controller, a view controller has a set of events, known as the life cycle of a view controller. The life cycle of a view controller has a variety of events, including (but not limited to) the following:

» `viewDidLoad`: Called after the controller's view is loaded into memory

» `loadView`: Creates the view that the controller manages

» `viewWillAppear`: Notifies the view controller that its view is about to be added to a view hierarchy

» `viewDidAppear`: Notifies the view controller that its view was added to a view hierarchy

» `viewWillDisappear`: Notifies the view controller that its view is about to be removed from a view hierarchy

» `viewDidDisappear`: Notifies the view controller that its view was removed from a view hierarchy

» `didReceiveMemoryWarning`: Sent to the view controller when the app receives a memory warning

The following code shows how to handle the various events of a view controller.

```
import UIKit

class ViewController: UIViewController {

    override func viewDidLoad() {
        super.viewDidLoad()
    }

    override func loadView() {
        super.loadView()
    }

    override func viewWillAppear(_ animated: Bool) {
        super.viewWillAppear(animated)
    }

    override func viewDidAppear(_ animated: Bool) {
        super.viewDidAppear(animated)
    }

    override func viewWillDisappear(_ animated: Bool) {
        super.viewWillDisappear(animated)
    }

    override func viewDidDisappear(_ animated: Bool) {
        super.viewDidDisappear(animated)
    }

    override func didReceiveMemoryWarning() {
        super.didReceiveMemoryWarning()
    }
}
```

The various events are fired during the lifetime of the view controller. For example, you often initialize your variables during the viewDidLoad event (it fires only once when the view controller is first loaded). If you needed to update the view whenever the view controller appears, you would perform the updates in the viewDidAppear event (fired every time the view comes to the foreground). Or if you need to build the UI dynamically during loading time, you can do it in the loadView event.

Understanding the SwiftUI view life cycle

Compared to the UIViewController life cycles, the life cycle of a view in SwiftUI is much simpler and more straightforward. In SwiftUI, there is no concept of a view controller. Instead, everything is a View.

In SwiftUI, View has only two events:

» onAppear

» onDisappear

You can attach these two events to any views, and SwiftUI will execute them when they occur.

Working with the onAppear and onDisappear events

When a view appears, the onAppear event will be fired. Likewise, when the view disappears, the onDisappear event will be fired.

In Chapter 6, I illustrate the use of the onAppear event:

```
func fetchData() {
    ...
}

var body: some View {
    List(articles, id: \.url) { item in
        VStack(alignment: .leading) {
            Text(item.title)
                .font(.headline)
            Text(item.description ?? "")
                .font(.footnote)
        }
    }.onAppear(perform: fetchData)
}
```

When the List view first appears, it will fire the onAppear event, which you then use to call the fetchData() function to load data from the web. For that example, it's quite straightforward to understand when the onAppear event fires.

A more involved example would be one comprising a NavigationView and a TabView. Figure 9-2 shows an example where the ContentView contains a TabView, which in turn also contains a NavigationView.

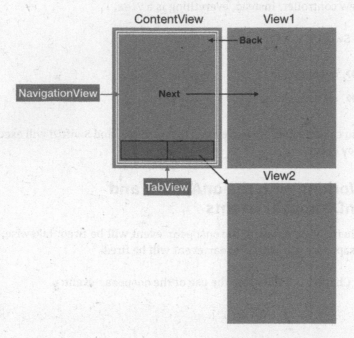

FIGURE 9-2:
Three views
in SwiftUI
embedded within
NavigationView
and TabView.

The following code snippet shows the implementation of the three views that you've just seen. To understand when the onAppear and onDisappear events are fired when the user moves from one screen to another, you insert print statements, as shown in the following code:

```
import SwiftUI

struct View1: View {
    var body: some View {
        Text("View1")
        .onAppear{
            print("onAppear in View1")
        }
        .onDisappear{
            print("onDisappear in View1")
        }
    }
}
```

```
struct View2: View {
    var body: some View {
        Text("View2")
        .onAppear{
            print("onAppear in View2")
        }
        .onDisappear{
            print("onDisappear in View2")
        }
    }
}

struct ContentView: View {
    var body: some View {
        TabView {
            NavigationView{
                NavigationLink(destination: View1()) {
                    Text("Next")
                }
            }.onAppear{
                print("onAppear in ContentView")
            }
            .onDisappear{
                print("onDisappear in ContentView")
            }
            .tabItem {
                Image(systemName:
                    "viewfinder.circle.fill")
                Text("ContentView")
            }

            View2()
            .tabItem {
                Image(systemName: "camera.viewfinder")
                Text("View2")
            }
        }
        .onAppear{
            print("onAppear in TabView")
        }
        .onDisappear{
            print("onDisappear in TabView")
        }
    }
}
```

When the app is first loaded (see Figure 9-3), you see the following outputs:

```
onAppear in TabView
onAppear in ContentView
```

FIGURE 9-3:
The ContentView
and the TabView
showing.

You can see that TabView first appeared, followed by ContentView. When you click the Next button, it navigates to View1 (see Figure 9-4).

The following statement in bold shows the additional statement printed:

```
onAppear in TabView
onAppear in ContentView
onAppear in View1
```

Even though ContentView is now hidden, it hasn't disappeared yet (because there is no output indicating its disappearance).

FIGURE 9-4:
Navigating to
View1.

Now, click the Back button to go back to ContentView. This time, you see the following additional output:

```
onAppear in TabView
onAppear in ContentView
onAppear in View1
onDisappear in View1
```

So View1 has disappeared. Click the View2 item on the tab bar (see Figure 9-5). As you can see, View2 is now loaded.

Here's the output:

```
onAppear in TabView
onAppear in ContentView
onAppear in View1
onDisappear in View1
onDisappear in ContentView
onAppear in View2
```

Now ContentView has disappeared and View2 appears.

FIGURE 9-5:
Displaying View2
through the
tab bar.

Finally, click ContentView item on the tab bar and notice that View2 has disappeared and ContentView has appeared again:

```
onAppear in TabView
onAppear in ContentView
onAppear in View1
onDisappear in View1
onDisappear in ContentView
onAppear in View2
onDisappear in View2
onAppear in ContentView
```

As you can see from the example, the onAppear event allows you to know when a view comes onscreen. This is useful in cases where you want to load data on demand. Suppose you have a tabbed application with five tab items and each of these tab pages separately loads data from the web. It would be useful to load the data only when the user views a particular page. Otherwise, the entire app would feel sluggish when it tries to load all the data at the same time when the app starts up.

Instantiating properties of a view

The preceding section explains the events life cycle of a view in SwiftUI. Besides understanding when the two events are fired, it's also important to understand how SwiftUI processes a `View` when it's created and the sequences in which properties and binding objects are processed.

In earlier chapters, I show you that the `View` is a `struct`. Very often, views have properties, which allows you to pass in additional information to customize the behaviors of views.

Consider the following simple example of a `View` named `MyView`:

```
struct MyView: View {

    var greetings: String

    var body: some View {
        Text(greetings)
    }
}
```

In the `MyView` struct, you have a property named `greetings`. It is of type `String`, but it hasn't been initialized yet.

When you try to use `MyView`, as in the following code snippet,

```
struct ContentView: View {
    var body: some View {
        VStack{
            MyView("Hello, World!")
        }
    }
}
```

You get the error: `Missing argument label 'greetings:' in call`. This is because you need to initialize the value of the `greetings` property in `MyView`, which is the first thing the compiler tries to do when instantiating the struct.

To fix this, pass in the argument for the `greetings` property when calling `MyView`, like this:

```
MyView(greetings: "Hello, World!")
```

Using initializers in a view

Structs can also have initializers (constructors). If `MyView` has an explicit initializer, like the following:

```
struct MyView: View {
    var greetings: String

    init(_ str:String) {
        self.greetings = str
    }

    var body: some View {
        Text(greetings)
    }
}
```

Then `greetings` must be initialized via the initializer for `MyView`:

```
MyView("Hello, World!")
```

Using binding variables in a view

If `MyView` has a `@Binding` variable, like this:

```
struct MyView: View {

    @Binding var text: String

    var greetings: String
    var body: some View {
        Text(greetings)
    }
}
```

Then you have to initialize it through the parameters:

```
struct ContentView: View {
    @State var text: String = ""
    var body: some View {
        MyView(greetings: "Hello, World!", text: $text)
    }
}
```

Note that the binding variable argument must come after the `greetings` argument.

If `MyView` has an explicit initializer, you have to specify the type of the `Binding` object in your initializer, like this:

```swift
struct MyView: View {

    @Binding var text: String

    var greetings: String

    init(_ str:String, _ text: Binding<String>) {
        self.greetings = str
        self._text = text
    }

    var body: some View {
        Text(greetings)
    }
}
```

Observe that the `text` `@Binding` variable has an underscore (`_`) in the initializer:

```swift
        self._text = text
```

And now when you create an instance of the `MyView` struct, you can bind the state variable through the initializer, like this:

```swift
MyView("Hello, World!", $text)
```

Using the UIViewRepresentable Protocol for UIKit Views

In the process of using SwiftUI to build your UI, you'll likely encounter cases where the widget that you want to use is not available (yet). In this case, you need to use the views in `UIKit`. And this is where the `UIViewRepresentable` protocol comes in.

The `UIViewRepresentable` protocol is a wrapper for a `UIKit` view that you can use in your SwiftUI app. To use a view from `UIKit`, you need to adhere to the following steps:

1. **Create a struct that conforms to the** `UIViewRepresentable` **protocol.**

2. **Define the** `makeUIView()` **method.**

   This method returns the view that you're wrapping.

3. **Define the** `updateUIView()` **method.**

   This method will be called whenever data for the view that you're wrapping has changed.

The best way to understand this is to use a concrete example. The following sections show you two examples:

>> How to use the `UIActivityIndicator` view from `UIKit` to display a spinning indicator

>> How to use the `WKWebView` from the `WebKit` to display a web browser

ActivityIndicator

In `UIKit`, you use the `UIActivityIndicator` class for displaying an activity indicator (a spinner). However, in the current version of SwiftUI, the activity indicator has not been ported to SwiftUI yet. So, to use it, you need to wrap it using the `UIViewRepresentable` protocol.

First, create a struct that conforms to the `UIViewRepresentable` protocol:

```
struct ActivityIndicator: UIViewRepresentable {
}
```

Then, you need to implement the `makeUIView()` and `updateUIView()` methods:

```
struct ActivityIndicator: UIViewRepresentable {

    func makeUIView(context: Context) ->
        UIActivityIndicatorView {

        // returns an instance of UIActivityIndicatorView
        let view = UIActivityIndicatorView()
        return view
    }
```

```
func updateUIView( activityIndicator:
    UIActivityIndicatorView, context: Content) {

    // start animating the activity indicator
    activityIndicator.startAnimating()
}

}
```

That's it. To use it, you can just make an instance of the `ActivityIndicator` struct in `ContentView`:

```
struct ContentView: View {
    var body: some View {
        ActivityIndicator()
    }
}
```

Figure 9-6 shows the activity indicator spinning.

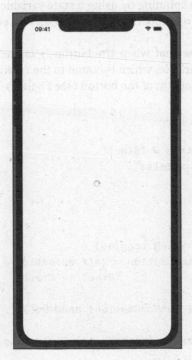

FIGURE 9-6:
The activity
indicator spinning
continuously.

Obviously, an activity indicator that spins nonstop is not very useful. There should be a way to start the spinning as well as stop it. To do so, you can use a @Binding object:

```
struct ActivityIndicator: UIViewRepresentable {

    @Binding var isAnimating: Bool

    func makeUIView(context: Context) ->
        UIActivityIndicatorView {
        let view = UIActivityIndicatorView()
        return view
    }

    func updateUIView(_ activityIndicator:
        UIActivityIndicatorView, context: Context) {
        isAnimating ? activityIndicator.startAnimating() :
            activityIndicator.stopAnimating()
    }
}
```

You can now start and stop the spinning by using a state variable. You'll bind the state variable to the isAnimating property of the ActivityIndicator.

The following statements show that when the button is tapped, it toggles the value of the animating state variable, which is bound to the isAnimating binding object; it will also change the caption of the button (see Figure 9-7):

```
struct ContentView: View {

    @State var buttonCaption = "Start"
    @State var animating = false

    var body: some View {
        VStack{
            Button(action: {
                self.animating.toggle()
                self.buttonCaption = self.animating ?
                                    "Stop" : "Start"
            }){
                Text(self.buttonCaption).padding()
            }
            ActivityIndicator(isAnimating: $animating)
        }
    }
}
```

FIGURE 9-7:
You can now start
or stop the
activity indicator.

WebView

Another popular view that you'll often want to use in SwiftUI is the web browser. Technically, it's not part of the UIKit framework, but you can use the UIView Representable protocol to wrap the WKWebView (from the WebKit framework) for use in SwiftUI.

The following code snippet shows the WKWebView wrapped using the UIView Representable protocol:

```swift
import SwiftUI
import WebKit

struct WebView: UIViewRepresentable {
    let request: URLRequest

    func makeUIView(context: Context) -> WKWebView  {
        return WKWebView()
    }
```

```
    func updateUIView(_ uiView: WKWebView, context: Context) {
        uiView.load(request)
    }
}
```

You can now use it in your `ContentView`:

```
struct ContentView: View {
    var body: some View {
        WebView(request: URLRequest(url: URL(string: "https://
            www.apple.com")!))
    }
}
```

Figure 9-8 shows the `WebView` struct display Apple's home page.

FIGURE 9-8: Loading Apple's home page using the WebView struct.

Using the UIViewControllerRepresentable Protocol for UIKit View Controllers

Besides being able to use the views in UIKit from within SwiftUI, you can also use the various UIKit view controllers in SwiftUI through the UIViewController Representable protocol.

The UIViewControllerRepresentable protocol provides the wrappers for using view controllers in UIKit. The UIImagePickerController is a view controller that interfaces with the user's media library. Specifically, it allows your application to access the photos in the Photos application, record movies, take pictures, and more.

I'll recap how this is done in the old-fashioned way. To select a user from the Photos application, you need to do the following:

1. **Make your** ViewController **conform to the** UINavigationControllerDelegate **and** UIImagePickerControllerDelegate **protocols.**

2. **Implement the** imagePickerController(_:didFinishPickingMedia WithInfo:) **method.**

    This method will be called when the user selects a photo from the Photos application.

3. **Create an instance of the** UIImagePickerController **class and set its** delegate **to the view controller.**

    This is to ensure that the appropriate methods (such as imagePickerControl ler(_:didFinishPickingMediaWithInfo:)) in the view controller can handle the events fired by the UIImagePickerController instance.

Here is the code snippet for using the UIImagePickerController in Storyboard in Xcode:

```
import UIKit

class ViewController: UIViewController,
    UINavigationControllerDelegate,
    UIImagePickerControllerDelegate {

    @IBOutlet weak var imageView: UIImageView!
```

```
@IBAction func btnClick(_ sender: Any) {
    selectPhoto()
}

override func viewDidLoad() {
    super.viewDidLoad()
}

func selectPhoto() {
    let photoPicker = UIImagePickerController()
    photoPicker.delegate = self
    self.present(photoPicker,
                 animated: true,
                 completion: nil)
}

func imagePickerController(
    _ picker: UIImagePickerController,
    didFinishPickingMediaWithInfo info:
    [UIImagePickerController.InfoKey : Any]) {

    if let uiImage = info[.originalImage]
        as? UIImage {
        self.imageView.image = uiImage
    }
    picker.dismiss(animated: true)
}
}
```

What you want to do now is wrap the UIImagePickerController in SwiftUI, using the UIViewControllerRepresentable protocol.

Creating the ImagePickerViewController

First, create a struct named ImagePickerViewController that conforms to the UIViewControllerRepresentable protocol:

```
struct ImagePickerViewController:
    UIViewControllerRepresentable {

}
```

Then, add in the two methods that you need to implement — makeUIViewContro
ller(context:) and updateUIViewController(_:context:):

```
struct ImagePickerViewController:
    UIViewControllerRepresentable {

    func makeUIViewController(
        context: UIViewControllerRepresentableContext
        <ImagePickerViewController>) ->
        UIImagePickerController {

        let imagePicker = UIImagePickerController()
        return imagePicker
    }

    func updateUIViewController(
        _ uiViewController: UIImagePickerController,
        context: UIViewControllerRepresentableContext
        <ImagePickerViewController>) {
    }
}
```

In the makeUIViewController(context:) method, you create an instance of the
UIImagePickerController and return it. You leave the other method empty.

You can now try to use the ImagePickerViewController struct in your
ContentView:

```
import SwiftUI

struct ContentView: View {

    // display the ImagePicker
    @State private var displayImagePicker = false

    var body: some View {
        VStack {
            Button("Select Photo") {
                self.displayImagePicker = true
            }
        }
```

```
        .sheet(isPresented: $displayImagePicker)
        {
            ImagePickerViewController()
        }
    }
}
```

As usual, you'll use a state variable and bind it to the sheet() modifier. When the sheet is displayed, you create an instance of the ImagePickerViewController struct.

Figure 9-9 shows that clicking the Select Photo button displays the Image Picker, where you can select a photo.

FIGURE 9-9:
Testing the Image Picker.

Select a photo and the Image Picker will close. However, notice that at this point, the Image Picker doesn't notify you that an image has been selected.

Handling events using coordinators

In order for the UIViewController to notify you of events so that you can handle them, you need to use coordinators.

In SwiftUI, coordinators act as delegates for your UIKit view controllers. When a view controller needs to fire an event, the coordinator acts as the delegate, providing the methods to handle the events.

Delegation is a design pattern that enables a class or structure to hand off (or delegate) some of its responsibilities to an instance of another type.

Using our same example, create a class named Coordinator (nest it within the ImagePickerViewController struct), and make it inherit from the NSObject base class, and at the same time conform to the UINavigationControllerDelegate and UIImagePickerControllerDelegate protocols:

```
struct ImagePickerViewController:
    UIViewControllerRepresentable {

    class Coordinator: NSObject,
        UINavigationControllerDelegate,
        UIImagePickerControllerDelegate {

        // content to be implemented
    }

    func makeUIViewController(
        context: UIViewControllerRepresentableContext
        <ImagePickerViewController>) ->
        UIImagePickerController {

        let imagePicker = UIImagePickerController()
        imagePicker.delegate = context.coordinator
        return imagePicker
    }

    func updateUIViewController(
        _ uiViewController: UIImagePickerController,
        context: UIViewControllerRepresentableContext
        <ImagePickerViewController>) {
    }
}
```

Also, observe that you set the imagePicker's delegate to the coordinator. This specifies that the coordinator will contain the methods to handle events fired by the UIImagePickerController.

At this juncture, the compiler will complain with the following: Type 'Image PickerViewController' does not conform to protocol 'UIViewController Representable'. To fix this, add a method named makeCoordinator(), like this:

```
struct ImagePickerViewController:
    UIViewControllerRepresentable {

    class Coordinator: NSObject,
        UINavigationControllerDelegate,
        UIImagePickerControllerDelegate {

    }

    func makeCoordinator() ->
        ImagePickerViewController.Coordinator {
        Coordinator()
    }

    func makeUIViewController(
        context: UIViewControllerRepresentableContext
        <ImagePickerViewController>) ->
        UIImagePickerController {

        let imagePicker = UIImagePickerController()
        return imagePicker
    }

    func updateUIViewController(
        _ uiViewController: UIImagePickerController,
        context: UIViewControllerRepresentableContext
        <ImagePickerViewController>) {
    }
}
```

SwiftUI automatically calls the makeCoordinator() method. For now, you just need to create an instance of the Coordinator class.

Defining the methods in the Coordinator class

You can now start to define the methods in the Coordinator class. You'll define two methods:

- An initializer

- The `imagePickerController(_:didFinishPickingMediaWithInfo:)` method, which will be fired when the user selects a photo

Add the following statements in bold:

```
struct ImagePickerViewController:
    UIViewControllerRepresentable {

    @Binding var image: UIImage?

    func makeCoordinator() ->
        ImagePickerViewController.Coordinator {
        Coordinator(self)
    }

    class Coordinator: NSObject,
        UINavigationControllerDelegate,
        UIImagePickerControllerDelegate {

        var parent: ImagePickerViewController

        init(_ parent: ImagePickerViewController) {
            self.parent = parent
        }

        func imagePickerController(
            _ picker: UIImagePickerController,
            didFinishPickingMediaWithInfo info:
                [UIImagePickerController.InfoKey : Any]) {
            if let uiImage = info[.originalImage]
                as? UIImage {
                parent.image = uiImage
            }
            picker.dismiss(animated: true)
        }
    }

    func makeUIViewController(
        context: UIViewControllerRepresentableContext
        <ImagePickerViewController>) ->
        UIImagePickerController {
```

```
            let imagePicker = UIImagePickerController()
            imagePicker.delegate = context.coordinator
            return imagePicker
        }

        func updateUIViewController(
            _ uiViewController: UIImagePickerController,
            context: UIViewControllerRepresentableContext
            <ImagePickerViewController>) {
        }
    }
```

Observe the following:

>> You added a parent property to store an instance of the
   ImagePickerViewController struct.

>> In the initializer (init()), you used the parent property to save a copy of
   the ImagePickerViewController struct, which you passed in through the
   makeCoordinator() method.

>> When the user has selected an image, you get the image and cast it as
   UIImage. You then assign the UIImage instance to a @Binding object
   named image.

Using the updated ImagePickerViewController

To use the updated ImagePickerViewController, add the following statements in
bold to the ContentView:

```
struct ContentView: View {
    @State private var photoImage: Image?
    @State private var photoUIImage: UIImage?

    // display the ImagePicker
    @State private var displayImagePicker = false

    func getImage() {
        if let image = photoUIImage {
            photoImage = Image(uiImage: image)
        }
    }
```

```
    var body: some View {
        VStack {
            Button("Select Photo") {
                self.displayImagePicker = true
            }
            photoImage?
                .resizable()
                .scaledToFit()
        }
        .sheet(isPresented: $displayImagePicker,
            onDismiss: getImage)
        {
            ImagePickerViewController(
                image: self.$photoUIImage)
        }
    }
}
```

You created two new state variables:

>> photoImage is used for displaying the photo on the screen.

>> photoUIImage is used for storing the data of the photo.

When you call the ImagePickerViewController(), you now bind the photo UIImage state variable to the @Binding image property in the ImagePicker ViewController struct. This is to allow you to retrieve the photo that the user has selected (in UIImage format).

You also added the onDismiss parameter to the sheet() modifier. When the sheet is dismissed, it calls the method that you specify in the onDismiss parameter. In this case, it calls the getImage() function, which converts the UIImage data to an Image.

Once the photoImage state variable contains an Image, the photo selected by the user will be displayed.

You can now test the application. Figure 9-10 shows the image displaying in the ContentView after the user has selected an image.

FIGURE 9-10:
Displaying the image selected using the Image Picker.

4
Performing Animations and Drawings

IN THIS PART . . .

Learn how to draw using the various shape views in SwiftUI and apply special effects to them.

Create fun animations to make your apps more lively.

Put together all that you've learned by creating a complete project, from start to deployment.

Chapter **10**

Drawings and Special Effects

One of the core strengths of iOS is its superior graphic and animation capabilities. As an iOS developer, you can leverage Apple's key frameworks for drawings and animations: Core Animation and Metal. However, some frameworks can be pretty low level. In SwiftUI, you can make use of these frameworks without getting yourself knee-deep in the details of these application programming interfaces (APIs).

In this chapter, I show you how to:

» Draw basic shapes using the five built-in shapes in SwiftUI

» Perform clippings on views

» Draw your own custom shapes

» Use the special effects on views

Drawing Using the Five Built-in Shapes

SwiftUI comes with five built-in basic shapes that are most commonly used by developers for drawing:

>> Rectangle

>> Rounded rectangle

>> Circle

>> Capsule

>> Ellipse

Rectangles

To draw a rectangle, use the Rectangle struct:

```
struct ContentView: View {
    var body: some View {
        Rectangle()
            .frame(width: 300, height: 200)


    }
}
```

Figure 10-1 shows the rectangle.

Filling a rectangle with color and drawing a border around it

To fill the rectangle with a color and draw a border around it, use the fill() and border() modifiers, respectively (see Figure 10-2):

```
Rectangle()
    .fill(Color.yellow)
    .frame(width: 300, height: 200)
    .border(Color.black, width: 3)
```

FIGURE 10-1:
Drawing a
rectangle.

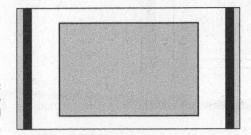

FIGURE 10-2:
The rectangle
with the filled
color and border.

The order of the modifiers is important. For example, if you call the `frame()` modifier first, like the following:

```
Rectangle()
    .frame(width: 300, height: 200)
    .fill(Color.yellow)
    .border(Color.black, width: 3)
```

An error will occur. You get the `Value of type 'some View' has no member 'fill'` error for the `fill()` modifier. So, make sure that you fill the rectangle with color before you change its size and apply the border.

Sometimes, even if the order of the modifiers doesn't cause syntax errors, you may get a very different effect depending on the order of the modifiers applied. Consider the following example:

```
Rectangle()
    .fill(Color.yellow)
    .frame(width: 300, height: 200)
    .padding(EdgeInsets(
        top: 10,
        leading: 20,
        bottom: 10,
        trailing: 20))
    .border(Color.black, width: 3)
```

Here, I inserted a `padding()` modifier before the `border()` modifier. The result is as shown in Figure 10-3. Notice that a rectangle is wrapped with the specified padding before the border is drawn around the padding.

FIGURE 10-3:
The rectangle with the padding applied before the border is drawn around it.

Contrast this with the case where the `padding()` modifier comes *after* the `border()` modifier:

```
Rectangle()
    .fill(Color.yellow)
    .frame(width: 300, height: 200)
    .border(Color.black, width: 3)
    .padding(EdgeInsets(
        top: 10,
        leading: 20,
        bottom: 10,
        trailing: 20))
```

The result is that the border is drawn first before the padding is added to the rectangle. Figure 10-4 shows the result (the blue border surrounding the rectangle is drawn by the preview canvas).

FIGURE 10-4:
The border is
applied first to
the rectangle
before the
padding is
applied.

Rotating the rectangle

To rotate the rectangle, use the `rotationEffect()` modifier:

```
Rectangle()
    .fill(Color.yellow)
    .frame(width: 300, height: 200)
    .border(Color.black, width: 3)
    .rotationEffect(Angle(degrees: 45))
```

Figure 10-5 shows the rectangle rotated 45 degrees clockwise.

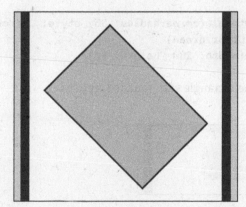

FIGURE 10-5:
The rectangle
rotated
45 degrees
clockwise.

Scaling the rectangle

To scale the rectangle, use the `scaleEffect()` modifier:

```
Rectangle()
    .fill(Color.yellow)
    .frame(width: 300, height: 200)
```

```
        .border(Color.black, width: 3)
        .rotationEffect(Angle(degrees: 45))
        .scaleEffect(0.5)
```

Figure 10-6 shows the rectangle reduced in size by 50 percent.

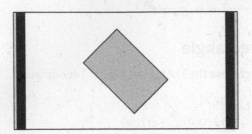

FIGURE 10-6:
The rectangle
reduced in size by
50 percent.

Rounded rectangles

If you need to draw a rectangle with rounded corners, use the RoundedRectangle struct:

```
RoundedRectangle(cornerRadius: 25, style: .circular)
    .fill(Color.green)
    .frame(width: 200, height: 80)
```

Figure 10-7 shows the rectangle with rounded corners.

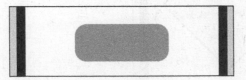

FIGURE 10-7:
Drawing a
rounded
rectangle.

The style parameter allows you to choose between classic rounded corners (.circular) or Apple's slightly smoother alternative (.continuous).

Filling a rounded rectangle with a gradient

Besides filling a shape with solid color, you can also apply a gradient fill:

```
RoundedRectangle(cornerRadius: 25, style: .circular)
    .fill(LinearGradient(
        gradient: Gradient(colors: [.yellow, .green]),
```

```
        startPoint: .leading,
        endPoint: .trailing
        ))
    .frame(width: 200, height: 80)
```

Figure 10-8 shows the rectangle filled with a linear gradient.

FIGURE 10-8:
Filling a rounded
rectangle with a
linear gradient.

Drawing a rounded rectangle without fill

If you simply want to draw a rounded rectangle without any fill (see Figure 10-9), use the RoundedRectangle() struct together with the stroke() modifier:

```
RoundedRectangle(cornerRadius: 25)
    .stroke(lineWidth: 2)
    .frame(width: 200, height: 80)
```

FIGURE 10-9:
A rounded
rectangle without
any fill.

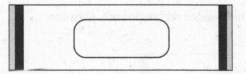

Drawing a rounded rectangle with a border

The border() modifier draws a border around the rectangle. However, it can't be used directly on the RoundedRectangle() struct:

```
RoundedRectangle(cornerRadius: 25, style: .circular)
    .fill(LinearGradient(
        gradient: Gradient(colors: [.yellow, .green]),
        startPoint: .leading,
        endPoint: .trailing
        ))
    .frame(width: 200, height: 80)
    .border(Color.black, width: 3)
```

The effect of applying the border() modifier to the RoundedRectangle is as shown in Figure 10-10.

FIGURE 10-10:
Applying the
border modifier
to Rounded
Rectangle
doesn't display a
border around
the corners.

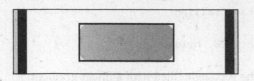

Instead, use the `overlay()` modifier to layer a secondary view over the Rounded Rectangle view:

```
RoundedRectangle(cornerRadius: 25, style: .circular)
    .fill(LinearGradient(
        gradient: Gradient(colors: [.yellow, .green]),
        startPoint: .leading,
        endPoint: .trailing
        ))
    .frame(width: 200, height: 80)
    .overlay(
        RoundedRectangle(cornerRadius: 25)
        .stroke(lineWidth: 2)
    )
```

Figure 10-11 shows the rounded rectangle with a border.

FIGURE 10-11:
Correctly applying
a border around
a rounded
rectangle.

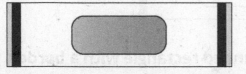

If you want the border to be a dotted line (see Figure 10-12), specify the style parameter with a `StrokeStyle` struct:

```
RoundedRectangle(cornerRadius: 25, style: .circular)
    .fill(LinearGradient(
        gradient: Gradient(colors: [.yellow, .green]),
        startPoint: .leading,
        endPoint: .trailing
        ))
    .frame(width: 200, height: 80)
    .overlay(
        RoundedRectangle(cornerRadius: 25)
```

```
            .stroke(style: StrokeStyle(
                lineWidth: 4, dash: [15,0]))
    )
```

FIGURE 10-12:
Changing the
border to a
dotted line.

Circles

To draw a circle (see Figure 10-13), use the `Circle` struct:

```
Circle()
    .fill(Color.yellow)
    .frame(width: 150, height: 150)
```

FIGURE 10-13:
Drawing a circle.

Filling a circle with a radial gradient

Besides filling a shape with a linear gradient, you can also fill it with a radial gradient. This is especially useful for the circle, as the following example shows:

```
Circle()
    .fill(RadialGradient(
            gradient: Gradient(colors: [.red, .yellow]),
            center: .center,
            startRadius: 0,
            endRadius: 75))
    .frame(width: 150, height: 150)
```

Figure 10-14 shows the circle filled with the radial gradient.

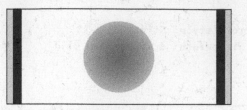

FIGURE 10-14:
Filling a circle
with a radial
gradient fill.

Filling a circle with an angular gradient

Another gradient fill that you can use is the angular gradient (also known as a conic gradient):

```
Circle()
    .fill(AngularGradient(
            gradient: Gradient(colors: [.red, .yellow]),
            center: .center))
    .frame(width: 150, height: 150)
```

Figure 10-15 shows the circle filled with an angular gradient.

FIGURE 10-15:
Filling a circle
with an angular
gradient.

Capsules

The next built-in shape in SwiftUI is the capsule. A capsule is a rounded rectangle where the corner radius is half the length of the capsule's smallest edge.

TIP

The easiest way to visualize how a capsule looks is to take a look at the vitamin capsule that you may have in your medicine cabinet.

To draw a capsule, use the Capsule struct:

```
Capsule()
    .fill(Color.green)
    .frame(width: 300, height: 100)
```

Figure 10-16 shows the capsule.

FIGURE 10-16:
Drawing a
capsule.

If you set the width of the capsule the same as the height, you get a circle (see Figure 10-17):

```
Capsule()
    .fill(Color.green)
    .frame(width: 300, height: 300)
```

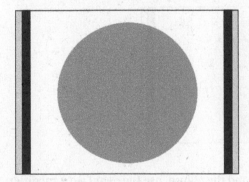

FIGURE 10-17:
A capsule with
equal width and
height is a circle.

Ellipses

The final built-in shape is the ellipse. The Ellipse struct draws an ellipse with the specified dimension:

```
Ellipse()
    .fill(Color.yellow)
    .frame(width: 200, height: 80)
```

Figure 10-18 shows the ellipse.

FIGURE 10-18:
Drawing an
ellipse.

The following code shows the ellipse filled with an angular gradient (see Figure 10-19):

```
Ellipse()
    .fill(AngularGradient(
        gradient: Gradient(
            colors: [.red, .yellow, .green, .blue,
                    .purple, .red]),
        center: .center,
        angle: Angle(degrees: -90)))
    .frame(width: 200, height: 250)
```

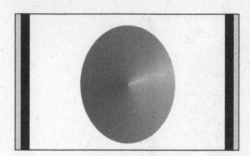

FIGURE 10-19:
Filling an ellipse with an angular gradient.

To draw a border around the ellipse, use the overlay() modifier:

```
Ellipse()
    .fill(AngularGradient(
        gradient: Gradient(
            colors: [.red, .yellow, .green, .blue,
                    .purple, .red]),
        center: .center,
        angle: Angle(degrees: -90)))
.frame(width: 200, height: 250)
.overlay(
    Ellipse()
    .stroke(lineWidth: 5)
)
```

Figure 10-20 shows an ellipse drawn with a border around it.

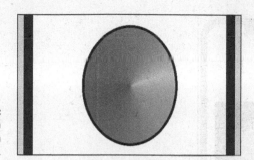

FIGURE 10-20:
Drawing an
ellipse with a
border.

Clipping with the Basic Shapes

The previous section shows how to draw with the five built-in shapes in SwiftUI. You aren't limited to *drawing* with these shapes; you can also use them to apply clippings to a view. By clipping a view, you're essentially preserving the part of the view covered by the shape, while eliminating the other parts of the view.

To understand how clipping works, consider the following example of an Image view:

```
Image("Einstein")
    .resizable()
    .aspectRatio(contentMode: .fill)
    .frame(width: 370.0, height: 480.0)
```

TIP

For this example, you need to have an image named Einstein in the Assets. xcassets file. You can also use your own black-and-white image.

Figure 10-21 shows the image displayed by the Image view.

To clip the image with a circle, use the clipShape() modifier with the Circle struct:

```
Image("Einstein")
    .resizable()
    .aspectRatio(contentMode: .fill)
    .frame(width: 370.0, height: 480.0)
    .clipShape(Circle())
```

Figure 10-22 shows the image clipped with the circle shape.

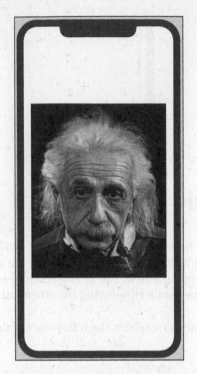

FIGURE 10-21:
Displaying an image using the Image view.

FIGURE 10-22:
Clipping the image with a circle.

If you want to display a shadow around the circle, use the `overlay()` modifier and supply it with a `Circle` struct; then apply the `shadow()` modifier:

```
Image("Einstein")
    .resizable()
    .aspectRatio(contentMode: .fill)
    .frame(width: 370.0, height: 480.0)
    .clipShape(Circle())
```

```
        .overlay(
            Circle()
                .stroke(Color.white,lineWidth:4)
                .shadow(radius: 10))
```

Figure 10-23 shows the image clipped with a circle with a shadow around it.

FIGURE 10-23:
Displaying a
shadow around
the image clipped
with a circle.

You can also clip with the Capsule struct (see Figure 10-24):

```
Image("Einstein")
    .resizable()
    .aspectRatio(contentMode:  .fill)
    .frame(width: 370.0, height: 480.0)
    .clipShape(Capsule())
```

FIGURE 10-24:
Clipping the
image with the
capsule shape.

You can also clip with the Ellipse struct (see Figure 10-25).

```
Image("Einstein")
    .resizable()
    .aspectRatio(contentMode: .fill)
    .frame(width: 370.0, height: 480.0)
    .clipShape(Ellipse())
```

FIGURE 10-25:
Clipping the
image with the
ellipse shape.

What about clipping it with a square shape? For this, you have to first set the size of the square using the frame() modifier, followed by the clipped() modifier:

```
Image("Einstein")
    .resizable()
    .aspectRatio(contentMode: .fill)
    .frame(width: 370.0, height: 480.0)
    .frame(width: 300, height: 300,
        alignment: .center)
    .clipped()
```

Figure 10-26 shows the image clipped with a square shape.

FIGURE 10-26:
Clipping the
image with the
square shape.

Drawing Custom Shapes

If none of the built-in shapes satisfies your requirements, you can draw your own custom shapes by implementing the Shape protocol. In this section, I show you how to draw your own desired shape using the Shape protocol.

First, create a struct named MyShape and make sure it implements the Shape protocol:

```
struct MyShape: Shape {
}
```

The Shape protocol requires you to implement just one method, path, with one single parameter, rect, of type CGRect:

```
struct MyShape: Shape {
    func path(in rect: CGRect) -> Path {

    }
}
```

The path() function returns a struct of type Path. Basically, it says, "Given a rectangle, what do you want to draw?" The Path is a series of drawing instructions, such as, "Draw a line from this point to that point," "Draw an arc from this point to that point," and so on.

Let's add the following statements so that we can create an instance of the Path structure and return it. In addition, let's print out the coordinates of the rectangle available for our shape to draw:

```
struct MyShape: Shape {
    func path(in rect: CGRect) -> Path {
        var path = Path()
```

```
            print(rect)
            return path
        }
    }
```

To use the MyShape struct, add an instance of it to the ContentView:

```
struct ContentView: View {
    var body: some View {
        MyShape()
    }
}
```

When you run the preceding code on the iPhone simulator (or real device), you should see the following output (press ⌘+Shift+C to show the Output window):

```
(0.0, 0.0, 414.0, 818.0)
```

You can also view the output by right-clicking the Live Preview button and selecting Debug Preview.

TIP

The values are printed in the following format: x and y coordinates of the upper-left corner, followed by the width and height of the rectangle. In particular, the width and height are the dimensions of the custom shape that you're going to draw.

The values that you see depend on the device that you're testing on. For example, the preceding output is obtained when you test the application on an iPhone 11 Pro Max. If you test the application on the iPhone SE (2nd generation), you get an output of (0.0, 0.0, 375.0, 647.0).

TIP

You can change the dimension of the shape using the frame() modifier:

```
struct ContentView: View {
    var body: some View {
        MyShape()
            .frame(width: 200, height: 100,
                    alignment: .center)
    }
}
```

The preceding yields the following output:

```
(0.0, 0.0, 200.0, 100.0)
```

Drawing lines

To see how to draw your own custom shapes, let's start by drawing lines. Add the following statements in bold to the `MyShape` struct:

```
struct MyShape: Shape {
    func path(in rect: CGRect) -> Path {
        let topCenter = CGPoint(x: rect.width / 2, y: 0)
        let bottomLeft = CGPoint(x: 0, y: rect.height)
        let bottomRight = CGPoint(
            x: rect.width, y: rect.height)

        var path = Path()
        print(rect)
        return path
    }
}
```

The preceding statements define a number of constants representing the various points in the `rect`. Figure 10-27 shows the various points.

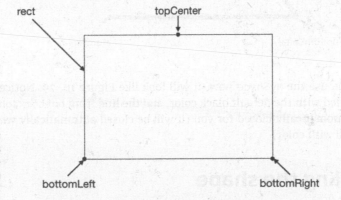

FIGURE 10-27:
The constants representing the various points on the rectangle.

You can now start to draw within the `rect`:

```
struct MyShape: Shape {
    func path(in rect: CGRect) -> Path {
        let topCenter = CGPoint(x: rect.width / 2, y: 0)
        let bottomLeft = CGPoint(x: 0, y: rect.height)
        let bottomRight = CGPoint(
            x: rect.width, y: rect.height)

        var path = Path()
```

```
        path.move(to:topCenter)
        path.addLine(to: bottomLeft)
        path.addLine(to: bottomRight)

        print(rect)
        return path
    }
}
```

You first move to topCenter and from there draw a line to bottomLeft. Then, from bottomLeft, you draw a line to bottomRight (see Figure 10-28).

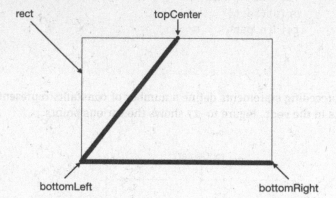

FIGURE 10-28:
Drawing two lines
in the rectangle.

If you use the MyShape now, it will look like Figure 10-29. Notice that the shape is filled with the default black color, and the line from bottomRight to topCenter is automatically closed for you (it will be closed automatically when the shape is filled with color).

Filling the shape

Like all the built-in shapes, you can fill your own custom shape with colors using the fill() modifier. Figure 10-30 shows the shape filled with yellow:

```
MyShape()
    .fill(Color.yellow)
    .frame(width: 200, height: 150,
           alignment: .center)
```

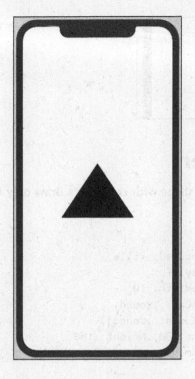

FIGURE 10-29:
The initial custom shape.

FIGURE 10-30:
Filling the custom shape with yellow.

You can also fill it with a linear gradient (see Figure 10-31):

```
MyShape()
    .fill(LinearGradient(
        gradient: Gradient(
            colors: [.yellow, .green]),
        startPoint: .leading,
        endPoint: .trailing
    ))
    .frame(width: 200, height: 150,
        alignment: .center)
```

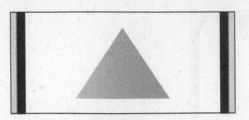

Drawing a border

Instead of filling the custom shape with color, let's draw only the outline of it using the stroke() modifier:

```
MyShape()
    .stroke(Color.red, style:
        StrokeStyle(
            lineWidth: 10,
            lineCap: .round,
            lineJoin: .round))
    .frame(width: 200, height: 150,
        alignment: .center)
```

Figure 10-32 shows the output.

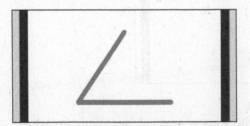

Remember that you didn't draw a line from bottomRight to topCenter. This is why you see an incomplete triangle. To fix this, draw a line from bottomRight to topCenter:

```
var path = Path()
path.move(to:topCenter)
path.addLine(to: bottomLeft)
path.addLine(to: bottomRight)
path.addLine(to: topCenter)
```

Figure 10-33 shows the complete triangle.

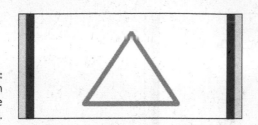

FIGURE 10-33:
The custom
shape with the
line added.

Drawing an arc

Besides drawing lines, you can also draw an arc, which is part of a circle. Add the following statements in bold to the MyShape struct:

```
struct MyShape: Shape {
    func path(in rect: CGRect) -> Path {
        let topCenter = CGPoint(x: rect.width / 2, y: 0)
        let bottomLeft = CGPoint(x: 0, y: rect.height)
        let bottomRight = CGPoint(x: rect.width, y: rect.height)

        var path = Path()
        path.move(to:topCenter)
        path.addLine(to: bottomLeft)
        path.addLine(to: bottomRight)
        path.addLine(to: topCenter)

        path.addArc(
            center: topCenter,
            radius: rect.width/2,
            startAngle: .degrees(20),
            endAngle: .degrees(160),
            clockwise: true)
        path.addLine(to: topCenter)

        print(rect)
        return path
    }
}
```

Figure 10-34 shows how MyShape looks after adding the arc.

The addArc() function in the Path structure can sometimes be confusing. First, remember that the starting angle is always at the 3 o'clock position. In the preceding code, you specified the clockwise parameter to true, and the start angle at 20 degrees and end angle at 160 degrees. As such, you would expect the arc to be drawn below the circle. However, due to the way SwiftUI measures the coordinates, the outcome is just the opposite.

Figure 10-35 shows some of the examples of the addArc() function in use.

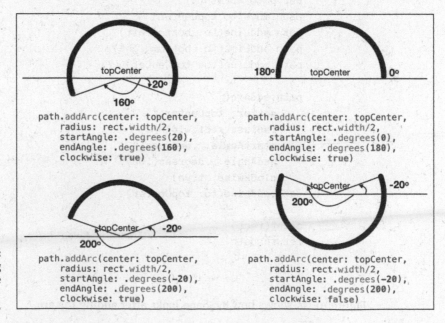

If you're observant, you'll also notice that after you draw the three lines (the triangle), there is a line connecting the tip of the triangle to the starting point of the arc (see Figure 10-36). This line is drawn for you because SwiftUI automatically draws a line connecting the last drawn point to the new starting point.

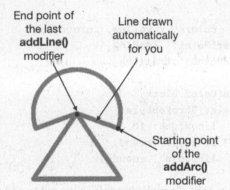

FIGURE 10-36:
SwiftUI
automatically
draws a line
connecting the
last drawn point
to the new
starting point.

End point of
the last
addLine()
modifier

Line drawn
automatically
for you

Starting point
of the
addArc()
modifier

Also notice that we added the last statement to draw a line to topCenter:

```
path.addArc(
    center: topCenter,
    radius: rect.width/2,
    startAngle: .degrees(20),
    endAngle: .degrees(160),
    clockwise: true)
path.addLine(to: topCenter)
```

The last statement draws a line from the end of the arc to topCenter. Without it, your shape will look like Figure 10-37.

FIGURE 10-37:
How the custom
shape will look
after adding the
last line.

Combining fill and stroke

In the midst of trying out the examples in this section, you may have tried filling up the shape with some colors (or gradients) and trying to draw a border around it at the same time, like this:

```
MyShape()
    .fill(LinearGradient(
        gradient: Gradient(
```

```
             colors: [.yellow, .green]),
          startPoint: .leading,
          endPoint: .trailing
      ))
      .stroke(Color.black,
          style: StrokeStyle(
              lineWidth: 10,
              lineCap: .round,
              lineJoin: .round))
```

Unfortunately, this won't work. To make it work, you need to add an overlay to the shape, like this:

```
MyShape()
    .fill(LinearGradient(
        gradient: Gradient(
            colors: [.yellow, .green]),
        startPoint: .leading,
        endPoint: .trailing
    ))
    .overlay(
        MyShape()
        .stroke(Color.black,
                style: StrokeStyle(
                    lineWidth: 10,
                    lineCap: .round,
                    lineJoin: .round))
    )
    .frame(width: 200, height: 150,
        alignment: .center)
```

Figure 10-38 shows the shape with the fill and border added.

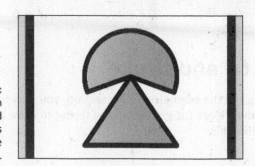

FIGURE 10-38:
Filling the custom
shape and
drawing borders
around it at the
same time.

One final point to note before I end this section: So far, your `MyShape` struct has the following instructions to use the various functions in the `Path` structure to draw lines and an arc:

```
var path = Path()
path.move(to:topCenter)
path.addLine(to: bottomLeft)
path.addLine(to: bottomRight)
path.addLine(to: topCenter)

path.addArc(
    center: topCenter,
    radius: rect.width/2,
    startAngle: .degrees(20),
    endAngle: .degrees(160),
    clockwise: true)
path.addLine(to: topCenter)

print(rect)
return path
```

You can combine the preceding instructions into a single block, like this:

```
return Path { path in
    path.move(to:topCenter)
    path.addLine(to: bottomLeft)
    path.addLine(to: bottomRight)
    path.addLine(to: topCenter)
    path.addArc(
        center: topCenter,
        radius: rect.width/2,
        startAngle: .degrees(20),
        endAngle: .degrees(160),
        clockwise: true)
    path.addLine(to: topCenter)
}
```

Using Special Effects in SwiftUI

Earlier in this chapter, I show you how to use the built-in shapes in SwiftUI, as well as how to draw your own custom shapes. This section explains how you can control the way your views are rendered in SwiftUI. In particular, I show you how to:

>> Use the different blend modes to combine two or more views to create a blended effect

>> Use blurs to apply a Gaussian blur to your views

>> Use saturation to adjust the amount of color used in views

Blend modes

Earlier you use the Image view to display an image of Einstein. Let's now wrap it using a ZStack view. In addition to the Image view, you'll add a Rectangle view filled with yellow:

```
struct ContentView: View {
    var body: some View {
        ZStack {
            Image("Einstein")
                .resizable()
                .aspectRatio(contentMode: .fill)
            Rectangle()
                .fill(Color.yellow)
                .blendMode(.multiply)
        }
        .frame(width: 370.0, height: 480.0)
    }
}
```

You'll add the blendMode() modifier to the Rectangle struct and use the multiply mode. The multiply mode multiplies the RGB channel numbers (from 0 to 1) for each pixel from the top layer with the values for the corresponding pixel from the bottom layer. The result is a darker image (see Figure 10-39), because multiplying a number smaller than 1 with another number also smaller than 1 will result in a number smaller than either initial value.

TIP

The default blend mode is normal, which means if you have multiple images in a ZStack, the last view on the ZStack is always on top, because there is no mixing of its colors with the layers underneath it.

Figure 10-40 shows the various blend modes applied to the Image view.

FIGURE 10-39:
Applying the
multiply blend
mode to the
Image view.

.blendMode(.darken)   .blendMode(.exclusion)

.blendMode(.lighten)   .blendMode(.hardLight)

FIGURE 10-40:
Applying the
different blend
modes to the
Image view.

The multiply blend mode is the most commonly used mode in image processing. As such, it has its own shortcut, the colorMultiply() modifier. Using this modifier, instead of embedding the Image view with another Rectangle view in a ZStack view, you can simply apply the colorMultiply() directly on the Image view:

```
Image("Einstein")
    .resizable()
    .colorMultiply(.yellow)
    .frame(width: 370.0, height: 480.0)
```

Another blend mode that is popular is the screen blend mode. With the screen blend mode, the values of the pixels in the two layers are inverted, multiplied, and then inverted. This is the direct opposite of the multiply blend mode and results in a brighter image.

Let's try out an example:

```
struct ContentView: View {
    var body: some View {

        VStack {
            ZStack {
                Circle()
                    .fill(Color.yellow)
                    .offset(x: -50, y: -50)
                Circle()
                    .fill(Color.green)
                Circle()
                    .fill(Color.red)
                    .offset(x: 50, y: 50)
            }
            .frame(width: 300, height: 200)
        }
    }
}
```

In this example, three circles are stacked on top of one another using the ZStack view (see Figure 10-41).

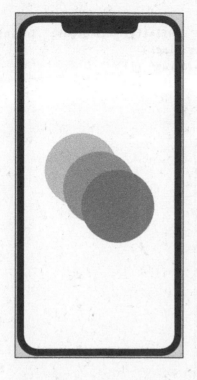

FIGURE 10-41:
Three circles
overlapping each
other.

With a white background (default), applying a `screen` blend mode will cause all the circles to turn white. Can you figure out why? With the background set to black, all the circles can now overlap each other, with the output shown in Figure 10-42.

```
struct ContentView: View {
    var body: some View {
        VStack {
            ZStack {
                Circle()
                    .fill(Color.yellow)
                    .offset(x: -50, y: -50)
                    .blendMode(.screen)
                Circle()
                    .fill(Color.green)
                    .blendMode(.screen)
                Circle()
                    .fill(Color.red)
                    .offset(x: 50, y: 50)
                    .blendMode(.screen)
            }
            .frame(width: 300, height: 200)
        }
```

```
        .frame(maxWidth: .infinity, maxHeight: .infinity)
        .background(Color.black)
        .edgesIgnoringSafeArea(.all)
    }
}
```

FIGURE 10-42:
Applying the
screen blend
mode to all
three circles.

**TECHNICAL
STUFF**

`Color.yellow`, `Color.red`, and `Color.green` are not the true yellow, red, and green, respectively. Apple has modified these colors so that they look good in Dark and Light modes. If you want to get the true red, blue, and green, you have to use their RGB values, such as this:

```
// true red
.fill(Color(red:1, green:0, blue:0))
```

TIP

If you leave out the last three statements in the earlier code snippet, you can still see the effect in Figure 10-42 when you run it on the iPhone Simulator (or real device) and turn on Dark mode.

Blurs

The best way to understand how the blur effect works is to try it out yourself. The following code snippet applies a blur effect (with a radius of 5) on the three circles in the ZStack view:

```
VStack {
    ZStack {
        Circle()
            .fill(Color.yellow)
            .offset(x: -50, y: -50)
            .blendMode(.screen)
        Circle()
            .fill(Color.green)
            .blendMode(.screen)
        Circle()
            .fill(Color.red)
            .offset(x: 50, y: 50)
            .blendMode(.screen)

    }
    .blur(radius: 5)
    .frame(width: 300, height: 200)
}
```

Figure 10-43 shows the blur effect with different radius values.

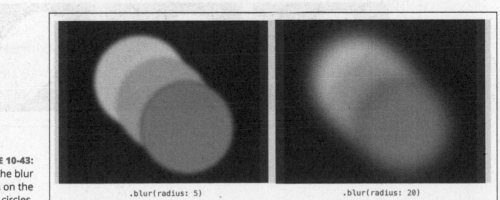

FIGURE 10-43: Applying the blur effects on the three circles.

Saturation

Saturation allows you to adjust the intensity of colors in a view. The following code snippet applies a saturation of 0.1 to the three circles in a ZStack view:

```
VStack {
    ZStack {
        Circle()
            .fill(Color.yellow)
            .offset(x: -50, y: -50)
            .blendMode(.screen)
        Circle()
            .fill(Color.green)
            .blendMode(.screen)
        Circle()
            .fill(Color.red)
            .offset(x: 50, y: 50)
            .blendMode(.screen)

    }
    .saturation(0.1)
    .frame(width: 300, height: 200)
}
```

Figure 10-44 shows the saturation effect with different saturation values.

FIGURE 10-44:
Applying the saturation effects to the three circles.

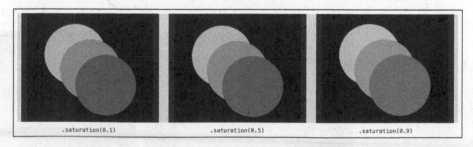

IN THIS CHAPTER

» Seeing how you can animate in SwiftUI

» Repeating an animation

» Stopping an animation

» Rotating views in 2D and 3D

» Creating your own custom progress indicator

Chapter **11**

Performing Animations in SwiftUI

I n Chapter 10, I show you how to draw different types of shapes in SwiftUI. To make your great-looking user interface (UI) even more interactive and appealing, it's useful to animate some of the components. For example, you may want to create your own custom progress indicator for the app that you're building. For this, you need to perform some animations. SwiftUI makes animating your views really simple. It hides the complexity of the work needed to handle complex animations and allows you to focus on what you want to animate.

In this chapter, I show you some of the techniques to perform animation in SwiftUI.

Understanding How to Animate

To animate a view in SwiftUI, apply the animation() modifier on it. SwiftUI animates any changes made to animatable properties of a view. For example, the various properties of a view — such as its color, opacity, rotation, size, and other properties — are all animatable. As usual, the best way to understand this concept is to use an example.

First, create a rounded button that shows the Confirm caption:

```
struct ContentView: View {

    var body: some View {
        Button(action: {
        }) {
            Text("Confirm")
            .bold()
        }
        .padding(40)
        .background(Color.green)
        .foregroundColor(.white)
        .clipShape(Circle())
    }
}
```

Figure 11-1 shows the rounded button.

FIGURE 11-1:
Displaying the
rounded Button
view.

Apply some scaling (zooming) to the button using the `scaleEffect()` modifier:

```swift
struct ContentView: View {
    @State private var scaleFactor: CGFloat = 1

    var body: some View {
        Button(action: {
        }) {
            Text("Confirm")
                .bold()
        }
        .onAppear(perform: {
            self.scaleFactor = 2.5
        })
        .padding(40)
        .background(Color.green)
        .foregroundColor(.white)
        .clipShape(Circle())
        .scaleEffect(scaleFactor)
    }
}
```

What you want to do here is zoom the button to two and a half times its original size. The scaling will be performed as soon as the `Button` view is shown. Figure 11-2 shows the button zoomed in to two and a half times its original size when it first appears.

What you really want is to slow down the scaling, so that users can see the zooming-in process. For this, you can use the `animation()` modifier on the `Button` view:

```swift
struct ContentView: View {
    @State private var scaleFactor: CGFloat = 1

    var body: some View {
        Button(action: {
        }) {
            Text("Confirm")
                .bold()
        }
        .onAppear(perform: {
            self.scaleFactor = 2.5
        })
        .padding(40)
```

```
        .background(Color.green)
        .foregroundColor(.white)
        .clipShape(Circle())
        .scaleEffect(scaleFactor)
        .animation(.default)
    }
}
```

FIGURE 11-2:
Zooming the
Button view two
and a half times.

The `.default` property actually belongs to the `Animation` struct, so you can rewrite the above statement as follows:

```
.animation(Animation.default)
```

When you now load the `Button` view again, the button zooms in two and a half times.

Specifying the type of animation

By default, the button will zoom in at a linear speed. You can also use the easeInOut() modifier if you want the animation to start slow, pick up speed, and then slow down again:

```
.animation(
    .easeInOut(duration: 2)
)
```

The duration parameter indicates how much time is given for the animation to complete. In this example, the zoom animation must complete in two seconds.

If you want to start fast and then slow down, use the easeOut() modifier:

```
.animation(
    .easeOut(duration: 2)
)
```

Both the easeInOut() and easeOut() modifiers are type methods of the Animation struct.

Repeating the animation

Many times, you want the animation to repeat a number of times. For this you can apply the repeatCount() modifier:

```
.animation(
    Animation.easeInOut(duration: 2)
        .repeatCount(2, autoreverses: true)
)
```

The easeInOut() is a type method of the Animation struct, and it returns an Animation struct. So, in this case, you call the repeatCount() modifier of the Animation struct to repeat the animation a number of times (twice, in this case). The autoreverses parameter allows you to reverse the animation, so for this particular case the size of the button changes from small to big, and then reverses and changes from big to small.

Figure 11-3 shows the animation that is repeated twice. Notice that at the end of the second animation, the button reverts back to the larger size as specified in the scaleFactor state variable:

```
.scaleEffect(scaleFactor) // changed to 2.5 in onAppear()
```

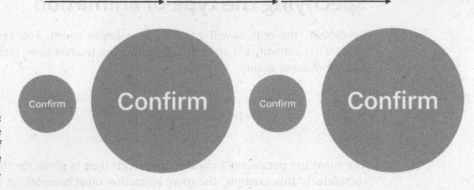

1   2   **Back to size specified in scaleFactor**

FIGURE 11-3:
Animating the
changing of
the scale of the
button.

If you want the animation to repeat forever, use the `repeatForever()` modifier:

```
.animation(
    Animation.easeInOut(duration: 2)
        .repeatForever(autoreverses: true)
)
```

Stopping the animation

Although you can animate nonstop, there are times where you need to stop the animation. Here's another example:

```
struct ContentView: View {
    @State private var opacity:Double = 1.0

    var body: some View {
        Button(action: {
        })
        {
        Text("Click Me")
            .fontWeight(.bold)
            .font(.title)
            .foregroundColor(.blue)
            .padding()
            .background(Color.yellow)
            .overlay(
                Rectangle()
                    .stroke(Color.blue, lineWidth: 5)
            )
            .opacity(opacity)
            .onAppear() {
```

```
            let baseAnimation =
                Animation.linear(duration: 1)
            withAnimation (
                baseAnimation.repeatForever(
                autoreverses: true))
            {
                self.opacity = 0.2
            }
        }
    }
}
```

The preceding code snippet shows a `Button` view with its opacity initially set to 1.0. When it appears, you perform a *linear animation* (animating with constant speed) to change the opacity of the button down to 0.2, all within a duration of 1 second. In the next 1 second, it then changes to fully opaque again.

Unlike the earlier example, this example does not use the `animation()` modifier for animation. Instead, you use the `withAnimation` block. The `withAnimation` block lets you explicitly tell SwiftUI what to animate.

Figure 11-4 shows the button fully opaque when it's loaded and then gradually changes its opacity to 0.2.

The animation is perpetual, so to stop it, you need to do some work. For this, you can use a Boolean state variable (let's call it `animate`) and use it to determine whether the animation should continue:

```
            withAnimation (self.animate ?
                baseAnimation.repeatForever(
                    autoreverses: true) :
                Animation.default) {
                self.opacity = 0.2
            }
```

In the preceding code snippet, if the `animate` state variable is `true`, you'll perform the animation perpetually, or you can set the animation to `default` (which will only perform the animation once).

FIGURE 11-4:
Dimming the
Button view.

The following code snippet stops the animation when the button is tapped and sets the opacity of the button back to 1:

```swift
struct ContentView: View {
    @State private var opacity:Double = 1.0
    @State private var animate = true

    var body: some View {
        Button(action: {
            self.animate = false
            self.opacity = 1.0
        })
        {
        Text("Click Me")
            .fontWeight(.bold)
            .font(.title)
            .foregroundColor(.blue)
            .padding()
            .background(Color.yellow)
            .overlay(
                Rectangle()
                    .stroke(Color.blue, lineWidth: 5)
            )
```

```
            .opacity(opacity)
            .onAppear() {
                let baseAnimation =
                    Animation.linear(duration: 1)
                withAnimation (self.animate ?
                    baseAnimation.repeatForever(
                        autoreverses: true) :
                    Animation.default) {
                    self.opacity = 0.2
                }
            }
        }
    }
}
```

REMEMBER

Remember to follow the Apple Human Interface Guidelines (HIG) when it comes to animating your UI. This also applies to custom animations. See `https://developer.apple.com/design/human-interface-guidelines/ios/visual-design/animation` for the details.

Performing Your Own Animation

In addition to animating changes made to animatable properties of views, SwiftUI also allows you to specify your own animation, such as moving views or rotating views. In the following sections, I show you how to rotate views in two dimensions.

Rotating in 2D

To perform rotation in two dimensions, use the `rotationEffect()` modifier. The following code snippet displays a "wheel of fortune" image on the screen, together with a `Button` view:

```
struct ContentView: View {
    @State private var degrees = 0.0

    var body: some View {
        VStack{
            Image("wheel")
                .resizable()
                .frame(width: 400.0, height: 400.0)
                .rotationEffect(.degrees(degrees))
```

```
        Button("Spin") {
            let d = Double.random(in: 720...7200)
            withAnimation () {
                self.degrees += d
            }
        }
    }
}
```

When the button is tapped, a random number between 720 and 7,200 is generated and assigned to the `degrees` state variable. This state variable is bound to the `rotationEffect()` modifier, so when the button is tapped, the image will rotate. To rotate the image one complete turn takes 360 degrees. So, when you generate a value from 720 to 7,200, you're essentially making the image turn from 2 to 20 complete turns. The image on the left of Figure 11-5 shows the image before rotation. The image on the right shows the image rotated using the random number generator.

Image of wheel by MarioGS (https://commons.wikimedia.org/w/index. php?curid=29159295) used under a Creative Commons Attribution-Share Alike 3.0 Unported license (https://creativecommons.org/licenses/by-sa/3.0/deed.en)

FIGURE 11-5:
Spinning the wheel of fortune.

For this example, you really need to try it out to see the effects of the rotation.

If you try this code snippet, you'll find that the animation is very abrupt — it starts and ends with the same speed. A more natural way of spinning can be achieved using the easeInOut() modifier earlier in this chapter:

```
var body: some View {
    VStack{
        Image("wheel")
         .resizable()
         .frame(width: 400.0, height: 400.0)
         .rotationEffect(.degrees(degrees))

        Button("Spin") {
            let d = Double.random(in: 720...7200)
            let baseAnimation =
                Animation.easeInOut(duration: d / 360)
            withAnimation (baseAnimation) {
                self.degrees += d
            }
        }
    }
}
```

In the preceding addition, you use the easeInOut() modifier to perform the animation based on the number of complete rotations you need to perform (each turn is allocated 1 second). When the wheel is rotated now, it's more realistic, and at the same time each spin of the wheel takes a random amount of times to complete (more spins take more time).

Rotating in 3D

In addition to performing animations in 2D, you can also perform 3D animations using the rotation3DEffect() modifier. To understand how this modifier works, it's best to look at an example:

```
struct ContentView: View {
    var body: some View {
        Text("SwiftUI for Dummies")
            .font(.largeTitle)
    }
}
```

The preceding code shows a Text view displayed in large title format (see Figure 11-6).

FIGURE 11-6:
Displaying a
Text view.

Let's now apply a rotation3DEffect() modifier to the Text view:

```
struct ContentView: View {
    @State private var degrees = 45.0

    var body: some View {
        Text("SwiftUI for Dummies")
            .font(.largeTitle)
            .rotation3DEffect(.degrees(degrees),
                axis: (x: 1, y: 0, z: 0))
    }
}
```

In the preceding addition, you converted the value of the degrees state variable using the degrees() function (which returns an Angle struct), pass the result to the rotation3DEffect() modifier, and specify the axis to apply the rotation to. In this example, you specified the x-axis to apply the rotation. The result of this rotation is shown in Figure 11-7.

FIGURE 11-7:
Applying the
3D rotation to
the *x*-axis
(45 degrees).

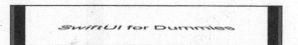

If you change the degrees to 75, then the result would look like Figure 11-8:

```
@State private var degrees = 75.0
```

FIGURE 11-8:
Applying the
3D rotation
to the *x*-axis
(75 degrees).

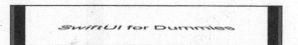

Now change the axis to *y* and the result is as shown in Figure 11-9:

```
struct ContentView: View {
    @State private var degrees = 75.0
    var body: some View {
        Text("SwiftUI for Dummies")
            .font(.largeTitle)
            .rotation3DEffect(.degrees(degrees),
                axis: (x: 0, y: 1, z: 0))
    }
}
```

FIGURE 11-9:
Applying the 3D
rotation to the
y-axis.

How about *z*-axis? Figure 11-10 shows the output:

```
struct ContentView: View {
    @State private var degrees = 45.0
    var body: some View {
        Text("SwiftUI for Dummies")
```

```
        .font(.largeTitle)
        .rotation3DEffect(.degrees(degrees),
            axis: (x: 0, y: 0, z: 1))
    }
}
```

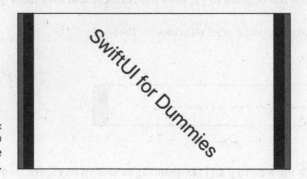

FIGURE 11-10:
Applying the 3D
rotation to the
z-axis.

Finally, how about all the three axes? Figure 11-11 shows the output:

```
struct ContentView: View {
    @State private var degrees = 45.0
    var body: some View {
        Text("SwiftUI for Dummies")
            .font(.largeTitle)
            .rotation3DEffect(.degrees(degrees),
                axis: (x: 1, y: 1, z: 1))
    }
}
```

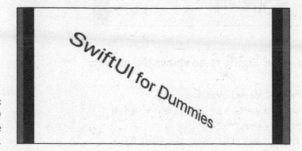

FIGURE 11-11:
Applying the 3D
rotation to the
three axes.

By now, you should have a pretty good grasp of how the rotation is applied to the three axes. Figure 11-12 shows a summary of the rotation made to the three axes:

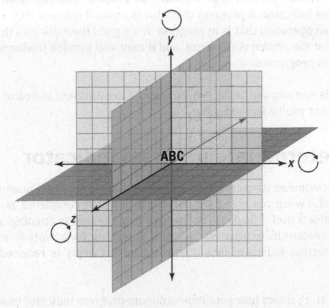

Now apply some 3D animation to the rotation:

```
struct ContentView: View {
    @State private var degrees = 0.0
    var body: some View {
        Text("SwiftUI for Dummies")
            .font(.largeTitle)
            .rotation3DEffect(.degrees(degrees),
                axis: (x: 1, y: 1, z: 1))
            .onAppear() {
                let baseAnimation =
                    Animation.easeInOut(duration: 3)
                withAnimation (baseAnimation) {
                    self.degrees += 360
                }
            }
    }
}
```

Now you're able to see the text rotate in 3D.

Creating a Custom Progress Indicator

Based on the concepts explained in this chapter, you can now build a custom progress indicator. A progress indicator is a visual element that informs the user about an operation that is in progress. It's a good feedback tool that reassures the user that the system is not hung, and it may also provide feedback on how far the task has progressed.

For this section, you build two variants of the progress indicator using the concepts that you've learned so far.

Indeterminate progress indicator

An *indeterminate progress indicator* expresses an unspecified amount of wait time. It's useful when you aren't sure when a task will be completed, but you'd still like to provide a useful feedback to the user that the task is ongoing. A good use case of an indeterminate progress indicator is waiting for a reply from a web service. The progress indicator should animate until a reply is received from the web service.

Figure 11-13 shows how your indeterminate progress indicator looks. It consists of a circular groove with a ball spinning within it. You can modify the speed in which the ball spins inside the groove.

Initial state of the progress indicator

The ball inside the progress indicator spinning within the groove

FIGURE 11-13:
The indeterminate progress indicator that you'll build.

For this progress indicator, create a new struct with the following code:

```
struct ProgressIndicator1: View {

    @Binding var degrees: Double
    @Binding var animate:Bool
```

```
    var body: some View {
        ZStack {
            Circle()
                .stroke(lineWidth: 20.0)
                .opacity(0.3)
                .foregroundColor(Color.green)

            Circle()
                .trim(from: 0, to: 0.001)
                .stroke(style: StrokeStyle(
                    lineWidth: 20.0,
                    lineCap: .round,
                    lineJoin: .round))
                .foregroundColor(Color.green)
                .rotationEffect(Angle(degrees: -90))
                .rotationEffect(Angle(degrees:
                    self.degrees))
                .animation(
                    self.animate ?
                        Animation.linear(
                        duration: 2)
                        .repeatForever(
                        autoreverses: false) :
                        Animation.default
                )
        }
    }
}
```

Here, you have the following:

>> A ZStack view to stack up two circles

>> An inner circle to represent the groove for the ball to travel on

>> An outer circle to represent the ball

The left side of Figure 11-14 shows the two circles and the starting angle of the second circle.

The trim() modifier displays the proportion of the circle to display. Its value is from 0 to 1. Figure 11-15 shows how the arguments for the trim() modifier affects the look of the circle.

FIGURE 11-14:
The layout of the
two circles, and
rotating the
starting point
90 degrees
counterclockwise.

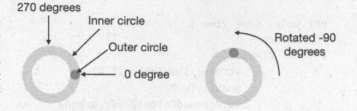

FIGURE 11-15:
The trim controls
the proportion of
the circle to
display, as well as
the starting point.

trim(from: 0, to: 0.001)   trim(from: 0, to: 0.25)   trim(from: 0.25, to: 0.75)

Notice that you applied the `rotationEffect()` modifier twice to the second circle. As the starting angle of the second circle starts from the 3 o'clock position, you need to rotate the second circle by 90 degrees counterclockwise (see the right side of Figure 11-14) so that it can start from the top 12 o'clock position.

The second `rotationEffect()` modifier allows you to rotate the second circle to a specific degree using a `@Binding degrees` variable. Finally, the `animation()` modifier allows you to control when to repeat the animation and when to stop the animation through the use of the `@Binding animate` variable.

Notice that you use `linear` animation for the circle, which means the ball will spin at a constant speed:

```
.animation(
        self.animate ?
            Animation.linear(
            duration: 2)
            .repeatForever(
            autoreverses: false) :
            Animation.default
    )
```

If you want, you can also change it to `easeInOut()`, like this:

```
.animation(
        self.animate ?
            Animation.easeInOut(
            duration: 2)
            .repeatForever(
```

```
                                    autoreverses: false) :
                                    Animation.default
                        )
```

You can now use it in your ContentView, like this:

```
import SwiftUI

struct ContentView: View {

    @State var degrees = 0.0
    @State var buttonCaption1 = "Start"
    @State var startProgressIndicator1 = true

    var body: some View {
        VStack {
            ProgressIndicator1(
                degrees: self.$degrees,
                animate: self.$startProgressIndicator1)
                    .frame(width: 100.0, height: 100.0)
                    .padding(40.0)

            Button(action: {
                switch self.buttonCaption1 {
                    case "Start":
                        self.startProgressIndicator1 =
                            true
                        self.degrees = 360
                    case "Stop" :
                        self.degrees = 0
                        self.startProgressIndicator1 =
                            false
                    default: break
                }
                self.buttonCaption1 =
                    self.buttonCaption1 == "Start" ?
                    "Stop" : "Start"
            })
            {
                Text(self.buttonCaption1)
            }
        }
    }
}
```

To use the `ProgressIndicator1`, you bind two state variables to it. The first state variable (`degrees`) controls how many degrees you want the progress indicator to rotate (360 for a full circle), while the second state variable (`startProgress Indicator1`) controls when the indicator starts or stops. Figure 11-16 shows the progress indicator at its initial position when it's first loaded. Clicking the Start button animates the progress indicator. When you click the Stop button, the indicator reverts back to its initial position at the top.

FIGURE 11-16:
Using the indeterminate progress indicator.

Determinate progress indicator

A *determinate progress indicator* shows how much a task has been completed and is useful if you know how much longer a task will take to complete. A good example of the use of a determinate progress indicator is when downloading files from the web. For example, if you're trying to load a 50MB file and based on the amount downloaded, you can use a determinate progress indicator to show the percentage of the file that has been downloaded.

To create the second type of progress indicator, create a new `struct` with the following code snippet:

```swift
struct ProgressIndicator2: View {
    @Binding var trim: CGFloat

    var body: some View {
        ZStack {
            Circle()
                .stroke(lineWidth: 20.0)
                .opacity(0.3)
                .foregroundColor(Color.green)

            Circle()
                .trim(from: 0, to: self.trim)
                .stroke(style: StrokeStyle(
                    lineWidth: 20.0,
                    lineCap: .round,
                    lineJoin: .round))
                .foregroundColor(Color.green)
                .rotationEffect(Angle(degrees: -90))

            Text(String(format: "%.0f %%",
                    min(self.trim, 1.0) * 100.0))
                .font(.headline)
                .bold()
        }
    }
}
```

Like the first progress indicator, you have two circles. For the second circle, this time around you'll vary the trim amount using a `@Binding` `trim` variable:

```swift
.trim(from: 0, to: self.trim)
```

Unlike the first progress indicator, you aren't animating the second circle — you only rotate it counterclockwise to set the starting point to the 12 o'clock position.

You also display a `Text` view in the middle of the two circles to display the percentage completed. The value to display is based on the value of the `trim` variable.

You can now use the new progress indicator in your ContentView:

```
import SwiftUI

struct ContentView: View {
    @State var proportion:CGFloat = 0.0
    @State var buttonCaption2 = "Start"
    @State var startProgressIndicator2 = false

    var body: some View {
        VStack {
            ProgressIndicator2(trim: self.$proportion)
                .frame(width: 100.0, height: 100.0)
                .padding(40.0)

            HStack{
                Button(action: {
                    self.proportion += 0.1
                    self.proportion =
                        min(self.proportion,1)
                })
                {
                    Text("+")
                    .padding()
                        .border(Color.black)
                }
                Button(action: {
                    self.proportion -= 0.1
                    self.proportion =
                        max(self.proportion,0)
                })
                {
                    Text("-")
                    .padding()
                    .border(Color.black)
                }
            }

            Button(action: {
                switch self.buttonCaption2 {
                    case "Start":
                        self.startProgressIndicator2 =
                            true
```

```
                case "Stop" :
                    self.startProgressIndicator2 =
                        false
                default: break
            }
            self.buttonCaption2 =
                self.buttonCaption2 == "Start"
                ? "Stop" : "Start"

            Timer.scheduledTimer(
                withTimeInterval: 0.1,
                repeats: true) {
                    timer in
                    self.proportion += 0.01
                    if self.proportion>1 {
                        self.proportion = 0
                    }
                    if !self.startProgressIndicator2 {
                        timer.invalidate()
                    }
                }
        })
        {
            Text(self.buttonCaption2)
        }
    }
}
}
```

For this second progress indicator, there are two ways you can use it:

>> Use the plus (+) or minus (–) button to increment or decrement the propor-
tion state variable manually, which is bound to the trim parameter of
ProgressIndicator2.

>> Use a Timer object to increment the proportion state variable at regular
time interval.

Figure 11-17 shows the progress indicator in action.

FIGURE 11-17:
Using the
determinate
progress
indicator.

Chapter **12**

Creating a Complete Project

n the previous chapters of this book, I show you the various components of SwiftUI and explain how it enables you to build compelling iOS applications quickly and easily. My approach has always been to examine the various parts of SwiftUI using independent examples so that you can easily jump into a specific topic of interest and start learning. However, nothing beats learning how to build a complete working application from start to finish, complete with deploying the app onto a real device. And that's exactly what you do in this chapter: Build a complete app from start to finish, and then see how to deploy it onto an iPhone.

Understanding What the App Does

In Chapter 6, I show you how to create a navigation and tabbed application. The app you'll build in this chapter makes use of the knowledge you acquire in

Chapter 6 to build a complete news reader application (so if you haven't read Chapter 6 yet, you'll probably want to do that now).

The app you'll build in this chapter is a news reader. The app has two tabs — one for showing a list of news headlines and another for showing a list of user preferences. The preferences tab allows users to select a specific news source from a list and select the content to display (just the headlines or everything). The preferences set by the user are persisted to storage so when the app is restarted, the preferences are preserved. The app also allows the user to share a news item.

Figure 12-1 shows the app displaying a list of news headlines from the news source Engadget. When reading a specific article, the user can share the article by tapping the Share button located at the top of the navigation bar. Figure 12-2 shows the preferences view, where users can select from a list of news sources.

FIGURE 12-1:
The app you build in this chapter.

FIGURE 12-2:
Selecting from a
list of news
sources.

Building the Project

Now that you have a good idea of what the app will do, you're ready to create the project. In Xcode, create a new single-view app and name it NewsReader (see Figure 12-3).

In the following sections, I walk you through creating the layouts; defining the news sources and observable objects; fetching the data; displaying the news headlines, images, and news; creating the share sheet and preferences view; and persisting the user's preferences. Whew!

Creating the layouts

After you've created the project, add three SwiftUI View items and one Swift File item to the project and name them as follows (see Figure 12-4):

>> `NewsView.swift` (SwiftUI View): Shows the details of each article

>> `MainView.swift` (SwiftUI View): Shows the list of news items

» `PreferencesView.swift` (SwiftUI View): Shows the preferences view

» `MainViewModel.swift` (Swift File): Provides the content (news headlines)

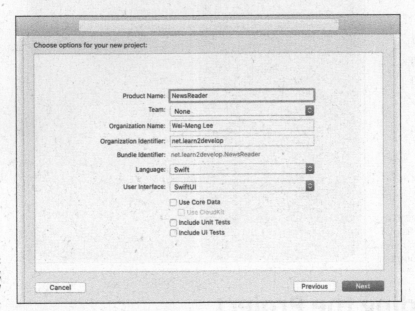

TIP

After the files are added to the project, you can rearrange their order simply by dragging them.

Because the application has two tabs, add the `TabView` item to the `ContentView.swift` file:

```swift
import SwiftUI

struct NewsView: View {
    var body: some View {
        TabView {
            MainView()
                .tabItem {
                    Image(systemName: "doc.richtext")
                    Text("News")
                }
            PreferencesView()
                .tabItem {
                    Image(systemName: "gear")
                    Text("Preferences")
                }
        }
    }
}
```

Figure 12-5 shows the app with the two tabs on the iPhone Simulator.

Hello, World!

Defining the news sources and observable objects

For the next step, you're going to add a Swift file to your project so that you can use it to store the various news sources to be used by the various views. This file will also contain two observable objects that can be shared by all the views.

Observable objects are discussed in more detail in Chapter 8.

TIP

Name the Swift file item NewsURL.swift (see Figure 12-6).

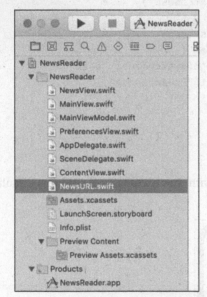

FIGURE 12-6:
Adding the
NewsURL.swift
file to your
project.

Add the following statements in bold to the NewsURL.swift file:

```
import Foundation

class NewsURLSources: ObservableObject {
    var sources = [
        "bloomberg": "Bloomberg",
        "buzzfeed": "Buzzfeed",
        "cbs-news": "CBS News",
        "engadget": "Engadget",
        "fortune": "Fortune",
        "abc-news":"ABC News",
        "ars-technica":"Ars Technica",
```

```
            "associated-press": "Associated Press",
            "bbc-news": "BBC News",
            "google-news": "Google News",
            "hacker-news": "Hacker News",
            "new-scientist": "New Scientist",
            "newsweek": "Newsweek",
            "new-york-magazine": "New York Magazine",
            "reuters": "Reuters",
            "techcrunch": "TechCrunch"
        ]
        var displayContentType =
            ["top-headlines","everything"]

        @Published var source  = "engadget"
        @Published var content = "top-headlines"
}
```

The sources is a dictionary that contains key/value pairs of news source IDs and their associated descriptive names.

The source and content observable objects represent the news source ID and the type of content to retrieve ("top-headlines" or "everything"), respectively.

To share the two observable objects with all the views in the application, add the following statements in bold to the SceneDelegate.swift file:

```
import UIKit
import SwiftUI

class SceneDelegate: UIResponder, UIWindowSceneDelegate {

    var window: UIWindow?

    var newsURLSources = NewsURLSources()

    func scene(_ scene: UIScene, willConnectTo session:
            UISceneSession, options connectionOptions:
            UIScene.ConnectionOptions) {

        let contentView = ContentView().environmentObject(newsUR
        LSources)

        // Use a UIHostingController as window root view
           controller.
```

```
        if let windowScene = scene as? UIWindowScene {
            let window = UIWindow(windowScene: windowScene)
            window.rootViewController =
                UIHostingController(rootView: contentView)
            self.window = window
            window.makeKeyAndVisible()
        }
    }
```

Now all the views in your application will be able to access the two observable objects and at the same time be updated automatically when these two objects change in value.

Fetching the data

You can now work on fetching the data. This part is covered in Chapter 6, so be sure to refer to that chapter if you want to understand how it works.

For this app, you use the free service provided by News API (https://newsapi.org). This is a JSON-based application programming interface (API) that provides you with breaking news headlines and allows you to search for articles from more than 30,000 news sources and blogs. To register for your own API key, go to https://newsapi.org/register.

If you've tried the examples in Chapter 6, you can use the same API key.

REMEMBER

Populate the MainViewModel.swift file with the following statements:

```
import Foundation

struct Result: Codable {
    var articles: [Article]
}

struct Article: Codable {
    var url: String
    var title: String
    var description: String?
    var urlToImage: String?
}
```

```
class MainViewModel: ObservableObject {
    @Published var articles = [Article]()

    func fetchData(newsUrl:String) {
        guard let url = URL(string: newsUrl) else {
            print("URL is not valid")
            return
        }
        let request = URLRequest(url: url)
        URLSession.shared.dataTask(with: request) {
            data, response, error in
            if let data = data {
                if let decodedResult = try?
                    JSONDecoder().decode(
                    Result.self, from: data) {
                    // decoding is successful
                    DispatchQueue.main.async {
                        // assign the decoded articles to
                        // the state variable
                        self.articles =
                            decodedResult.articles
                    }
                    return
                }
            }
            print("Error: \(error?.localizedDescription ??
        "Unknown error")")
        }.resume()
    }
}
```

Basically, the `fetchData()` function takes in a URL and downloads the JSON string containing the news feed. Then it decodes the JSON string into a struct of type `Result`. The decoded data is then assigned to the `articles` observable object, which will be used to display the list of news headlines.

Displaying the news headlines

With the code for fetching the news feed out of the way, you can now add the following statements in bold to the `MainView.swift` file:

```
struct MainView: View {
    @EnvironmentObject var newsURLChoices: NewsURLSources
```

```
        @ObservedObject private var mainViewModel =
            MainViewModel()

        var body: some View {
            return NavigationView {
                List(mainViewModel.articles, id: \.url) {
                    item in
                    NavigationLink(destination:
                        NewsView()
                    ) {
                        HStack(alignment: .top) {
                            VStack(alignment: .leading) {
                                Text(item.title)
                                    .font(.headline)
                                Text(item.description ?? "")
                                    .font(.footnote)
                            }
                        }
                    }
                }
                // the following five lines should all be in
                // one single line; formatted for clarity
                .onAppear {self.mainViewModel.fetchData(
                    newsUrl:"https://newsapi.org/v2/
                    \(self.newsURLChoices.content)?
                    sources=\(self.newsURLChoices.source)&
                    apiKey=API_KEY")
                }
                // the following three lines should all be in
                // one single line; formatted for clarity
                .navigationBarTitle(
                    "\(self.newsURLChoices.sources[
                    self.newsURLChoices.source]!)")
            }
        }
    }

    struct MainView_Previews: PreviewProvider {
        static var previews: some View {
            MainView().environmentObject(
                NewsURLSources.init())
        }
    }
```

Replace API_KEY with your own API key obtained from News API.

These statements call the fetchData() function in the MainViewModel class to fetch the news feed, and then use the mainViewModel.articles observable object to display the various news headlines using a List view.

You made use of the two observable objects — newsURLChoices.content and newsURLChoices.source — in your URL in order to determine the type of content to retrieve and the source of the news to fetch from.

An example of the URL to fetch the news feed looks like this:

```
https://newsapi.org/v2/top-headlines?sources=engadget&apiKey=API_KEY
```

The preceding URL fetches the top headlines from the Engadget site. If you want to fetch everything from the Engadget site, the URL would look like this:

```
https://newsapi.org/v2/everything?sources=engadget&apiKey=API_KEY
```

Figure 12-7 shows the news feed displayed in the iPhone Simulator.

FIGURE 12-7: Displaying the news headlines.

TIP

Click the Live Preview button, and you'll be able to load the data and display the news feed!

Displaying the images

Besides displaying the news titles and descriptions, you also want to display the images from the articles in each row in the List view. As described in Chapter 6, to display images that are located remotely, you need to use an external package. For this, choose File➪Swift Packages➪Add Package Dependency and enter https://github.com/dmytro-anokhin/url-image. Follow the steps to add the dependency to your project.

To display the image for each article, add the following statements in bold to the MainView.swift file:

```
import SwiftUI
import URLImage

...

struct MainView: View {
    ...

    var body: some View {
        NavigationView {
            List(mainViewModel.articles, id: \.url) {
                item in
                HStack(alignment: .top) {
                    URLImage(
                        ((URL(string:item.urlToImage ??
                            "https://picsum.photos/100") ??
                            nil)!),
                        delay: 0.25,
                        processors:
                            [Resize(size:
                                CGSize(width: 100.0,
                                       height: 100.0),
                                   scale:
                                UIScreen.main.scale)],
                        content: {
                            $0.image
                            .resizable()
                                .aspectRatio(
                                    contentMode:.fit)
                        .clipped()
```

```
                }
            ).frame(width: 100.0, height: 100.0)

            VStack(alignment: .leading) {
                Text(item.title)
                    .font(.headline)
                Text(item.description ?? "")
                    .font(.footnote)
            }
        }
    }
    .onAppear {
        ...
    }
    .navigationBarTitle(
        "\(self.newsURLChoices.sources[
            self.newsURLChoices.source]!)")
    }
  }
}
```

Figure 12-8 shows the List view showing the news headline plus the image for each row.

FIGURE 12-8:
Displaying an image for each news headline.

Displaying the news

When the user taps on each row, you want to display the details of the news in another view. To do that, you display the news details in the NewsView.swift file.

Add the following statements in bold to the NewsView.swift file:

```swift
import SwiftUI
import WebKit

struct WebView: UIViewRepresentable {
    let request: URLRequest

    func makeUIView(context: Context) -> WKWebView  {
        return WKWebView()
    }

    func updateUIView(_ uiView: WKWebView,
                        context: Context) {
        uiView.load(request)
    }
}

struct NewsView: View {
    let url: String

    var body: some View {
        WebView(request: URLRequest(url: URL(string:
            url)!))
        .navigationBarTitle("",
            displayMode: .inline)
    }
}

struct NewsView_Previews: PreviewProvider {
    static var previews: some View {
        NewsView(url: "https://www.dummies.com")
    }
}
```

TIP

Refer to Chapter 9 for more details on the UIViewRepresentable protocol.

In the MainView.swift file, add the following statements so that when an item in the List view is tapped, you use the NavigationLink() function to navigate the user to the NewsView view:

```
var body: some View {
    NavigationView {
        List(mainViewModel.articles, id: \.url) {
            item in
            NavigationLink(destination:
                NewsView(url:item.url)
            ) {
                HStack(alignment: .top) {
                    URLImage(
                        (( URL(string:item.urlToImage ??
                          "https://picsum.photos/100") ??
                            nil)!),
                        delay: 0.25,
                        processors:
                            [Resize(size:
                                CGSize(width: 100.0,
                                        height: 100.0),
                                    scale:
                                UIScreen.main.scale)],
                        content: {
                            $0.image
                            .resizable()
                                .aspectRatio(
                                    contentMode:.fit)
                            .clipped()
                        }
                    ).frame(width: 100.0, height: 100.0)

                    VStack(alignment: .leading) {
                        Text(item.title)
                            .font(.headline)
                        Text(item.description ?? "")
                            .font(.footnote)
                    }
                }
            }
        }
        .onAppear {
            ...
        }
        .navigationBarTitle(...)
    }
}
```

Figure 12-9 shows the details of the selected news item displayed using the `WebView`.

FIGURE 12-9: Displaying the details of the news item.

Creating the share sheet

When the user is viewing the selected news in the `WebView`, it would be useful to be able to share the URL of this page with other users. In iOS 13, you can easily accomplish this with the share sheet. The *share sheet* is an action sheet that shows the item you're sharing, with optional buttons at the bottom. Using the share sheet, you can easily share items of interest with other users through AirDrop, Messages, Mail, Notes, and other apps on your device.

Add the following statements in bold to the `NewsView.swift` file:

```swift
struct NewsView: View {
    let url: String

    func shareURLButton() {
        let url = URL(string:self.url)
        let avc = UIActivityViewController(
            activityItems: [url!],
            applicationActivities: nil)
```

```
        UIApplication.shared.windows.first?
            .rootViewController?.present(
            avc, animated: true, completion: nil)
    }

    var body: some View {
        WebView(request: URLRequest(url: URL(string:
            url)!))
        .navigationBarTitle("",
            displayMode: .inline)

        .navigationBarItems(trailing:
            Button(action: {
                self.shareURLButton()
            }) {
                Image(systemName: "square.and.arrow.up")
            }
        )
    }
}
```

The share button is an image displayed as a navigation bar item located at the upper-right corner of the navigation bar. To display the share sheet, use the UIActivityViewController class and pass the item that you want to share (a URL object in this case) as the first argument to its initializer.

The left side of Figure 12-10 shows the NewsView showing the share button at the upper-right corner of the navigation bar. When the share button is tapped, the share sheet is displayed (see the right side of Figure 12-10).

Creating the preferences view

One of the key features of the news reader app is the ability to switch the source of the headlines. In this section, you build a preferences view for the app so that the user can switch between news sources. In addition, the user will be able to change from loading only the top headlines to loading everything, and vice versa.

You'll use the Form and Section views to display two Picker views. The first Picker view allows the user to select the news source, while the second Picker view selects the content type to load.

FIGURE 12-10:
Displaying the
share sheet.

Add the following statements in bold to the `PreferencesView.swift` file:

```
import SwiftUI

struct PreferencesView: View {

    @State private var newsSource = -1
    @State private var contentToDisplay = 0

    @EnvironmentObject var newsURLChoices: NewsURLSources

    let keys =
        NewsURLSources().sources.map{$0.key}.sorted()
    let values =
        NewsURLSources().sources.map {$0.value}.sorted()

    var body: some View {
        return NavigationView {
            Form {
                Section(header: Text("News Sources")) {
                    Picker(selection: $newsSource,
                        label: Text(
                            "Display News from")) {
```

```
                        ForEach(0..<values.count) {
                            Text(self.values[$0])
                        }
                    }
                }
                Section (header:Text(
                    "Content to Display")) {
                    Picker(selection: $contentToDisplay,
                        label: Text("")) {
                        Text("Top Headlines").tag(0)
                        Text("Everything").tag(1)
                    }.pickerStyle(SegmentedPickerStyle())
                }
            }
            .padding()
            .navigationBarTitle("Preferences")
        }
    }
}
```

Figure 12-11 shows the preferences view loaded. When you tap the first `Picker` view, it displays a list of news sources. The second `Picker` view is displayed as a segmented control (due to the `SegmentedPickerStyle` struct applied).

FIGURE 12-11:
Displaying the preferences view.

Notice that when the preferences view is first loaded, no news source is selected, even though in the NewsURL.swift file you've defined Engadget to be the default news source. To fix this problem, you have to update the newsSource state variable when the view first appears. You can do this using the onAppear() function:

```
var body: some View {
    return NavigationView {
        Form {
            ...
        }
        .onAppear() {
            // update the news source
            if self.newsSource < 0 {
                self.newsSource =
                    self.keys.firstIndex(
                    of:self.newsURLChoices.source) ?? 0
            } else {
                self.newsURLChoices.source =
                    self.keys[self.newsSource]
            }
        }
        .padding()
        .navigationBarTitle("Preferences")
    }
}
```

After the user has selected a news source, it's also important to set the source observed object so that the List view can update to the newly selected news source. The onAppear() function will always be fired whenever the user navigates back from selecting a news source, so this is the ideal location to set the source observed object.

You need to fix one more issue. When the user has selected the content type to display, you need to save the setting to the content observable object. This can be done using the onDisappear() function, like this:

```
var body: some View {
    return NavigationView {
        Form {
            ...
        }
```

```
            .onAppear() {
                ...
            }
            .onDisappear() {
                self.newsURLChoices.content =
                    self.contentToDisplay == 0 ?
                    self.newsURLChoices.displayContentType[0]
                    :
                    self.newsURLChoices.displayContentType[1]
            }
            .padding()
            .navigationBarTitle("Preferences")
        }
    }
```

The onDisappear() function will always be fired when the user selects another tab item, so this is the ideal location to update the content observed object.

Figure 12-12 shows the preferences view when it's first loaded.

FIGURE 12-12: The preferences view with the selected news source.

Select a new news source (say, Ars Technica) and select Everything. Now click the News tab, and it will automatically refresh to the selected news source (see Figure 12-13).

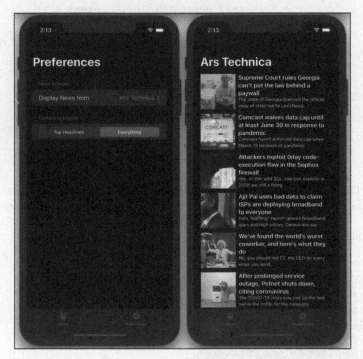

FIGURE 12-13:
Select a new news source and the List view will automatically display the headlines from the newly selected news source.

Persisting the user's preferences

So far, the user has been able to select the news source and change the content type of the news to be downloaded. But the user's preferences are not persisted to storage. If the app were restarted (whether because the OS killed the app to free memory resources or because the user terminated the app), the preferences settings would be lost. To solve this problem, use the UserDefaults class to persist the preferences settings as key/value pairs.

Add the following statements in bold to the PreferencesView.swift file:

```
    .onAppear() {
        // update the news source
        if self.newsSource < 0 {
            self.newsSource = self.keys.firstIndex(
                of:self.newsURLChoices.source) ?? 0
        } else {
```

```
            self.newsURLChoices.source =
                self.keys[self.newsSource]

            // write the news source using UserDefaults
            UserDefaults.standard.set(
                self.newsURLChoices.source,
                forKey: "source")
        }
        self.contentToDisplay =
            self.newsURLChoices.content=="top-headlines" ?
            0:1
    }
    .onDisappear() {
        self.newsURLChoices.content =
            self.contentToDisplay == 0 ?
            self.newsURLChoices.displayContentType[0]
            :
            self.newsURLChoices.displayContentType[1]

        // write the display content type using
        // UserDefaults
        UserDefaults.standard.set(
            self.newsURLChoices.content,
            forKey: "content")
    }
```

In the `SceneDelegate.swift` file, add the following statements in bold:

```
import UIKit
import SwiftUI

class SceneDelegate: UIResponder, UIWindowSceneDelegate {

    var window: UIWindow?

    var newsURLSources = NewsURLSources()

    func scene(_ scene: UIScene, willConnectTo session:
            UISceneSession, options connectionOptions:
            UIScene.ConnectionOptions) {

        // load the news source and content type from
        // UserDefaults
```

```
    newsURLSources.source =
        UserDefaults.standard.string(forKey: "source")
            ?? "engadget"
    newsURLSources.content =
        UserDefaults.standard.string(forKey:
            "content") ?? "top-headlines"
let contentView =
    ContentView().environmentObject(newsURLSources)

// Use a UIHostingController as window root view
    controller.
if let windowScene = scene as? UIWindowScene {
    let window = UIWindow(windowScene: windowScene)
    window.rootViewController =
    UIHostingController(rootView: contentView)
    self.window = window
    window.makeKeyAndVisible()
}
}
```

Now when you make changes to the preferences settings, the changes are persisted on storage. When the app is restarted, it will load the values of the last-saved settings.

Deploying the App

The final step to this entire project is to deploy the application onto an iPhone. To deploy an application from Xcode to an iPhone, you need to have a valid Apple ID. If you're a paid developer in the Apple Developer Program (https://developer.apple.com/programs), the process is straightforward, but membership is *not* a requirement.

Follow these steps to deploy your app:

1. In Xcode, select the NewsReader app under TARGETS and click the Signing & Capabilities tab on the right side of the window (see Figure 12-14).

2. From the Team drop-down list, select Add an Account.

3. If you have an existing Apple ID, enter it now and then click Next (see Figure 12-15).

    If you don't have an Apple ID, click the Create Apple ID button and follow the steps to create an Apple ID. When your Apple ID is created, go back to the window shown in Figure 12-15 and enter your Apple ID.

FIGURE 12-14:
Preparing to
deploy your app
to a real device.

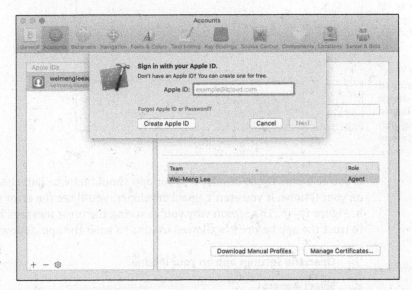

FIGURE 12-15:
Entering your
Apple ID.

4. Select your Apple ID from the Team drop-down list (see Figure 12-16).

TIP

If you see an error message on creating a provisioning profile, make sure your iPhone is connected to the Mac and that it's selected as the destination in Xcode (see Figure 12-17).

Xcode should now automatically create the provisioning profile for your iPhone. After this is done, you should be able to run (deploy) the app onto your iPhone by pressing ⌘+R in Xcode.

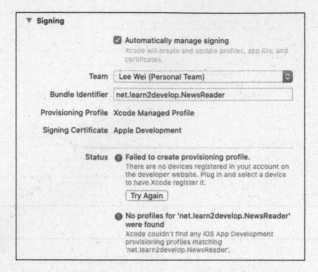

FIGURE 12-16:
Selecting your
Apple ID.

FIGURE 12-17:
Be sure to
select your device
name before
proceeding with
deployment.

If you're a paid Apple developer, your app should now be launched automatically on your iPhone. If you aren't a paid developer, you'll see the error message shown in Figure 12-18. The reason why you're seeing the error message is that you need to trust the app before it's allowed to run. To trust the app, follow these steps:

1. **Open the Settings app on your iPhone.**

2. **Select General.**

3. **Select Device Management.**

   You should see the developer app, as shown on the left side of Figure 12-19.

4. **Tap the developer app and then tap Trust (see the right side of Figure 12-19).**

   Now you'll be able to launch the app you created.

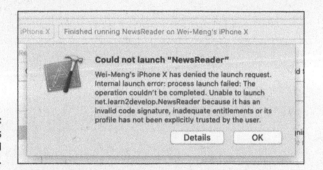

FIGURE 12-18:
Your app needs
to be trusted
before it can run.

FIGURE 12-19:
Trusting the app.

5

The Part of Tens

Discover the ten SwiftUI tips and tricks.

Find ten SwiftUI resources to make you a better SwiftUI developer.

Chapter **13**

Ten SwiftUI Tips and Tricks

S wiftUI makes creating your iOS applications easy and efficient. However, there are neat tricks that are not so obvious. In this chapter, you learn some of these tips and tricks so that you can become a better SwiftUI developer.

Resuming Live Preview

My number-one pet peeve about SwiftUI is that the Live Preview feature in Xcode doesn't always work. Very often, changes made to your code will cause the automatic previewing feature to pause. Even though your code is perfectly correct and there is no error, the Live Preview just can't seem to update automatically.

Of course, you can click the Resume button to update the preview, but you waste precious time moving your mouse to click the button.

TIP

A better way is to press ⌘+Option+P. This causes the Live Preview to resume and update itself. Now that you know this trick, there is no reason to click the Resume button anymore!

You may also want to check out the list of shortcuts for working in Xcode available at `https://developer.apple.com/library/archive/documentation/IDEs/Conceptual/xcode_help-command_shortcuts/MenuCommands/MenuCommands014.html`.

TIP

Implementing Localization

Localizing your app allows you to target it for the international market. A common task in localization involves translating the user interface (UI) of your app to display strings in the local language. SwiftUI makes localization straightforward. But you need to perform a few steps to get it set up:

1. **Go to the Info page of your project and select the project name (see Figure 13-1).**

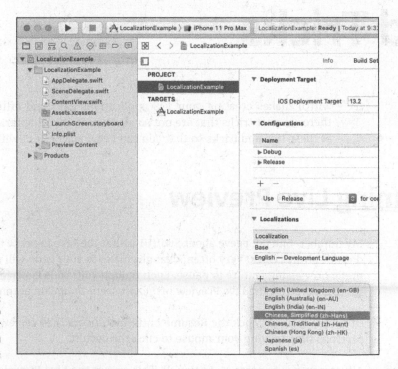

FIGURE 13-1:
Setting up localization for your project in Xcode.

2. **On the Info page, expand the Localizations section and click the plus sign (+) below it.**

Internationalization and *localization* are two terms that are often used interchangeably. However, they don't mean the same thing. Internationalization is an activity that you, the developer, perform by utilizing system-provided application programming interfaces (APIs). These modifications allow your app to be localized. Localization, on the other hand, is the process of translating an app's UI and resources into different languages.

3. **Select the language that you want to localize to.**

For this example, I'm selecting Chinese, Simplified (zh-Hans).

4. **In the pop-up that appears, click Finish.**

5. **In Xcode, choose File ⇨ New ⇨ File.**

6. **Select Strings File (see Figure 13-2) and click Next.**

FIGURE 13-2:
Adding a strings file item to your project.

7. **Name the file** Localizable.strings.

The file should now appear in your project.

8. **In the File Inspector window, click the Localize button (see Figure 13-3).**

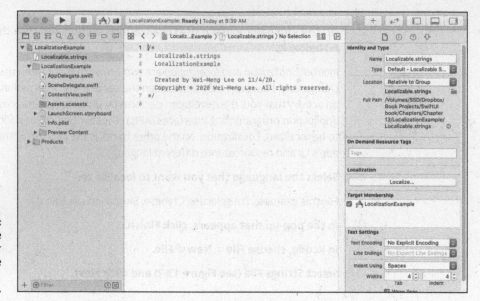

FIGURE 13-3:
Viewing the
File Inspector
window for the
Localizable.
strings file.

9. **In the pop-up window that appears, click Localize.**

You should now see an additional item named Chinese, Simplified appearing under the Localization section (see Figure 13-4).

10. **Expand the** `Localizable.strings` **item in your project to reveal the two files (see Figure 13-5),** `Localizable.strings` **(English) and** `Localizable.strings` **(Chinese, Simplified).**

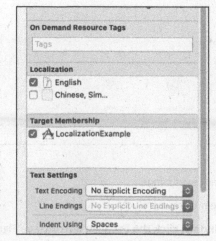

FIGURE 13-4:
The new
language should
now appear
under the
Localization
section.

FIGURE 13-5:
The two string
files for the two
languages,
English and
Simplified
Chinese.

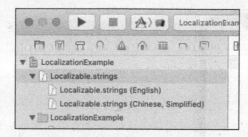

11. Add the following strings to the Localizable.strings (English) file:

```
"Hello, World!" = "Hello, World!";
```

12. Add the following strings to the Localizable.strings (Chinese, Simplified) file:

```
"Hello, World!" = "你好,世界!";
```

13. In the ContentView.swift file, add the following statements in bold:

```
import SwiftUI

struct ContentView: View {
    var body: some View {
        Text("Hello, World!")
            .font(.largeTitle)
    }
}
```

Your app is now localized. When you run the app on an iOS device with the language set to Simplified Chinese, it will automatically display the Text view in Chinese.

To test your application in the preview canvas, use the environment() modifier on the ContentView with the "zh" identifier:

```
struct ContentView_Previews: PreviewProvider {
    static var previews: some View {
        ContentView()
            .environment(\.locale, .init(identifier: "zh"))
    }
}
```

Figure 13-6 shows the Text view displaying in Chinese.

FIGURE 13-6:
Displaying the
Text view in
Simplified
Chinese.

你好，世界!

To change to English, use the "en" identifier:

```
ContentView()
    .environment(\.locale, .init(identifier: "en"))
```

Combining Text Views

Here is a neat little trick that you should know if you want to display the various words in a sentence in different colors and sizes. Instead of using the HStack view to group various Text views together, you can simply use the plus (+) operator to add different Text views together, like this:

```
struct ContentView: View {
    var body: some View {
        Text("Red ")
            .foregroundColor(.red)
            .font(.largeTitle)
        +
        Text("Green ")
```

```
            .foregroundColor(.green)
            .font(.body)
        +
        Text("Blue")
            .foregroundColor(.blue)
            .font(.title)
    }
}
```

How cool is that? Figure 13-7 shows the output.

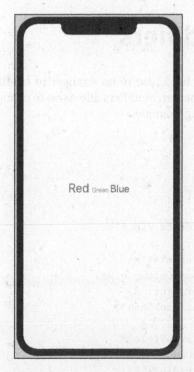

FIGURE 13-7:
Concatenating
different Text
views together.

If you want all the texts to be of the same font size, group them together using a
Group view and apply the font() modifier on the Group view:

```
struct ContentView: View {

    var body: some View {
        Group {
            Text("Red ")
                .foregroundColor(.red)
```

```
            +
        Text("Green ")
            .foregroundColor(.green)
            +
        Text("Blue")
            .foregroundColor(.blue)
        }
        .font(.largeTitle)
    }
}
```

Creating Custom Modifiers

If you've read the rest of this book, you're no stranger to modifiers in SwiftUI. They appear in almost every chapter. Modifiers allow you to change the behaviors of views. Consider the following example:

```
import SwiftUI

struct ContentView: View {
    var body: some View {
        VStack {
            Text("Leonardo da Vinci")
                .bold()
                .font(.largeTitle)
                .foregroundColor(.blue)
                .shadow(radius: 2)
            Text("Vincent van Gogh")
                .bold()
                .font(.largeTitle)
                .foregroundColor(.blue)
                .shadow(radius: 2)
        }
    }
}
```

Here, you apply the same set of modifiers to the two Text views. You often do that when you want to ensure consistencies in your UI (for example, applying the same set of UI styles when displaying certain information in your application). Instead of repeating the same set of modifiers again and again, wouldn't it be easier if you could just encapsulate all the modifiers into yet another modifier?

What you can do is create another struct that conforms to the `ViewModifier` protocol. This protocol requires you to implement a `body()` method that has a `Content` parameter. You then apply whatever modifiers you want to this `Content` argument and return it:

```
import SwiftUI

struct Title: ViewModifier {
    func body(content: Content) -> some View {
        content
            .font(.largeTitle)
            .foregroundColor(.blue)
            .shadow(radius: 2)
    }
}
```

To use the newly created `Title` struct on the `Text` view, apply the `modifier()` modifier and pass in the `Title` struct, like this:

```
struct ContentView: View {
    var body: some View {
        VStack {
            Text("Leonardo da Vinci")
                .bold()
                .modifier(Title())
            Text("Vincent van Gogh")
                .bold()
                .modifier(Title())
        }
    }
}
```

To make the `Title` struct look more like a true modifier, create an extension to the `View` protocol and give it a name — say, `titleStyle`:

```
import SwiftUI

extension View {
    func titleStyle() -> some View {
        self.modifier(Title())
    }
}
```

You can now apply the `titleStyle()` modifier to the two Text views:

```
struct ContentView: View {
    var body: some View {
        VStack {
            Text("Leonardo da Vinci")
                .bold()
                .titleStyle()

            Text("Vincent van Gogh")
                .bold()
                .titleStyle()
        }
    }
}
```

Displaying Multiple Alerts

Usually, in SwiftUI you apply a single `alert()` modifier to a single view. For example, when the user taps a button, you can display an alert by using the `alert()` modifier to the button. If you have multiple buttons, you can attach an `alert()` modifier to each button.

However, there are times when you need to display multiple different alerts for a single view. Applying multiple `alert()` modifiers to a single view will not work correctly, because the last modifier will override the earlier ones. To solve this problem, you can use a single `alert()` modifier, and use a `switch` statement within the modifier to decide which alert to display.

The following example shows a button that, when it's clicked, generates a random number of either 1 or 2 and uses it to decide which alert to display:

```
struct ContentView: View {
    @State private var displayAlert = false
    @State private var alertToDisplay = 0

    var body: some View {
```

```
        Button(action: {
            self.alertToDisplay = Int.random(in: 1...2)
            self.displayAlert = true
        }) {
            Text("Display Alert")
        }
        .alert(isPresented: $displayAlert) {
            switch alertToDisplay {
            case 1:
                return Alert(title: Text("Alert 1"),
                    message: Text("This is Alert 1"))
            default:
                return Alert(title: Text("Alert 2"),
                    message: Text("This is Alert 2"))
            }
        }
    }
}
```

Enabling Debug Preview

By default, the preview canvas doesn't display outputs printed using the `print()` function. This isn't useful, however, because often you want to use the `print()` function as a quick debugging option. The good news is, you can easily fix this.

In the preview canvas, right-click the Play button and select Debug Preview (see Figure 13-8).

Now if you tap the button, your code will print the output in the Output window:

```
struct ContentView: View {
    var body: some View {
        Button ("Tap Me") {
            print("Button was tapped...")
        }
    }
}
```

If the Output window is not shown in Xcode, press ⌘+Shift+C and it should appear.

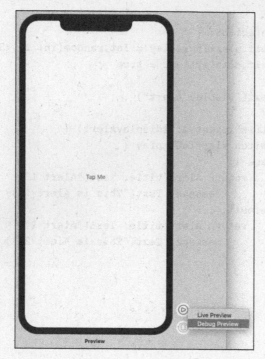

FIGURE 13-8:
Enabling the
Debug Preview
feature in the
preview canvas.

Previewing Using Different Devices

You're familiar with using the preview canvas to preview your app. By default, Xcode automatically picks an appropriate device based on your target (see Figure 13-9).

FIGURE 13-9:
The target set for
your project
(iPhone 11 Pro
Max, in this
example).

In Chapter 5, I show you how you can preview your app on different modes — Light mode and Dark mode — using the environment() modifier:

```
struct ContentView_Previews: PreviewProvider {
    static var previews: some View {
        Group {
            ContentView()
                .environment(\.colorScheme, .light)
```

```
            ContentView()
                .environment(\.colorScheme, .dark)
        }
    }
}
```

In addition to previewing in different modes, you can alter the size of the preview window, allowing you to have a glimpse of how your UI will look under different screen dimensions. You can do so using the previewLayout() modifier:

```
static var previews: some View {
    Group {
        ContentView()
            .environment(\.colorScheme, .light)
            .previewLayout((.fixed(width: 400,
                                   height: 600)))
        ContentView()
            .environment(\.colorScheme, .dark)
    }
}
```

Figure 13-10 shows the top preview displaying your UI in a dimension of 400 x 600 pixels. Note that clicking the Live Preview button will revert the preview back to the default size.

If you want to preview your UI on multiple devices, you can use a ForEach loop, supply a list of device names, and then use the previewDevice() modifier on the ContentView, like this:

```
static var previews: some View {
    ForEach(["iPhone 11", "iPhone SE"],
        id: \.self) { deviceName in
        ContentView()
            .environment(\.colorScheme,
                .light)
            .previewDevice(PreviewDevice(
                rawValue: deviceName))
            .previewDisplayName(deviceName)
    }
}
```

In addition to previewing the content of your app, you can resize the preview window using the resize handle in the bottom-right of the preview. You can look at different screen dimensions you want by dragging the resize handle (see Figure 13-10).

Figure 13-10 shows the same app (that displays a list of countries) running on two different screen dimensions. You can drag the resize handle of the preview frame to the desired size.

If you want to preview the sample app on specific iOS devices, you can apply the .previewDevice modifier together with the name of the device. To do this, use this statement:

FIGURE 13-10:
Previewing your
app in the
specified
dimensions.

Figure 13-11 shows the sample in Chapter 5 previewing on the iPhone 11 and the iPhone SE. Notice that you can display the name of the device using the previewDisplayName() modifier.

TIP

For a full list of devices that you can preview, check out the list at `https://developer.apple.com/documentation/swiftui/list/3270295-previewdevice`.

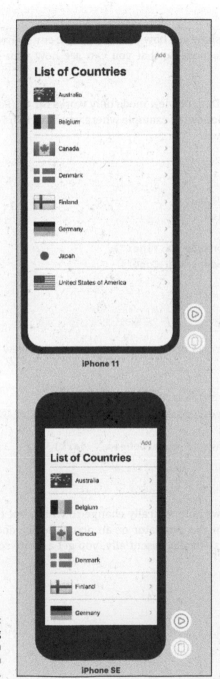

FIGURE 13-11:
Previewing the app on an iPhone 11 and an iPhone SE.

Dark Mode Only Works On NavigationView

In the preceding section, I show you how you can use the environment() modifier to set the preview to Dark mode so that you can see how your UI will look in Dark mode.

However, it seems like the Dark preview mode only works for the NavigationView. For example, consider the following example where you have two Text views contained within a VStack view:

```swift
import SwiftUI

struct ContentView: View {
    var body: some View {
        VStack {
            Text("Leonardo da Vinci")
            Text("Vincent van Gogh")
        }
    }
}
```

Suppose you use the environment() modifier to set the preview mode to dark, like this:

```swift
struct ContentView_Previews: PreviewProvider {
    static var previews: some View {
        ContentView()
            .environment(\.colorScheme, .dark)
    }
}
```

The words in the Text views automatically change to white, but the background remains white (running on the simulator or an actual device doesn't have this issue), as shown in Figure 13-12. So, essentially, you get a white screen.

FIGURE 13-12:
Previewing in
Dark mode but
the background
of the app is still
white.

To fix this problem, wrap the ContentView view using a ZStack and set its background to black, like this:

```
struct ContentView_Previews: PreviewProvider {
    static var previews: some View {
        ZStack {
            Color(.black)
            ContentView()
        }
        .edgesIgnoringSafeArea(.all)
        .environment(\.colorScheme, .dark)
    }
}
```

Figure 13-13 shows the text showing up on a black background.

FIGURE 13-13:
You can now
preview the Dark
mode correctly.

Extracting Subviews

Your UI may contain quite a large number of views. This is very common if you have a complicated UI. However, you can simplify your UI by extracting some of the views as subviews. Consider the following example from Chapter 3:

```
import SwiftUI

struct ContentView: View {
    var body: some View {
        HStack {
            Image("weimenglee")
                .resizable()
                .frame(width: CGFloat(120),
                    height: CGFloat(120))
                .cornerRadius(CGFloat(15),
                    antialiased: true)
            VStack {
                Text("Wei-Meng Lee")
                    .font(.largeTitle)
                    .bold()
```

```
                    Text("Founder")
                    Text("Developer Learning Solutions")
                        .italic()
                    Text("http://calendar.learn2develop.net")
                    Text("@weimenglee")
                }
            }
        }
    }
```

To break down the UI into smaller subviews so that your UI is more modular and manageable, follow these steps:

1. **In the preview canvas, select the** `Image` **view and press the ⌘ key.**

    You see a pop-up, as shown in Figure 13-14.

FIGURE 13-14:
Extracting views
as subviews in
the preview
canvas.

2. **Select Extract Subview.**

3. **Name the new view PhotoView (see Figure 13-15).**

```
The Image view will now be extracted as a new struct named
    PhotoView:
struct ContentView: View {
    var body: some View {
        HStack {
            PhotoView()
            VStack {
                Text("Wei-Meng Lee")
```

```
                              .font(.largeTitle)
                              .bold()
                      Text("Founder")
                      Text("Developer Learning Solutions")
                              .italic()
                      Text("http://calendar.learn2develop.net")
                      Text("@weimenglee")
                  }
              }
          }
      }

      struct PhotoView: View {
          var body: some View {
              Image("weimenglee")
                  .resizable()
                  .frame(width: CGFloat(120),
                         height: CGFloat(120))
                  .cornerRadius(CGFloat(15),
                               antialiased: true)
          }
      }
```

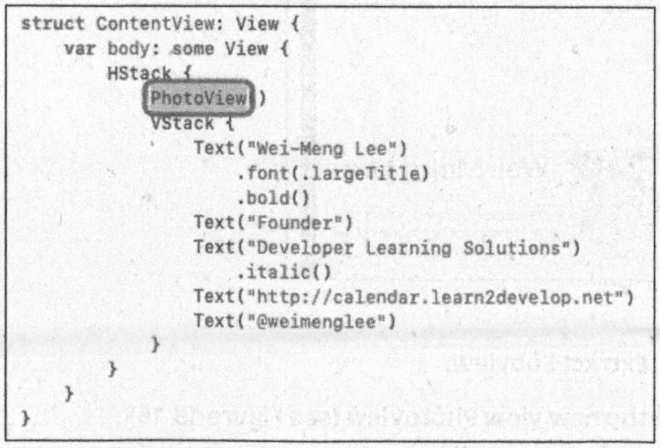

```
struct ContentView: View {
    var body: some View {
        HStack {
            PhotoView )
            VStack {
                Text("Wei-Meng Lee")
                    .font(.largeTitle)
                    .bold()
                Text("Founder")
                Text("Developer Learning Solutions")
                    .italic()
                Text("http://calendar.learn2develop.net")
                Text("@weimenglee")
            }
        }
    }
}
```

FIGURE 13-15:
Naming the newly
extracted
subview.

You can now also extract the VStack and save it as another struct named
DetailsView. Now your UI looks like the following, which is more
maintainable:

```
struct ContentView: View {
    var body: some View {
        HStack {
```

```
            PhotoView()
            DetailsView()
        }
    }
}

struct PhotoView: View {
...
}

struct DetailsView: View {
    var body: some View {
        VStack {
            Text("Wei-Meng Lee")
                .font(.largeTitle)
                .bold()
            Text("Founder")
            Text("Developer Learning Solutions")
                .italic()
            Text("http://calendar.learn2develop.net")
            Text("@weimenglee")
        }
    }
}
```

Displaying a Context Menu

One of the innovative features of iPhone is the support for Haptic Touch (which replaces the 3D Touch on older iPhones). Using Haptic Touch, you can long-press an item on your iPhone and a context-sensitive menu appears (if the app you're using supports it). You can support this feature in SwiftUI as well.

To attach a context menu to a view, use the contextMenu() modifier:

```
struct ContentView: View {
    var body: some View {
        Image("Mac Pro")
            .resizable()
            .frame(width: 300, height: 280)
            .contextMenu {
                Button(action: {
                    print("Save Image button tapped...")
```

```
		}) {
			Text("Save Image")
			Image(systemName:
				"tray.and.arrow.down")
		}
		Button(action: {
			print("Add to Cart button tapped...")
		}) {
			Text("Add to Cart")
			Image(systemName: "plus")
		}
	}
}
}
```

To create a context menu, you provide a list of Button views, and the content of each button is automatically wrapped using an HStack view. Now when you long-press the Image view, a context menu appears (see Figure 13-16).

FIGURE 13-16:
Implementing a
context menu on
an Image view.

Chapter **14**

Ten Great SwiftUI Resources

I hope this book covers all the important concepts you need to know to succeed in SwiftUI development, but I know you need more than just one single resource to stay ahead. In this chapter, I provide ten great SwiftUI resources that will be useful to you when you're ready to venture beyond the basics.

Apple

You may as well go straight to the source! Apple has a set of resources for learning SwiftUI, including tutorials, documentation, sample code, videos, and a forum. You can find it all at `https://developer.apple.com/tutorials/swiftui/resources`.

Of particular interest is the Tutorial section. As you scroll through each topic, you can follow the various steps in each section. Some of the figures are animated and interactive, which makes following the tutorials fun and effective. You can also jump directly to a specific topic that you're interested in and select the relevant section to start learning.

SwiftUI by Example

SwiftUI by Example (`www.hackingwithswift.com/quick-start/swiftui`) has a vast collection of tutorials on everything related to SwiftUI. If you search online for anything related to SwiftUI, chances are, you'll find an answer on Swift by Example. The code examples are very well written — straight to the point, without all the fluff.

100 Days of SwiftUI

Created by Paul Hudson, the same person behind SwiftUI by Example (see the preceding section), 100 Days of SwiftUI (`www.hackingwithswift.com/100/swiftui`) is a collection of videos, tutorials, tests, and more, designed to help beginners learn SwiftUI effectively. What's more, the course is entirely free! All you need is your motivation and focus to complete the 100 days of learning and coding.

Gosh Darn SwiftUI

Gosh Darn SwiftUI (`https://goshdarnswiftui.com`) is a curated list of questions and answers about SwiftUI. It also contains a quick reference to some of the commonly used views and controls in SwiftUI. I find it useful as a quick code reference when I need to refresh myself on how to use a particular view.

TIP

My editor wouldn't let me use the alternative URL for this same website. If you're curious, just replace `goshdarn` with `f___ing` (I can't spell out the whole word, but you can probably guess what word I'm talking about). You didn't hear it from me.

SwiftUI Hub

SwiftUI Hub (`https://swiftuihub.com/beginner-swiftui-tutorials`) is a collection of links to tutorials on SwiftUI. This site is useful if you're trying to learn a new topic in SwiftUI.

Awesome SwiftUI

Awesome SwiftUI (`https://github.com/chinsyo/awesome-swiftui`) is another curated list of awesome SwiftUI tutorials, libraries, videos, and articles. It contains tutorials and videos from the Apple Worldwide Developers Conference (WWDC), as well as related articles on SwiftUI. It also contains a list of GitHub code repositories of SwiftUI projects.

raywenderlich.com

raywenderlich.com has established itself in the iOS development world. It has a list of tutorials on SwiftUI (`www.raywenderlich.com/library?q=SwiftUI&sort_order=popularity`) that are worth a read. In addition, if you're already familiar with the Swift programming language, *SwiftUI by Tutorials* is a great book to get you started using SwiftUI to build an iOS app user interface (UI) declaratively. You can find the book at `https://store.raywenderlich.com/products/swiftui-by-tutorials`.

Swift Talk

Swift Talk (`https://talk.objc.io`) is a weekly video series on Swift programming. Although *Swift* is in its name, it contains a lot of interesting videos on SwiftUI, including ones that allow you to learn a particular topic in depth.

About SwiftUI

This site (`https://github.com/Juanpe/About-SwiftUI`) is another repository for all things SwiftUI. About SwiftUI contains a listing of documentations by Apple, WWDC videos, tutorials, books, courses, and articles, as well as code repositories created using SwiftUI.

Stack Overflow

No resource list would be complete if it didn't mention Stack Overflow, a question-and-answer site for professional and enthusiast programmers. In fact, if you don't know Stack Overflow, you aren't a programmer yet!

One of the top places to get your questions on SwiftUI answered is Stack Overflow (https://stackoverflow.com/search?q=swiftui). In fact, if you search the web for the answer to your question, chances are, Stack Overflow already has what you're looking for!

Code Snippets for Common SwiftUI Views

Throughout this book, I show the various SwiftUI views that you can use to build the user interface (UI) of an iPhone application. This appendix provides code snippets to demonstrate their use, so you can easily start using the views.

Content View

```
struct ContentView: View {
    var body: some View {
        Text("Hello World")
    }
}
```

Using Modifiers

```
Text("Hello, SwiftUI!")
    .font(.largeTitle)
    .bold()
    .foregroundColor(.red)
```

Image View

```
Image("weimenglee")
    .resizable()
    .frame(width: CGFloat(300.0),
        height:CGFloat(300))
```

```
        .clipShape(Circle())
        .overlay(Circle().stroke(
            Color.black, lineWidth: 5))
```

Text View

```
Text("Hello, world!")
    .fontWeight(.bold)
    .font(.title)
```

Button View

```
Button(action: {
    // action to perform
}) {
    Text("Submit")
}
```

VStack View

```
VStack {
    Text("Wei-Meng Lee")
    Text("Founder")
}
```

HStack View

```
HStack {
    Image("weimenglee")
        .resizable()
        .frame(width: CGFloat(120),
               height: CGFloat(120))
```

```
        .cornerRadius(CGFloat.(15),
            antialiased: true)
    VStack {
        Text("Wei-Meng Lee")
        Text("Founder")
    }
}
```

ZStack View

```
ZStack {
    Image("pdf")
        .resizable()
        .frame(width: 256, height: 256.0)
    Text("Watermark")
        .font(.largeTitle)
        .foregroundColor(.gray)
        .opacity(0.5)
        .rotationEffect(.degrees(-45))
}
```

TextField View

```
@State private var firstName: String = ""
TextField("First Name", text: $firstName)
    .border(Color.black)
```

SecureField View

```
@State private var password: String = ""
SecureField("Password", text: $password)
    .border(Color.black)
```

Toggle View

```
@State private var showFavorites = true
Toggle(isOn: $showFavorites) {
    Text("Show Favorites").bold()
}
    .padding()
    .background(showFavorites ?
        Color.yellow : Color.gray)
```

Slider View

```
@State private var sliderTemp = 23.0
Slider(value: $sliderTemp,
    in: 20.0...38.0)
```

Stepper View

```
@State private var qty = 1
Stepper(value: $qty, in: 0...10,
    label: {
        Text("Qty: \(qty)")
    }
)
```

Picker View

```
var typesOfCoffee =
    ["Caffè Americano", "Café Latte", "Cappuccino"]
@State private var selectedCoffee = 0
Picker(selection: $selectedCoffee,
    label: Text("Types of Coffee").bold()) {
    ForEach(0 ..< typesOfCoffee.count){
        Text(self.typesOfCoffee[$0]).tag($0)
    }
}
```

List View

```
// Adding Rows Statically
//========================
List {
    Text("Australia")
    Text("Canada")
    Text("United States of America")
}

// Adding Rows Programmatically
//==============================
// Example 1
@State var countries = [
    "Australia", "Canada", "United States of America"]
var body: some View {
    List {
        ForEach(countries, id: \.self) { (country) in
            Text(country)
        }
    }
}
```

```
// Example 2
var countries = [
    country(name: "Australia", flag: "Australia"),
    country(name: "Canada", flag: "Canada"),
    country(name: "United States of America",
            flag: "United States of America"),
]
// images of flags are stored in Assets.xcassets

var body: some View {
    List (countries, id:\.name) {(country) in
        HStack {
            Image(country.flag)
            Text(country.name)
        }
    }
}
```

NavigationView View

```
NavigationView{
    List {
        ForEach(countries, id: \.self) { (country) in
            Text(country)
        }
    }
    .navigationBarTitle("List of Countries")
}
```

NavigationLink View

```
NavigationView{
    List {
        ForEach(countries, id: \.self) { (country) in
            NavigationLink(destination:
                Text(country)
            ) {
                Text(country)
            }
        }
    }
    .navigationBarTitle("List of Countries")
}
```

Section View

```
List {
    Section(header: Text("Section I")) {
        Text("Item 1")
        Text("Item 2")
    }
    Section(header: Text("Section II")) {
        Text("Item 1")
        Text("Item 2")
    }
}
```

TabView View

```
struct TabView1: View {
    var body: some View {
        Text("TabView1")
    }
}
struct TabView2: View {
    var body: some View {
        Text("TabView2")
    }
}


struct ContentView: View {
    var body: some View {
        TabView {
            TabView1()
            .tabItem {
                Image(systemName: "doc.richtext")
                Text("News")
            }
            TabView2()
            .tabItem {
                Image(systemName: "info.circle")
                Text("About")
            }
        }
    }
}
```

Form and Section Views

```
Form {
    Section(header: Text("Sessions")) {
        Text("Hello")
        Text("World")
    }
    Section(header: Text("About this App")) {
        Text("Hello")
        Text("World")
    }
}
```

Rectangle View

```
Rectangle()
    .fill(Color.yellow)
    .frame(width: 300, height: 200)
    .border(Color.black, width: 3)
```

RoundedRectangle View

```
RoundedRectangle(cornerRadius: 25, style: .circular)
    .fill(Color.green)
    .frame(width: 200, height: 80)
```

Circle View

```
Circle()
    .fill(Color.yellow)
    .frame(width: 150, height: 150)
```

Capsule View

```
Capsule()
    .fill(Color.green)
    .frame(width: 300, height: 100)
```

Ellipse View

```
Ellipse()
    .fill(Color.yellow)
    .frame(width: 200, height: 80)
```

Index

Symbols

! character, 34, 35
... (closed range operator), 42, 43
: (colon operator), 26
, (comma), 56
$ character, 88, 95
. (dot) syntax, 44
// (forward slashes), 27
> (greater than) function, 55
-> operator, 39
< (lesser than) function, 54
() (parentheses), 40, 47
+ (plus) operator, 358
+= operator, 31
? character, 34, 36–37
_ (underscore), 247

A

About SwiftUI, 377
accelerate() method, 49, 56, 57
accessing built-in environment variables, 228–233
actions, adding, 77–78
addArc() function, 288
adding
  actions, 77–78
  elements to arrays, 31
  rows, 116–119, 123–124
  rows programmatically, 116–119
adjusting
  elements in arrays, 31
  items in dictionaries, 33
  style of List view, 136–138
alert() modifier, 362–363
Alert view, 210–211, 212
alerts, displaying multiple, 362–363

alignment parameter, 176–179, 187–188
angular gradients, filling circles with, 274
animation() modifier, 299, 301, 305
animations
  about, 299
  creating custom progress indicators, 314–322
  determinate progress indicator, 318–322
  indeterminate progress indicator, 314–318
  performing your own, 307–313
  process of, 299–302
  repeating, 303–304
  rotating in 2D, 307–309
  rotating in 3D, 309–313
  specifying type of, 303
  stopping, 304–307
  within a ZStack, 193–195
AppDelegate.swift file, 22–23
append() function, 31
Apple, 375
Apple Developer Program, 346, 375
Apple Human Interface Guidelines (HIG), 307
applications
  deploying, 346–349
  what they do, 323–325
arcs, drawings, 287–289
arguments, 39
Array type, 46
arrays, 30–32
ascending() function, 52, 53
assigning closures to variables, 52
Awesome SwiftUI, 377

B

Binding property, 150, 170
@Binding property wrapper, 218, 227, 246–247, 250

comma (,), 50

comments, 27–28

CompanyLabel view, 230–233

computed property, 47, 48

conforming
  to protocols, 56–57
  to View protocols, 64–65

constants, 26

Contact view, 104, 105

container views
  about, 195–197
  Divider view, 203–204
  Form view, 198–200, 339, 385
  Group view, 200–202, 359–360
  Section view, 198–200, 339, 384, 385

ContentView, 171, 214–218, 223, 224, 226,
    240, 241–244, 249, 261, 282, 317, 320, 365,
    369, 379

context menus, displaying, 373–374

contextMenu() modifier, 373–374

continue statement, 42

control transfer statements, 42

Coordinator class
  about, 256
  defining methods in, 258–260

coordinators, handling events using, 256–258

creating
  custom modifiers, 360–362
  custom progress indicators, 314–322
  custom views, 103–112
  details pages, 162–167
  ImagePickerViewController, 254–256
  layouts, 325–327
  navigation applications, 143–172
  news reader applications, 151–167
  preferences view, 339–344
  previews, 19–21
  projects, 323–349
  rows in List view, 119–120
  share sheets, 338–339
  tabbed applications, 143–172

customizing
  buttons, 76–77
  rows, 114–116

D

Dark mode
  NavigationView and, 368–370
  previewing in, 138–141

data
  basic types of, 28–30
  fetching, 330–331

datatask() method, 155

Debug Preview, enabling, 363–364

decode() function, 58, 155

default() function, 41, 211

defaultValue property, 231

defining
  classes, 47
  environment keys, 230–231
  methods in Coordinator class,
    258–260
  news sources, 328–330
  observable objects, 328–330
  protocols, 56
  vlews, 155–157

degrees() function, 310

delegation, 256

delete() function, 127

deleting rows, 126–128

deploying apps, 346–349

design time, previewing in Light/Dark modes
    during, 139–141

destructive() button, 211

details pages, creating, 162–167

DetailView(), 149, 225

determinate progress indicator,
    318–322

devices, previewing, 364–367

dictionaries
  about, 32–33
  displaying sections from, 134–136

greetings, 245, 246, 247
instantiating of views, 245
isEmpty, 37
lastTextBaseline, 188–190
leading, 79
row, 44, 45
self, 50–51
stored, 47–48
top, 188
Weight, 67
wrappedValue, 208
property wrappers, 207–209
@propertywrapper attribute, 208
protocol keyword, 56
protocols
    about, 55–56
    Codable, 57–59, 154
    conforming to, 56–57
    defining and using, 56
    some keyword, 59–60
publish() method, 194
@Published property wrapper, 220–221

R

radial gradients, filling circles with, 273–274
range operators, 43
raywenderlich.com, 377
reactive programming, 10
Rectangle view, 174–175, 292, 386
rectangles
    drawing using, 266–270
    filling, 266–269
    rotating, 269
    scaling, 269–270
Remember icon, 2
remove() function, 127
removeSpecialCharsFromString() function, 90
removing
    elements from arrays, 32
    items from dictionaries, 33

repeatCount() modifier, 303
repeating animations, 303–304
Repeat–While loop, 42
resizable() modifier, 73–74
resizing images, 73–75
resources, Internet
    About SwiftUI, 377
    Apple Developer Program, 346, 375
    Apple Human Interface Guidelines (HIG), 307
    Awesome SwiftUI, 377
    Cheat Sheet, 3
    Gosh Darn SwiftUI, 376
    JSON validator, 152
    News API, 152, 330
    raywenderlich.com, 377
    Stack Overflow, 378
    Swift Talk, 377
    SwiftUI by Example, 376
    SwiftUI by Tutorials, 377
    SwiftUI Hub, 376
    URLImage view, 159
    Xcode shortcuts, 354
resources, recommended, 375–378
Resume button, 15
resuming Live Preview, 353–354
retrieving
    elements from arrays, 31
    elements from dictionaries, 32–33
return keyword, 39, 54, 64–65
returning values, 39
rotating
    in 2D, 307–309
    in 3D, 309–313
    rectangles, 269
rotation3DEffect() modifier, 309–313
rotationEffect() modifier, 269, 307–309, 316
rounded rectangles
    drawing using, 270–273
    drawing with borders, 271–272
    filling with gradients, 270–271

About the Author

Wei-Meng Lee is a technologist and founder of Developer Learning Solutions (http://calendar.learn2develop.net), a company specializing in hands-on training on the latest technologies.

Wei-Meng has many years of training experiences, and his training courses place special emphasis on the learning-by-doing approach. His hands-on approach to learning programming makes understanding the subject much easier than reading books, tutorials, and documentations.

His name regularly appears in online and print publications, such as DevX.com, MobiForge.com, and *CODE Magazine.* He is also the author of *Python Machine Learning* (Wiley), *Learning WatchKit Programming* (Addison-Wesley), *Beginning Swift Programming* (Wrox), and *Beginning iOS 5 Application Development* (Wrox).

When not coding, you can find Wei-Meng speaking at meetups and conferences such as NDC Oslo, NDC London, NDC Copenhagen, and RigaDevDays.

Dedication

I dedicate this book with love to my dearest wife, Sze Wa, and daughter, Chloe, who have to endure my irregular work schedule and for their companionship when I am trying to meet writing deadlines!

Author's Acknowledgments

Writing a book is always exciting, but along with it come long hours of hard work, straining to get things done accurately and correctly. To make a book possible, a lot of unsung heroes work tirelessly behind the scene. For this, I would like to take this opportunity to thank a number of special people who made this book possible.

First, I want to thank Executive Editor Steven Hayes, who approached me (through the recommendation of Katie Mohr, whom I worked with on my earlier book *C# 2008 Programmer's Reference*) with the idea of writing a book on SwiftUI. At that time, I wasn't sure if I was ready to work on another book, because I had just finished writing *Python Machine Learning.* However, as they say, old habits die hard, and before I could say no I was already working on the outline of the book. Thank you, Steven and Katie, for giving me this opportunity and for your trust in me!

Next, a huge thanks to Elizabeth Kuball, my project editor, who is always a pleasure to work with. Elizabeth has been instrumental in getting this book out on time. With her guidance, I was able to stick to the original schedule and ensure that I keep up with my writing momentum. A sincere thank-you, Elizabeth!

Equally important is my technical editor, Siamak Ashrafi. Ash gave a lot of ideas and advice during the technical review process. I learned a tremendous amount from him. Thank you, Ash!

Last, but not least, I want to thank my parents, my wife, and my lovely girl, for all the support they have given me. They have selflessly adjusted their schedules to accommodate my busy schedule when I was working on this book. I love you all!

Publisher's Acknowledgments

Executive Editor: Steven Hayes
Project Editor: Elizabeth Kuball
Copy Editor: Elizabeth Kuball
Technical Editor: Siamak Ashrafi

Production Editor: Siddique Shaik
Cover Image: © Sergey Peterman/Getty Images